HUMAN ACTION

A Treatise on Economics

Volume 1

LUDWIG VON MISES

Human Action

A *Treatise on Economics*

 LUDWIG VON MISES

Edited by Bettina Bien Greaves

Volume 1

LIBERTY FUND   *Indianapolis*

Editorial Additions © 2007 Liberty Fund, Inc.
All Rights Reserved
First published in 1949 by Yale University Press with a revised edition in 1963. In
1966, Henry Regnery Company published the third revised edition in agreement
with Yale. The fourth revised edition (and the edition used for this setting) was
published in 1996 by The Foundation for Economic Education, Inc. in cooperation with Bettina Bien Greaves.
Mises Made Easier: A Glossary for Ludwig von Mises' HUMAN ACTION © 1990
Bettina Bien Greaves and reprinted with permission.

Front cover photograph of Ludwig von Mises used by permission
of the Ludwig von Mises Institute, Auburn, Alabama

Frontispiece courtesy of Bettina Bien Greaves

Printed in the United States of America

11 10 09 08 07   C   5   4   3   2   1
11 10 09 08 07   P   5   4   3   2   1

Library of Congress Cataloging-in-Publication Data
Von Mises, Ludwig, 1881–1973
   Human action: a treatise on economics / Ludwig von Mises; edited by Bettina Bien Greaves.
      p.   cm. — (Liberty Fund library of the works of Ludwig von Mises)
      Originally published: 4th rev. ed., Irvington-on-Hudson, N. Y.: Foundation for
   Economic Education, c1996.
      Includes bibliographical references and index.
      ISBN-13: 978-0-86597-630-6 (hardcover: 4 volume set: alk. paper)
      ISBN-10: 0-86597-630-9 (hardcover: 4 volume set: alk. paper)
      ISBN-13: 978-0-86597-631-3 (pbk.: 4 volume set: alk. paper)
      ISBN-10: 0-86597-631-7 (pbk.: 4 volume set: alk. paper)
      [etc.]
         1. Economics   2. Commerce.   I. Greaves, Bettina Bien.   II. Title.
      HB171.V63   2007
      330—dc22

                                                                                    2005025025

Vol. 1 ISBNS: 978-0-86597-674-0 (hc)   978-0-86597-678-8 (pb)

Liberty Fund, Inc.
8335 Allison Pointe Trail, Suite 300
Indianapolis, Indiana 46250-1684

This edition of Mises's *Human Action* is reproduced from the Foundation for Economic Education's 4th edition which was a reprint of the 3rd 1966 Henry Regnery edition. In this book Mises cited many foreign language works in footnotes. Whenever feasible, if English-language translations are available, the editor has referenced the pertinent pages in those English translations. Also when the meaning of foreign words and phrases are not readily apparent from the context, English translations of those foreign terms have been inserted, in brackets, immediately following.

For the benefit of scholars who have read, studied, and cited Mises's *Human Action* over many years, this Liberty Fund edition has been typeset, insofar as possible, to preserve the pagination of the 3rd (1966) and 4th (1996) editions, which were identical. As it was not always possible to keep the page divisions exactly the same, a careful scrutiny will detect minor discrepancies on pages 206–207, 234–235, 373–374, 404–407, 468–478, 564–565, and 689–690.

Because the vocabulary Mises used in *Human Action* included many words and phrases which will be unfamiliar to modern readers, this Liberty Fund Edition reproduces Percy L. Greaves, Jr.'s *Mises Made Easier: A Glossary to Ludwig von Mises' HUMAN ACTION*, first published in 1974. This glossary defines and explains technical terms and historical references and includes translations of all foreign-language words and phrases in *Human Action*.

Mises' contribution was very simple, yet at the same time extremely profound. He pointed out that the whole economy is the result of what individuals do. Individuals act, choose, cooperate, compete, and trade with one another. In this way Mises explained how complex market phenomena develop. Mises did not simply describe economic phenomena — prices, wages, interest rates, money, monopoly and even the trade cycle — he explained them as the outcomes of countless conscious, purposive actions, choices, and preferences of individuals, each of whom was trying as best as he or she could under the circumstances to attain various wants and ends and to avoid undesired consequences. Hence the title Mises chose for his economic treatise, *Human Action*. Thus also, in Mises' view, Adam Smith's "invisible hand" was explainable on the basis of logic and utilitarian principles as the outcome of the countless actions of individuals.

Sprinkled throughout Mises' scholarly and erudite explanations of market operations are many colorful descriptions of economic phenomena. For instance, on the difference between economic and political power: "A 'chocolate king' has no power over the consumers, his patrons. He provides them with chocolate of the best quality and at the cheapest price. He does not rule the consumers, he serves them. The consumers . . . are free to stop patronizing his shops. He loses his 'kingdom' if the consumers prefer to spend their pennies elsewhere." (p. 300) On why people trade: "The inhabitants of the Swiss Jura prefer to manufacture watches instead of growing wheat. Watchmaking is for them the cheapest way to acquire wheat. On the other hand the growing of wheat is the cheapest way for the Canadian farmer to acquire watches." (p. 431) For Mises a price is a ratio arrived at on the market by the competitive bids of consumers for money on the one hand and some particular good or service on the other. A government may issue decrees, but "A government can no more determine prices than a goose can lay hen's eggs." (pp. 433–34)

In Mises' view, the inequality of men was the beginning of peaceful interpersonal social cooperation and the source of all the advantages it brings: "The liberal champions of equality under the law were fully aware of the fact that men are born unequal and that it is precisely their inequality that generates social cooperation and civilization. Equality under the law was in their opinion not designed to correct the inexorable facts of the universe and to make natural inequality disappear. It was, on the contrary, the device to secure for the whole of mankind the maximum of benefits it can derive from it. . . . Equality under the law is in their eyes good because it best serves the interests of all. It leaves it to the voters to decide who should hold public office and to the consumers to decide who should direct production activities." (p. 915)

Mises' 1949 comments on Social Security and government debt read as if they had been written yesterday: "Paul in the year 1940 saves by paying one hundred dollars to the national social security institution. He receives in exchange a claim which is virtually an unconditional government IOU. If the government spends the hundred dollars for current expenditures, no additional capital comes into existence, and no increase in the productivity of labor results. The government's IOU is a check drawn upon the future taxpayer. In 1970 a certain Peter may have to fulfill the government's promise although he himself does not derive any benefit from the fact that Paul in 1940 saved one hundred dollars. . . . The trumpery argument that the public debt is no burden because 'we owe it to ourselves' is delusive. The Pauls of 1940 do not owe it to themselves. It is the Peters of 1970 who owe it to the Pauls of 1940. . . . The statesmen of 1940 solve their problems by shifting them to the statesmen of 1970. On that date the statesmen of 1940 will be either dead or elder statesmen glorying in their wonderful achievement, social security." (p. 921)

In the "Foreword to the Third Edition" of *Human Action*, Mises mentioned the Italian and Spanish translations of this book. Since then it has been translated by Tao-Ping Hsia into Chinese (1976/77), by Raoul Audouin into French (1985), by Donald Stewart, Jr., into Portuguese (1990), and by Toshio Murata into Japanese (1991). Its German-language precursor, *Nationalökonomie* (1940) has also been republished (1980).

The publishers of this new edition of *Human Action* have tried to correct the typos that inevitably creep into almost any book, especially one of this size. They have also included a completely new index, which they hope will help make the ideas in this book more readily accessible to readers.

Bettina Bien Greaves
Irvington-on-Hudson, New York
February 1996

FOREWORD TO THE THIRD EDITION

It gives me great satisfaction to see this book, handsomely printed by a distinguished publishing house, appear in its third revised edition.

Two terminological remarks may be in order.

First, I employ the term "liberal" in the sense attached to it everywhere in the nineteenth century and still today in the countries of continental Europe. This usage is imperative because there is simply no other term available to signify the great political and intellectual movement that substituted free enterprise and the market economy for the precapitalistic methods of production; constitutional representative government for the absolutism of kings or oligarchies; and freedom of all individuals for slavery, serfdom, and other forms of bondage.

Secondly, in the last decades the meaning of the term "psychology" has been more and more restricted to the field of experimental psychology, a discipline that resorts to the research methods of the natural sciences. On the other hand, it has become usual to dismiss those studies that previously had been called psychological as "literary psychology" and as an unscientific way of reasoning. Whenever reference is made to "psychology" in economic studies, one has in mind precisely this literary psychology, and therefore it seems advisable to introduce a special term for it. I suggested in my book *Theory and History* (New Haven, 1957, pp. 264–74) the term "thymology," and I used this term also in my recently published essay *The Ultimate Foundation of Economic Science* (Princeton, 1962). However, my suggestion was not meant to be retroactive and to alter the use of the term "psychology" in books previously published, and so I continue in this new edition to use the term "psychology" in the same way I used it in the first edition.

Two translations of the first edition of *Human Action* have come out: an Italian translation by Mr. Tullio Bagiotti, Professor at the Università Bocconi in Milano, under the title *L'Azione Umana, Trattato di economia*, published by the Unione Tipografico-Editrice Torinese in 1959; and a Spanish-language translation by Mr. Joaquin Reig Albiol under the title *La Acción Humana (Tratado de Economía)*, published in two volumes by Fundación Ignacio Villalonga in Valencia (Spain) in 1960.

I feel indebted to many good friends for help and advice in the preparation of this book.

First of all I want to remember two deceased scholars, Paul Mantoux and William E. Rappard, who by giving me the opportunity of teaching at the famous Graduate Institute of International Studies in Geneva, Switzerland, provided me with the time and the incentive to start work upon a long-projected plan.

I want to express my thanks for very valuable and helpful suggestions to Mr. Arthur Goddard, Mr. Percy Greaves, Doctor Henry Hazlitt, Professor Israel M. Kirzner, Mr. Leonard E. Read, Mr. Joaquin Reig Albiol and Doctor George Reisman.

But most of all I want to thank my wife for her steady encouragement and help.

Ludwig von Mises
New York
March, 1966

CONTENTS

VOLUME 1

Introduction

1   Economics and Praxeology

Economics is the youngest of all sciences. In the last two hundred years, it is true, many new sciences have emerged from the disciplines familiar to the ancient Greeks. However, what happened here was merely that parts of knowledge which had already found their place in the complex of the old system of learning now became autonomous. The field of study was more nicely subdivided and treated with new methods; hitherto unnoticed provinces were discovered in it, and people began to see things from aspects different from those of their precursors. The field itself was not expanded. But economics opened to human science a domain previously inaccessible and never thought of. The discovery of a regularity in the sequence and interdependence of market phenomena went beyond the limits of the traditional system of learning. It conveyed knowledge which could be regarded neither as logic, mathematics, psychology, physics, nor biology.

Philosophers had long since been eager to ascertain the ends which God or Nature was trying to realize in the course of human history. They searched for the law of mankind's destiny and evolution. But even those thinkers whose inquiry was free from any theological tendency failed utterly in these endeavors because they were committed to a faulty method. They dealt with humanity as a whole or with other holistic concepts like nation, race, or church. They set up quite arbitrarily the ends to which the behavior of such wholes is bound to lead. But they could not satisfactorily answer the question regarding what factors compelled the various acting individuals to behave in such a way that the goal aimed at by the whole's inexorable evolution was attained. They had recourse to desperate shifts: miraculous interference of the Deity either by revelation or by the delegation of God-sent prophets and consecrated leaders, preestablished harmony, predestination, or the operation of a mystic and fabulous "world soul" or "national soul." Others spoke of a "cunning of nature" which implanted in man impulses driving him unwittingly along precisely the path Nature wanted him to take.

2   INTRODUCTION

Other philosophers were more realistic. They did not try to guess the designs of Nature or God. They looked at human things from the viewpoint of government. They were intent upon establishing rules of political action, a technique, as it were, of government and statesmanship. Speculative minds drew ambitious plans for a thorough reform and reconstruction of society. The more modest were satisfied with a collection and systematization of the data of historical experience. But all were fully convinced that there was in the course of social events no such regularity and invariance of phenomena as had already been found in the operation of human reasoning and in the sequence of natural phenomena. They did not search for the laws of social cooperation because they thought that man could organize society as he pleased. If social conditions did not fulfill the wishes of the reformers, if their utopias proved unrealizable, the fault was seen in the moral failure of man. Social problems were considered ethical problems. What was needed in order to construct the ideal society, they thought, were good princes and virtuous citizens. With righteous men any utopia might be realized.

The discovery of the inescapable interdependence of market phenomena overthrew this opinion. Bewildered, people had to face a new view of society. They learned with stupefaction that there is another aspect from which human action might be viewed than that of good and bad, of fair and unfair, of just and unjust. In the course of social events there prevails a regularity of phenomena to which man must adjust his actions if he wishes to succeed. It is futile to approach social facts with the attitude of a censor who approves or disapproves from the point of view of quite arbitrary standards and subjective judgments of value. One must study the laws of human action and social cooperation as the physicist studies the laws of nature. Human action and social cooperation seen as the object of a science of given relations, no longer as a normative discipline of things that ought to be — this was a revolution of tremendous consequences for knowledge and philosophy as well as for social action.

For more than a hundred years, however, the effects of this radical change in the methods of reasoning were greatly restricted because people believed that they referred only to a narrow segment of the total field of human action, namely, to market phenomena. The classical economists met in the pursuit of their investigations an obstacle which they failed to remove, the apparent antinomy of value. Their theory of value was defective, and forced them to restrict the scope of their science. Until the late nineteenth century political economy remained a science of the "economic" aspects of human action, a theory of wealth and selfishness. It dealt with human action only to the extent that it is actuated by what was—very unsatisfactorily—described as the profit motive, and it asserted that there is in addition other human action whose treatment is the task of other disciplines. The transformation of thought which the classical economists had initiated was brought to its consummation only by modern subjectivist economics, which converted the theory of market prices into a general theory of human choice.

For a long time men failed to realize that the transition from the classical theory of value to the subjective theory of value was much more than the substitution of a more satisfactory theory of market exchange for a less satisfactory one. The general theory of choice and preference goes far beyond the horizon which encompassed the scope of economic problems as circumscribed by the economists from Cantillon, Hume, and Adam Smith down to John Stuart Mill. It is much more than merely a theory of the "economic side" of human endeavors and of man's striving for commodities and an improvement in his material well-being. It is the science of every kind of human action. Choosing determines all human decisions. In making his choice man chooses not only between various material things and services. All human values are offered for option. All ends and all means, both material and ideal issues, the sublime and the base, the noble and the ignoble, are ranged in a single row and subjected to a decision which picks out one thing and sets aside another. Nothing that men aim at or want to avoid remains outside of this arrangement into a unique scale of gradation and preference. The modern theory of value widens the scientific horizon and enlarges the field of economic studies. Out of the political economy of the classical school emerges the general theory of human action, *praxeology*.[1] The economic or catallactic problems[2] are embedded in a more general science, and can no longer be served from this connection. No treatment of economic problems proper can avoid starting from acts of choice; economics becomes a part, although the hitherto best elaborated part, of a more universal science, praxeology.

1. The term *praxeology* was first used in 1890 by Espinas. Cf. his article "Les Origines de la technologie," *Revue Philosophique*, XVth year, XXX, 114–15, and his book published in Paris in 1897, with the same title.
2. The term *Catallactics or the Science of Exchanges* was first used by Whately. Cf. his book *Introductory Lectures on Political Economy* (London, 1831), p. 6.

2   The Epistemological Problem of a General Theory of Human Action

In the new science everything seemed to be problematic. It was a stranger in the traditional system of knowledge; people were perplexed and did not know how to classify it and to assign it its proper place. But on the other hand they were convinced that the inclusion of economics in the catalogue of knowledge did not require a rearrangement or expansion of the total scheme. They considered their catalogue system complete. If economics did not fit into it, the fault could only rest with the unsatisfactory treatment that the economists applied to their problems.

It is a complete misunderstanding of the meaning of the debates concerning the essence, scope, and logical character of economics to dismiss them as the scholastic quibbling of pedantic professors. It is a widespread misconception that while pedants squandered useless talk about the most appropriate method of procedure, economics itself, indifferent to these idle disputes, went quietly on its way. In the *Methodenstreit* between the Austrian economists and the Prussian Historical School, the self-styled "intellectual bodyguard of the House of Hohenzollern," and in the discussions between the school of John Bates Clark and American Institutionalism much more was at stake than the question of what kind of procedure was the most fruitful one. The real issue was the epistemological foundations of the science of human action and its logical legitimacy. Starting from an epistemological system to which praxeological thinking was strange and from a logic which acknowledged as scientific — besides logic and mathematics — only the empirical natural sciences and history, many authors tried to deny the value and usefulness of economic theory. Historicism aimed at replacing it by economic history; positivism recommended the substitution of an illusory social science which should adopt the logical structure and pattern of Newtonian mechanics. Both these schools agreed in a radical rejection of all the achievements of economic thought. It was impossible for the economists to keep silent in the face of all these attacks.

The radicalism of this wholesale condemnation of economics was very soon surpassed by a still more universal nihilism. From time immemorial men in thinking, speaking, and acting had taken the uniformity and immutability of the logical structure of the human mind as an unquestionable fact. All scientific inquiry was based on this assumption. In the discussions about the epistemological character of economics, writers, for the first time in human history, denied this proposition too. Marxism asserts that a man's thinking is determined by his class affiliation. Every social class has a logic of its own. The product of thought cannot be anything else than an "ideological disguise" of the selfish class interests of the thinker. It is the task of a "sociology of knowledge" to unmask philosophies and scientific theories and to expose their "ideological" emptiness. Economics is a "bourgeois" makeshift, the economists are "sycophants" of capital. Only the classless society of the socialist utopia will substitute truth for "ideological" lies.

This polylogism was later taught in various other forms also. Historicism asserts that the logical structure of human thought and action is liable to change in the course of historical evolution. Racial polylogism assigns to each race a logic of its own. Finally there is irrationalism, contending that reason as such is not fit to elucidate the irrational forces that determine human behavior.

Such doctrines go far beyond the limits of economics. They question not only economics and praxeology but all other human knowledge and human reasoning in general. They refer to mathematics and physics as well as to economics. It seems therefore that the task of refuting them does not fall to any single branch of knowledge but to epistemology and philosophy. This furnishes apparent justification for the attitude of those economists who quietly continue their studies without bothering about epistemological problems and the objections raised by polylogism and irrationalism. The physicist does not mind if someone stigmatizes his theories as bourgeois, Western or Jewish; in the same way the economist should ignore detraction and slander. He should let the dogs bark and pay no heed to their yelping. It is seemly for him to remember Spinoza's dictum: *Sane sicut lux se ipsam et tenebras manifestat, sic veritas norma sui et falsi est.* [Indeed, just as light defines itself and darkness, so truth sets the standard for itself and falsity.]

However, the situation is not quite the same with regard to economics as it is with mathematics and the natural sciences. Polylogism and irrationalism attack praxeology and economics. Although they formulate their statements in a general way to refer to all branches of knowledge, it is the sciences of human action that they really have in view. They say that it is an illusion to believe that scientific research can achieve results valid for people of all eras, races, and social classes, and they take pleasure in disparaging certain physical and biological theories as bourgeois or Western. But if the solution of practical problems requires the application of these stigmatized doctrines, they forget their criticism. The technology of Soviet Russia utilizes without scruple all the results of bourgeois physics, chemistry, and biology just as if they were valid for all classes. The Nazi engineers and physicians did not disdain to utilize the theories, discoveries, and inventions of people of "inferior" races and nations. The behavior of people of all races, nations, religions, linguistic groups, and social classes clearly proves that they do not endorse the doctrines of polylogism and irrationalism as far as logic, mathematics, and the natural sciences are concerned.

But it is quite different with praxeology and economics. The main motive for the development of the doctrines of polylogism, historicism, and irrationalism was to provide a justification for disregarding the teachings of economics in the determination of economic policies. The socialists, racists, nationalists, and étatists failed in their endeavors to refute the theories of the economists and to demonstrate the correctness of their own spurious doctrines. It was precisely this frustration that prompted them to negate the logical and epistemological principles upon which all human reasoning both in mundane activities and in scientific research is founded.

It is not permissible to dispose of these objections merely on the ground of the political motives which inspired them. No scientist is entitled to assume beforehand that a disapprobation of his theories must be unfounded because his critics are imbued by passion and party bias. He is bound to reply to every censure without any regard to its underlying motives or its background. It is no less impermissible to keep silent in the face of the often asserted opinion that the theorems of economics are valid only under hypothetical assumptions never realized in life and that they are therefore useless for the mental grasp of reality. It is strange that some schools seem to approve of this opinion and nonetheless quietly proceed to draw their curves and to formulate their equations. They do not bother about the meaning of their reasoning and about its reference to the world of real life and action.

This is, of course, an untenable attitude. The first task of every scientific inquiry is the exhaustive description and definition of all conditions and assumptions under which its various statements claim validity. It is a mistake to set up physics as a model and pattern for economic research. But those committed to this fallacy should have learned one thing at least: that no physicist ever believed that the clarification of some of the assumptions and conditions of physical theorems is outside the scope of physical research. The main question that economics is bound to answer is what the relation of its statements is to the reality of human action whose mental grasp is the objective of economic studies.

It therefore devolves upon economics to deal thoroughly with the assertion that its teachings are valid only for the capitalistic system of the shortlived and already vanished liberal period of Western civilization. It is incumbent upon no branch of learning other than economics to examine all the objections raised from various points of view against the usefulness of the statements of economic theory for the elucidation of the problems of human action. The system of economic thought must be built up in such a way that it is proof against any criticism on the part of irrationalism, historicism, panphysicalism, behaviorism, and all varieties of polylogism. It is an intolerable state of affairs that while new arguments are daily advanced to demonstrate the absurdity and futility of the endeavors of economics, the economists pretend to ignore all this.

It is no longer enough to deal with the economic problems within the traditional framework. It is necessary to build the theory of catallactics upon the solid foundation of a general theory of human action, praxeology. This procedure will not only secure it against many fallacious criticisms but clarify many problems hitherto not even adequately seen, still less satisfactorily solved. There is, especially, the fundamental problem of economic calculation.

3 Economic Theory and the Practice of Human Action

It is customary for many people to blame economics for being backward. Now it is quite obvious that our economic theory is not perfect. There is no such thing as perfection in human knowledge, nor for that matter in any other human achievement. Omniscience is denied to man. The most elaborate theory that seems to satisfy completely our thirst for knowledge may one day be amended or supplanted by a new theory. Science does not give us absolute and final certainty. It only gives us assurance within the limits of our mental abilities and the prevailing state of scientific thought. A scientific system is but one station in an endlessly progressing search for knowledge. It is necessarily affected by the insufficiency inherent in every human effort. But to acknowledge these facts does not mean that present-day economics is backward. It merely means that economics is a living thing—and to live implies both imperfection and change.

The reproach of an alleged backwardness is raised against economics from two different points of view.

There are on the one hand some naturalists and physicists who censure economics for not being a natural science and not applying the methods and procedures of the laboratory. It is one of the tasks of this treatise to explode the fallacy of such ideas. In these introductory remarks it may be enough to say a few words about their psychological background. It is common with narrow-minded people to reflect upon every respect in which other people differ from themselves. The camel in the fable takes exception to all other animals for not having a hump, and the Ruritanian criticizes the Laputanian for not being a Ruritanian. The research worker in the laboratory considers it as the sole worthy home of inquiry, and differential equations as the only sound method of expressing the results of scientific thought. He is simply incapable of seeing the epistemological problems of human action. For him economics cannot be anything but a kind of mechanics.

Then there are people who assert that something must be wrong with the social sciences because social conditions are unsatisfactory. The natural sciences have achieved amazing results in the last two or three hundred years, and the practical utilization of these results has succeeded in improving the general standard of living to an unprecedented extent. But, say these critics, the social sciences have utterly failed in the task of rendering social conditions more satisfactory. They have not stamped out misery and starvation, economic crises and unemployment, war and tyranny. They are sterile and have contributed nothing to the promotion of happiness and human welfare.

These grumblers do not realize that the tremendous progress of technological methods of production and the resulting increase in wealth and welfare were feasible only through the pursuit of those liberal policies which were the practical application of the teachings of economics. It was the ideas of the classical economists that removed the checks imposed by age-old laws, customs, and prejudices upon technological improvement and freed the genius of reformers and innovators from the straitjackets of the guilds, government tutelage, and social pressure of various kinds. It was they that reduced the prestige of conquerors and expropriators and demonstrated the social benefits derived from business activity. None of the great modern inventions would have been put to use if the mentality of the pre-capitalistic era had not been thoroughly demolished by the economists. What is commonly called the "industrial revolution" was an offspring of the ideological revolution brought about by the doctrines of the economists. The economists exploded the old tenets: that it is unfair and unjust to outdo a competitor by producing better and cheaper goods; that it is iniquitous to deviate from the traditional methods of production; that machines are an evil because they bring about unemployment; that it is one of the tasks of civil government to prevent efficient businessmen from getting rich and to protect the less efficient against the competition of the more efficient; that to restrict the freedom of entrepreneurs by government compulsion or by coercion on the part of other social powers is an appropriate means to promote a nation's well-being. British political economy and French Physiocracy were the pacemakers of modern capitalism. It is they that made possible the progress of the applied natural sciences that has heaped benefits upon the masses.

What is wrong with our age is precisely the widespread ignorance of the role which these policies of economic freedom played in the technological evolution of the last two hundred years. People fell prey to the fallacy that the improvement of the methods of production was contemporaneous with the policy of laissez faire only by accident. Deluded by Marxian myths, they consider modern industrialism an outcome of the operation of mysterious "productive forces" that do not depend in any way on ideological factors. Classical economics, they believe, was not a factor in the rise of capitalism, but rather its product, its "ideological superstructure," i.e., a doctrine designed to defend the unfair claims of the capitalistic exploiters. Hence the abolition of capitalism and the substitution of socialist totalitarianism for a market economy and free enterprise would not impair the further progress of technology. It would, on the contrary, promote technological improvement by removing the obstacles which the selfish interests of the capitalists place in its way.

The characteristic feature of this age of destructive wars and social disintegration is the revolt against economics. Thomas Carlyle branded economics a "dismal science," and Karl Marx stigmatized the economists as "the sycophants of the bourgeoisie." Quacks — praising their patent medicines and short cuts to an earthly paradise — take pleasure in scorning economics as "orthodox" and "reactionary." Demagogues pride themselves on what they call their victories over economics. The "practical" man boasts of his contempt for economics and his ignorance of the teachings of "armchair" economists. The economic policies of the last decades have been the outcome of a mentality that scoffs at any variety of sound economic theory and glorifies the spurious doctrines of its detractors. What is called "orthodox" economics is in most countries barred from the universities and is virtually unknown to the leading statesmen, politicians, and writers.

The blame for the unsatisfactory state of economic affairs can certainly not be placed upon a science which both rulers and masses despise and ignore.

It must be emphasized that the destiny of modern civilization as developed by the white peoples in the last two hundred years is inseparably linked with the fate of economic science. This civilization was able to spring into existence because the peoples were dominated by ideas which were the application of the teachings of economics to the problems of economic policy. It will and must perish if the nations continue to pursue the course which they entered upon under the spell of doctrines rejecting economic thinking.

It is true that economics is a theoretical science and as such abstains from any judgment of value. It is not its task to tell people what ends they should aim at. It is a science of the means to be applied for the attainment of ends chosen, not, to be sure, a science of the choosing of ends. Ultimate decisions, the valuations and the choosing of ends, are beyond the scope of any science. Science never tells a man how he should act; it merely shows how a man must act if he wants to attain definite ends.

It seems to many people that this is very little indeed and that a science limited to the investigation of the *is* and unable to express a judgment of value about the highest and ultimate ends is of no importance for life and action. This too is a mistake. However, the exposure of this mistake is not a task of these introductory remarks. It is one of the ends of the treatise itself.

4   Résumé

It was necessary to make these preliminary remarks in order to explain why this treatise places economic problems within the broad frame of a general theory of human action. At the present stage both of economic thinking and of political discussions concerning the fundamental issues of social organization, it is no longer feasible to isolate the treatment of catallactic problems proper. These problems are only a segment of a general science of human action and must be dealt with as such.

Human Action

CHAPTER 1

Acting Man

1 Purposeful Action and Animal Reaction

Human action is purposeful behavior. Or we may say: Action is will put into operation and transformed into an agency, is aiming at ends and goals, is the ego's meaningful response to stimuli and to the conditions of its environment, is a person's conscious adjustment to the state of the universe that determines his life. Such paraphrases may clarify the definition given and prevent possible misinterpretations. But the definition itself is adequate and does not need complement or commentary.

Conscious or purposeful behavior is in sharp contrast to unconscious behavior, i.e., the reflexes and the involuntary responses of the body's cells and nerves to stimuli. People are sometimes prepared to believe that the boundaries between conscious behavior and the involuntary reaction of the forces operating within man's body are more or less indefinite. This is correct only as far as it is sometimes not easy to establish whether concrete behavior is to be considered voluntary or involuntary. But the distinction between consciousness and unconsciousness is nonetheless sharp and can be clearly determined.

The unconscious behavior of the bodily organs and cells is for the acting *ego* no less a datum than any other fact of the external world. Acting man must take into account all that goes on within his own body as well as other data, e.g., the weather or the attitudes of his neighbors. There is, of course, a margin within which purposeful behavior has the power to neutralize the working of bodily factors. It is feasible within certain limits to get the body under control. Man can sometimes succeed through the power of his will in overcoming sickness, in compensating for the innate or acquired insufficiency of his physical constitution, or in suppressing reflexes. As far as this is possible, the field of purposeful action is extended. If a man abstains from controlling the involuntary reaction of cells and nerve centers, although he would be in a position to do so, his behavior is from our point of view purposeful.

The field of our science is human action, not the psychological events which result in an action. It is precisely this which distinguishes the general theory of human action, praxeology, from psychology. The theme of psychology is the internal events that result or can result in a definite action. The theme of praxeology is action as such. This also settles the relation of praxeology to the psychoanalytical concept of the subconscious. Psychoanalysis too is psychology and does not investigate action but the forces and factors that impel a man toward a definite action. The psychoanalytical subconscious is a psychological and not a praxeological category. Whether an action stems from clear deliberation, or from forgotten memories and suppressed desires which from submerged regions, as it were, direct the will, does not influence the nature of the action. The murderer whom a subconscious urge (the *Id*) drives toward his crime and the neurotic whose aberrant behavior seems to be simply meaningless to an untrained observer both act; they like anybody else are aiming at certain ends. It is the merit of psychoanalysis that it has demonstrated that even the behavior of neurotics and psychopaths is meaningful, that they too act and aim at ends, although we who consider ourselves normal and sane call the reasoning determining their choice of ends nonsensical and the means they choose for the attainment of these ends contrary to purpose.

The term *unconscious*, as used by praxeology, and the terms *subconscious* and *unconscious*, as applied by psychoanalysis, belong to two different systems of thought and research. Praxeology no less than other branches of knowledge owes much to psychoanalysis. The more necessary is it then to become aware of the line which separates praxeology from psychoanalysis.

Action is not simply giving preference. Man also shows preference in situations in which things and events are unavoidable or are believed to be so. Thus a man may prefer sunshine to rain and may wish that the sun would dispel the clouds. He who only wishes and hopes does not interfere actively with the course of events and with the shaping of his own destiny. But acting man chooses, determines, and tries to reach an end. Of two things both of which he cannot have together he selects one and gives up the other. Action therefore always involves both taking and renunciation.

To express wishes and hopes and to announce planned action may be forms of action in so far as they aim in themselves at the realization of a certain purpose. But they must not be confused with the actions to which they refer. They are not identical with the actions they announce, recommend, or reject. Action is a real thing.

ACTING MAN ❧ 13

What counts is a man's total behavior, and not his talk about planned but not realized acts. On the other hand action must be clearly distinguished from the application of labor. Action means the employment of means for the attainment of ends. As a rule one of the means employed is the acting man's labor. But this is not always the case. Under special conditions a word is all that is needed. He who gives orders or interdictions may act without any expenditure of labor. To talk or not to talk, to smile or to remain serious, may be action. To consume and to enjoy are no less action than to abstain from accessible consumption and enjoyment.

Praxeology consequently does not distinguish between "active" or energetic and "passive" or indolent man. The vigorous man industriously striving for the improvement of his condition acts neither more nor less than the lethargic man who sluggishly takes things as they come. For to do nothing and to be idle are also action, they too determine the course of events. Wherever the conditions for human interference are present, man acts no matter whether he interferes or refrains from interfering. He who endures what he could change acts no less than he who interferes in order to attain another result. A man who abstains from influencing the operation of physiological and instinctive factors which he could influence also acts. Action is not only doing but no less omitting to do what possibly could be done.

We may say that action is the manifestation of a man's will. But this would not add anything to our knowledge. For the term *will* means nothing else than man's faculty to choose between different states of affairs, to prefer one, to set aside the other, and to behave according to the decision made in aiming at the chosen state and forsaking the other.

2   The Prerequisites of Human Action

We call contentment or satisfaction that state of a human being which does not and cannot result in any action. Acting man is eager to substitute a more satisfactory state of affairs for a less satisfactory. His mind imagines conditions which suit him better, and his action aims at bringing about this desired state. The incentive that impels a man to act is always some uneasiness.[1] A man perfectly content with the state of his affairs would have no incentive to change things. He would have neither wishes nor desires; he would be perfectly

---

1. Cf. Locke, *An Essay Concerning Human Understanding*, ed. Fraser (Oxford, 1984), 1, 331–33; Leibniz, *Nouveaux essais sur l'entendement humain*, ed. Flammarion, p. 119.

happy. He would not act; he would simply live free from care.

But to make a man act, uneasiness and the image of a more satisfactory state alone are not sufficient. A third condition is required: the expectation that purposeful behavior has the power to remove or at least to alleviate the felt uneasiness. In the absence of this condition no action is feasible. Man must yield to the inevitable. He must submit to destiny.

These are the general conditions of human action. Man is the being that lives under these conditions. He is not only *Homo sapiens*, but no less *Homo agens*. Beings of human descent who either from birth or from acquired defects are unchangeably unfit for any action (in the strict sense of the term and not merely in the legal sense) are practically not human. Although the statutes and biology consider them to be men, they lack the essential feature of humanity. The newborn child too is not an acting being. It has not yet gone the whole way from conception to the full development of its human qualities. But at the end of this evolution it becomes an acting being.

On Happiness

In colloquial speech we call a man "happy" who has succeeded in attaining his ends. A more adequate description of his state would be that he is happier than he was before. There is however no valid objection to a usage that defines human action as the striving for happiness.

But we must avoid current misunderstandings. The ultimate goal of human action is always the satisfaction of the acting man's desire. There is no standard of greater or lesser satisfaction other than individual judgments of value, different for various people and for the same people at various times. What makes a man feel uneasy and less uneasy is established by him from the standard of his own will and judgment, from his personal and subjective valuation. Nobody is in a position to decree what should make a fellow man happier.

To establish this fact does not refer in any way to the antitheses of egoism and altruism, of materialism and idealism, of individualism and collectivism, of atheism and religion. There are people whose only aim is to improve the condition of their own ego. There are other people with whom awareness of the troubles of their fellow men causes as much uneasiness as or even more uneasiness than their own wants. There are people who desire nothing else than the satisfaction of their appetites for sexual intercourse, food, drinks, fine homes, and other material things. But other men care more for the satisfactions commonly called "higher" and "ideal." There are individuals eager to adjust their actions to the requirements of social cooperation; there are, on the other hand, refractory people who defy the rules of social life. There are people for whom the ultimate goal of the earthly pilgrimage is the preparation for a life of bliss. There are other people who do not believe in the teachings of any religion and do not allow their actions to be influenced by them.

Praxeology is indifferent to the ultimate goals of action. Its findings are valid for all kinds of action irrespective of the ends aimed at. It is a science of means, not of ends. It applies the term happiness in a purely formal sense. In the praxeological terminology the proposition: man's unique aim is to attain happiness, is tautological. It does not imply any statement about the state of affairs from which man expects happiness.

The idea that the incentive of human activity is always some uneasiness and its aim always to remove such uneasiness as far as possible, that is, to make the acting men feel happier, is the essence of the teachings of Eudaemonism and Hedonism. Epicurean ἀταραξία [(ataraxia, Greek) complete peace of mind] is that state of perfect happiness and contentment at which all human activity aims without ever wholly attaining it. In the face of the grandeur of this cognition it is of little avail only that many representatives of this philosophy failed to recognize the purely formal character of the notions *pain* and *pleasure* and gave them a material and carnal meaning. The theological, mystical, and other schools of a heteronomous ethic did not shake the core of Epicureanism because they could not raise any other objection than its neglect of the "higher" and "nobler" pleasures. It is true that the writings of many earlier champions of Eudaemonism, Hedonism, and Utilitarianism are in some points open to misinterpretation. But the language of modern philosophers and still more that of the modern economists is so precise and straightforward that no misinterpretation can possibly occur.

On Instincts and Impulses

One does not further the comprehension of the fundamental problem of human action by the methods of instinct-sociology. This school classifies the various concrete goals of human action and assigns to each class a special instinct as its motive. Man appears as a being driven by various innate instincts and dispositions. It is assumed that this explanation demolishes once for all the odious teachings of economics and utilitarian ethics. However, Feuerbach has already justly observed that every instinct is an instinct to happiness.[2] The method of instinct-psychology and instinct-sociology consists in an arbitrary classification of the immediate goals of action and in a hypostasis of each. Whereas praxeology says that the goal of an action is to remove

2. Cf. Feuerbach, *Sämmtliche Werke*, ed. Bolin and Jodl (Stuttgart, 1907), X, 231.

a certain uneasiness, instinct-psychology says it is the satisfaction of an instinctive urge.

Many champions of the instinct school are convinced that they have proved that action is not determined by reason, but stems from the profound depths of innate forces, impulses, instincts, and dispositions which are not open to any rational elucidation. They are certain they have succeeded in exposing the shallowness of rationalism and disparage economics as "a tissue of false conclusions drawn from false psychological assumptions."[3] Yet rationalism, praxeology, and economics do not deal with the ultimate springs and goals of action, but with the means applied for the attainment of an end sought. However unfathomable the depths may be from which an impulse or instinct emerges, the means which man chooses for its satisfaction are determined by a rational consideration of expense and success.[4]

He who acts under an emotional impulse also acts. What distinguishes an emotional action from other actions is the valuation of input and output. Emotions disarrange valuations. Inflamed with passion, man sees the goal as more desirable and the price he has to pay for it as less burdensome than he would in cool deliberation. Men have never doubted that even in the state of emotion means and ends are pondered and that it is possible to influence the outcome of this deliberation by rendering more costly the yielding to the passionate impulse. To punish criminal offenses committed in a state of emotional excitement or intoxication more mildly than other offenses is tantamount to encouraging such excesses. The threat of severe retaliation does not fail to deter even people driven by seemingly irresistible passion.

We interpret animal behavior on the assumption that the animal yields to the impulse which prevails at the moment. As we observe that the animal feeds, cohabits, and attacks other animals or men, we speak of its instincts of nourishment, of reproduction, and of aggression. We assume that such instincts are innate and peremptorily ask for satisfaction.

But it is different with man. Man is not a being who cannot help yielding to the impulse that most urgently asks for satisfaction. Man is a being capable of subduing his instincts, emotions, and impulses; he can rationalize his behavior. He renounces the satisfaction of a burning impulse in order to satisfy other desires. He is not a puppet of his appetites. A man does not ravish every female that stirs his senses; he does not devour every piece of food that entices him; he does not knock down every fellow he would like to kill. He arranges

---

3. Cf. William McDougall, *An Introduction to Social Psychology* (14th ed. Boston, 1921), p. 11.
4. Cf. Mises, *Epistemological Problems of Economics*, trans. by G. Reisman (New York, 1960), pp. 52 ff.

his wishes and desires into a scale, he chooses; in short, he acts. What distinguishes man from beasts is precisely that he adjusts his behavior deliberatively. Man is the being that has inhibitions, that can master his impulses and desires, that has the power to suppress instinctive desires and impulses.

It may happen that an impulse emerges with such vehemence that no disadvantage which its satisfaction may cause appears great enough to prevent the individual from satisfying it. In this case too there is choosing. Man decides in favor of yielding to the desire concerned.[5]

3   Human Action as an Ultimate Given

Since time immemorial men have been eager to know the prime mover, the cause of all being and of all change, the ultimate substance from which everything stems and which is the cause of itself. Science is more modest. It is aware of the limits of the human mind and of the human search for knowledge. It aims at tracing back every phenomenon to its cause. But it realizes that these endeavors must necessarily strike against insurmountable walls. There are phenomena which cannot be analyzed and traced back to other phenomena. They are the ultimate given. The progress of scientific research may succeed in demonstrating that something previously considered as an ultimate given can be reduced to components. But there will always be some irreducible and unanalyzable phenomena, some ultimate given.

Monism teaches that there is but one ultimate substance, dualism that there are two, pluralism that there are many. There is no point in quarreling about these problems. Such metaphysical disputes are interminable. The present state of our knowledge does not provide the means to solve them with an answer which every reasonable man must consider satisfactory.

Materialist monism contends that human thoughts and volitions are the product of the operation of bodily organs, the cells of the brain and the nerves. Human thought, will, and action are solely brought about by material processes which one day will be completely explained by the methods of physical and chemical inquiry. This too is a metaphysical hypothesis, although its supporters consider it as an unshakable and undeniable scientific truth.

Various doctrines have been advanced to explain the relation be-

5. In such cases a great role is played by the circumstance that the two satisfactions concerned — that expected from yielding to the impulse and that expected from the avoidance of its undesirable consequences — are not simultaneous. Cf. below, pp. 479–490.

tween mind and body. They are mere surmises without any reference to observed facts. All that can be said with certainty is that there are relations between mental and physiological processes. With regard to the nature and operation of this connection we know little if anything.

Concrete value judgments and definite human actions are not open to further analysis. We may fairly assume or believe that they are absolutely dependent upon and conditioned by their causes. But as long as we do not know how external facts—physical and physiological—produce in a human mind definite thoughts and volitions resulting in concrete acts, we have to face an insurmountable *methodological dualism*. In the present state of our knowledge the fundamental statements of positivism, monism and panphysicalism are mere metaphysical postulates devoid of any scientific foundation and both meaningless and useless for scientific research. Reason and experience show us two separate realms: the external world of physical, chemical, and physiological phenomena and the internal world of thought, feeling, valuation, and purposeful action. No bridge connects—as far as we can see today—these two spheres. Identical external events result sometimes in different human responses, and different external events produce sometimes the same human response. We do not know why.

In the face of this state of affairs we cannot help withholding judgment on the essential statements of monism and materialism. We may or may not believe that the natural sciences will succeed one day in explaining the production of definite ideas, judgments of value, and actions in the same way in which they explain the production of a chemical compound as the necessary and unavoidable outcome of a certain combination of elements. In the meantime we are bound to acquiesce in a methodological dualism.

Human action is one of the agencies bringing about change. It is an element of cosmic activity and becoming. Therefore it is a legitimate object of scientific investigation. As—at least under present conditions—it cannot be traced back to its causes, it must be considered as an ultimate given and must be studied as such.

It is true that the changes brought about by human action are but trifling when compared with the effects of the operation of the great cosmic forces. From the point of view of eternity and the infinite universe man is an infinitesimal speck. But for man human action and its vicissitudes are the real thing. Action is the essence of his nature and existence, his means of preserving his life and raising himself above the level of animals and plants. However perishable and evanescent all human efforts may be, for man and for human science they are of primary importance.

4   Rationality and Irrationality; Subjectivism and Objectivity of Praxeological Research

Human action is necessarily always rational. The term *rational action* is therefore pleonastic and must be rejected as such. When applied to the ultimate ends of action, the terms *rational* and *irrational* are inappropriate and meaningless. The ultimate end of action is always the satisfaction of some desires of the acting man. Since nobody is in a position to substitute his own value judgments for those of the acting individual, it is vain to pass judgment on other people's aims and volitions. No man is qualified to declare what would make another man happier or less discontented. The critic either tells us what he believes he would aim at if he were in the place of his fellow; or, in dictatorial arrogance blithely disposing of his fellow's will and aspirations, declares what condition of this other man would better suit himself, the critic.

It is usual to call an action irrational if it aims, at the expense of "material" and tangible advantages, at the attainment of "ideal" or "higher" satisfactions. In this sense people say, for instance — sometimes with approval, sometimes with disapproval — that a man who sacrifices life, health, or wealth to the attainment of "higher" goods — like fidelity to his religious, philosophical, and political convictions or the freedom and flowering of his nation — is motivated by irrational considerations. However, the striving after these higher ends is neither more nor less rational or irrational than that after other human ends. It is a mistake to assume that the desire to procure the bare necessities of life and health is more rational, natural, or justified than the striving after other goods or amenities. It is true that the appetite for food and warmth is common to men and other mammals and that as a rule a man who lacks food and shelter concentrates his efforts upon the satisfaction of these urgent needs and does not care much for other things. The impulse to live, to preserve one's own life, and to take advantage of every opportunity of strengthening one's vital forces is a primal feature of life, present in every living being. However, to yield to this impulse is not — for man — an inevitable necessity.

While all other animals are unconditionally driven by the impulse to preserve their own lives and by the impulse of proliferation, man has the power to master even these impulses. He can control both his sexual desires and his will to live. He can give up his life when the conditions under which alone he could preserve it seem intolerable. Man is capable of dying for a cause or of committing suicide. To live is for man the outcome of a choice, of a judgment of value.

It is the same with the desire to live in affluence. The very existence of ascetics and of men who renounce material gains for the sake of clinging to their convictions and of preserving their dignity and self-respect is evidence that the striving after more tangible amenities is not inevitable but rather the result of a choice. Of course, the immense majority prefer life to death and wealth to poverty.

It is arbitrary to consider only the satisfaction of the body's physiological needs as "natural" and therefore "rational" and everything else as "artificial" and therefore "irrational." It is the characteristic feature of human nature that man seeks not only food, shelter, and cohabitation like all other animals, but that he aims also at other kinds of satisfaction. Man has specifically human desires and needs which we may call "higher" than those which he has in common with the other mammals.[6]

When applied to the means chosen for the attainment of ends, the terms rational and irrational imply a judgment about the expediency and adequacy of the procedure employed. The critic approves or disapproves of the method from the point of view of whether or not it is best suited to attain the end in question. It is a fact that human reason is not infallible and that man very often errs in selecting and applying means. An action unsuited to the end sought falls short of expectation. It is contrary to purpose, but it is rational, i.e., the outcome of a reasonable — although faulty — deliberation and an attempt — although an ineffectual attempt — to attain a definite goal. The doctors who a hundred years ago employed certain methods for the treatment of cancer which our contemporary doctors reject were — from the point of view of present-day pathology — badly instructed and therefore inefficient. But they did not act irrationally; they did their best. It is probable that in a hundred years more doctors will have more efficient methods at hand for the treatment of this disease. They will be more efficient but not more rational than our physicians.

The opposite of action is not *irrational behavior*, but a reactive response to stimuli on the part of the bodily organs and instincts which cannot be controlled by the volition of the person concerned. To the same stimulus man can under certain conditions respond both by reactive response and by action. If a man absorbs a poison, the organs

6. On the errors involved in the iron law of wages see below, pp. 603 f; on the misunderstanding of the Malthusian theory see below, pp. 667–72.

react by setting up their forces of antidotal defense; in addition, action may interfere by applying counterpoison.

With regard to the problem involved in the antithesis, rational and irrational, there is no difference between the natural sciences and the social sciences. Science always is and must be rational. It is the endeavor to attain a mental grasp of the phenomena of the universe by a systematic arrangement of the whole body of available knowledge. However, as has been pointed out above, the analysis of objects into their constituent elements must sooner or later necessarily reach a point beyond which it cannot go. The human mind is not even capable of conceiving a kind of knowledge not limited by an ultimate given inaccessible to further analysis and reduction. The scientific method that carries the mind up to this point is entirely rational. The ultimate given may be called an irrational fact.

It is fashionable nowadays to find fault with the social sciences for being purely rational. The most popular objection raised against economics is that it neglects the irrationality of life and reality and tries to press into dry rational schemes and bloodless abstractions the infinite variety of phenomena. No censure could be more absurd. Like every other branch of knowledge, economics goes as far as it can be carried by rational methods. Then it stops by establishing the fact that it is faced with an ultimate given, i.e., a phenomenon which cannot—at least in the present state of our knowledge—be further analyzed.[7]

The teachings of praxeology and economics are valid for every human action without regard to its underlying motives, causes, and goals. The ultimate judgments of value and the ultimate ends of human action are given for any kind of scientific inquiry; they are not open to any further analysis. Praxeology deals with the ways and means chosen for the attainment of such ultimate ends. Its object is means, not ends.

In this sense we speak of the subjectivism of the general science of human action. It takes the ultimate ends chosen by acting man as data, it is entirely neutral with regard to them, and it refrains from passing any value judgments. The only standard which it applies is whether or not the means chosen are fit for the attainment of the ends aimed at. If Eudaemonism says happiness, if Utilitarianism and economics say utility, we must interpret these terms in a subjectivistic way as that which acting man aims at because it is desirable in his eyes. It is in this formalism that the progress of the modern meaning of Eudaemonism, Hedonism, and Utilitarianism consists as opposed to

7. We shall see later (pp. 49–58) how the empirical social sciences deal with the ultimate given.

the older material meaning and the progress of the modern subjectivistic theory of value as opposed to the objectivistic theory of value as expounded by classical political economy. At the same time it is in this subjectivism that the objectivity of our science lies. Because it is subjectivistic and takes the value judgments of acting man as ultimate data not open to any further critical examination, it is itself above all strife of parties and factions, it is indifferent to the conflicts of all schools of dogmatism and ethical doctrines, it is free from valuations and preconceived ideas and judgments, it is universally valid and absolutely and plainly human.

5   Causality as a Requirement of Action

Man is in a position to act because he has the ability to discover causal relations which determine change and becoming in the universe. Acting requires and presupposes the category of causality. Only a man who sees the world in the light of causality is fitted to act. In this sense we may say that causality is a category of action. The category *means and ends* presupposes the category *cause and effect*. In a world without causality and regularity of phenomena there would be no field for human reasoning and human action. Such a world would be a chaos in which man would be at a loss to find any orientation and guidance. Man is not even capable of imagining the conditions of such a chaotic universe.

Where man does not see any causal relation, he cannot act. This statement is not reversible. Even when he knows the causal relation involved, man cannot act if he is not in a position to influence the cause.

The archetype of causality research was: where and how must I interfere in order to divert the course of events from the way it would go in the absence of my interference in a direction which better suits my wishes? In this sense man raises the question: who or what is at the bottom of things? He searches for the regularity and the "law," because he wants to interfere. Only later was this search more extensively interpreted by metaphysics as a search after the ultimate cause of being and existence. Centuries were needed to bring these exaggerated and extravagant ideas back again to the more modest question of where one must interfere or should one be able to interfere in order to attain this or that end.

The treatment accorded to the problem of causality in the last decades has been, due to a confusion brought about by some eminent physicists, rather unsatisfactory. We may hope that this unpleasant chapter in the history of philosophy will be a warning to future philosophers.

There are changes whose causes are, at least for the present time, unknown to us. Sometimes we succeed in acquiring a partial knowledge so that we are able to say: in 70 per cent of all cases A results in B, in the remaining cases in C, or even in D, E, F, and so on. In order to substitute for this fragmentary information more precise information it would be necessary to break up A into its elements. As long as this is not achieved, we must acquiesce in what is called a statistical law. But this does not affect the praxeological meaning of causality. Total or partial ignorance in some areas does not demolish the category of causality.

The philosophical, epistemological, and metaphysical problems of causality and of imperfect induction are beyond the scope of praxeology. We must simply establish the fact that in order to act, man must know the casual relationship between events, processes, or states of affairs. And only as far as he knows this relationship, can his action attain the ends sought. We are fully aware that in asserting this we are moving in a circle. For the evidence that we have correctly perceived a causal relation is provided only by the fact that action guided by this knowledge results in the expected outcome. But we cannot avoid this vicious circular evidence precisely because causality is a category of action. And because it is such a category, praxeology cannot help bestowing some attention on this fundamental problem of philosophy.

6   The Alter Ego

If we are prepared to take the term causality in its broadest sense, teleology can be called a variety of causal inquiry. Final causes are first of all causes. The cause of an event is seen as an action or quasi-action aiming at some end.

Both primitive man and the infant, in a naïve anthropomorphic attitude, consider it quite plausible that every change and event is the outcome of the action of a being acting in the same way as they themselves do. They believe that animals, plants, mountains, rivers, and fountains, even stones and celestial bodies, are, like themselves, feeling, willing, and acting beings. Only at a later stage of cultural development does man renounce these animistic ideas and substitute the mechanistic world view for them. Mechanicalism proves to be so satisfactory a principle of conduct that people finally believe it capable of solving all the problems of thought and scientific research. Materialism and panphysicalism proclaim mechanicalism as the essence of all knowledge and the experimental and mathematical methods of the natural sciences as the sole scientific mode of thinking. All changes are to be comprehended as motions subject to the laws of mechanics.

The champions of mechanicalism do not bother about the still unsolved problems of the logical and epistemological basis of the principles of causality and imperfect induction. In their eyes these principles are sound because they work. The fact that experiments in the laboratory bring about the results predicted by the theories and that machines in the factories run in the way predicted by technology proves, they say, the soundness of the methods and findings of modern natural science. Granted that science cannot give us truth — and who knows what truth really means? — at any rate it is certain that it works in leading us to success.

But it is precisely when we accept this pragmatic point of view that the emptiness of the panphysicalist dogma becomes manifest. Science, as has been pointed out above, has not succeeded in solving the problems of the mind-body relations. The panphysicalists certainly cannot contend that the procedures they recommend have ever worked in the field of interhuman relations and of the social sciences. But it is beyond doubt that the principle according to which an *Ego* deals with every human being as if the other were a thinking and acting being like himself has evidenced its usefulness both in mundane life and in scientific research. It cannot be denied that it works.

It is beyond doubt that the practice of considering fellow men as beings who think and act as I, the Ego, do has turned out well; on the other hand the prospect seems hopeless of getting a similar pragmatic verification for the postulate requiring them to be treated in the same manner as the objects of the natural sciences. The epistemological problems raised by the comprehension of other people's behavior are no less intricate than those of causality and incomplete induction. It may be admitted that it is impossible to provide conclusive evidence for the propositions that my logic is the logic of all other people and by all means absolutely the only human logic and that the categories of my action are the categories of all other people's action and by all means absolutely the categories of all human action. However, the pragmatist must remember that these propositions work both in practice and in science, and the positivist must not overlook the fact that in addressing his fellow men he presupposes — tacitly and implicitly — the intersubjective validity of logic and thereby the reality of the realm of the alter Ego's thought and action, of his eminent human character.[8]

8. Cf. Alfred Schütz, *Der sinnhafte Aufbau der sozialen Welt* (Vienna, 1932), p. 18.

Thinking and acting are the specific human features of man. They are peculiar to all human beings. They are, beyond membership in the zoological species *Homo sapiens*, the characteristic mark of man as man. It is not the scope of praxeology to investigate the relation of thinking and acting. For praxeology it is enough to establish the fact that there is only one logic that is intelligible to the human mind, and that there is only one mode of action which is human and comprehensible to the human mind. Whether there are or can be somewhere other beings — superhuman or subhuman — who think and act in a different way, is beyond the reach of the human mind. We must restrict our endeavors to the study of human action.

This human action which is inextricably linked with human thought is conditioned by logical necessity. It is impossible for the human mind to conceive logical relations at variance with the logical structure of our mind. It is impossible for the human mind to conceive a mode of action whose categories would differ from the categories which determine our own actions.

There are for man only two principles available for a mental grasp of reality, namely, those of teleology and causality. What cannot be brought under either of these categories is absolutely hidden to the human mind. An event not open to an interpretation by one of these two principles is for man inconceivable and mysterious. Change can be conceived as the outcome either of the operation of mechanistic causality or of purposeful behavior; for the human mind there is no third way available.[9] It is true, as has already been mentioned, that teleology can be viewed as a variety of causality. But the establishment of this fact does not annul the essential differences between the two categories.

The panmechanistic world view is committed to a methodological monism; it acknowledges only mechanistic causality because it attributes to it alone any cognitive value or at least a higher cognitive value than to teleology. This is a metaphysical superstition. Both principles of cognition — causality and teleology — are, owing to the limitations of human reason, imperfect and do not convey ultimate knowledge. Causality leads to a *regressus in infinitum* which reason can never exhaust. Teleology is found wanting as soon as the question is raised of what moves the prime mover. Either method stops short at an ultimate given which cannot be analyzed and interpreted. Reasoning and scientific inquiry can never bring full ease of mind, apodictic certainty, and perfect cognition of all things. He who seeks

9. Cf. Karel Engliš, *Begründung der Teleologie als Form des empirischen Erkennens* (Brünn, 1930), pp. 15 ff.

this must apply to faith and try to quiet his conscience by embracing a creed or a metaphysical doctrine.

If we do not transcend the realm of reason and experience, we cannot help acknowledging that our fellow men act. We are not free to disregard this fact for the sake of a fashionable prepossession and an arbitrary opinion. Daily experience proves not only that the sole suitable method for studying the conditions of our nonhuman environment is provided by the category of causality; it proves no less convincingly that our fellow men are acting beings as we ourselves are. For the comprehension of action there is but one scheme of interpretation and analysis available, namely, that provided by the cognition and analysis of our own purposeful behavior.

The problem of the study and analysis of other people's action is in no way connected with the problem of the existence of a *soul* or of an *immortal soul*. As far as the objections of empiricism, behaviorism, and positivism are directed against any variety of the soul-theory, they are of no avail for our problem. The question we have to deal with is whether it is possible to grasp human action intellectually if one refuses to comprehend it as meaningful and purposeful behavior aiming at the attainment of definite ends. Behaviorism and positivism want to apply the methods of the empirical natural sciences to the reality of human action. They interpret it as a response to stimuli. But these stimuli themselves are not open to description by the methods of the natural sciences. Every attempt to describe them must refer to the meaning which acting men attach to them. We may call the offering of a commodity for sale a "stimulus." But what is essential in such an offer and distinguishes it from other offers cannot be described without entering into the meaning which the acting parties attribute to the situation. No dialectical artifice can spirit away the fact that man is driven by the aim to attain certain ends. It is this purposeful behavior — viz., action — that is the subject matter of our science. We cannot approach our subject if we disregard the meaning which acting man attaches to the situation, i.e., the given state of affairs, and to his own behavior with regard to this situation.

It is not appropriate for the physicist to search for final causes because there is no indication that the events which are the subject matter of physics are to be interpreted as the outcome of actions of a being, aiming at ends in a human way. Nor is it appropriate for the praxeologist to disregard the operation of the acting being's volition and intention; they are undoubtedly given facts. If he were to disregard it, he would cease to study human action. Very often — but not always — the events concerned can be investigated both from the point of view of praxeology and from that of the natural sciences. But he who deals with the discharging of a firearm from the physical and chemical point of view is not a praxeologist. He neglects the very problems which the science of purposeful human behavior aims to clarify.

On the Serviceableness of Instincts

The proof of the fact that only two avenues of approach are available for human research, causality or teleology, is provided by the problems raised in reference to the serviceableness of instincts. There are types of behavior which on the one hand cannot be thoroughly interpreted with the casual methods of the natural sciences, but on the other hand cannot be considered as purposeful human action. In order to grasp such behavior we are forced to resort to a makeshift. We assign to it the character of a quasi-action; we speak of serviceable instincts.

We observe two things: first the inherent tendency of a living organism to respond to a stimulus according to a regular pattern, and second the favorable effects of this kind of behavior for the strengthening or preservation of the organism's vital forces. If we were in a position to interpret such behavior as the outcome of purposeful aiming at certain ends, we would call it action and deal with it according to the teleological methods of praxeology. But as we found no trace of a conscious mind behind this behavior, we suppose that an unknown factor—we call it *instinct*—was instrumental. We say that the instinct directs quasi-purposeful animal behavior and unconscious but nonetheless serviceable responses of human muscles and nerves. Yet, the mere fact that we hypostatize the unexplained element of this behavior as a force and call it instinct does not enlarge our knowledge. We must never forget that this word instinct is nothing but a landmark to indicate a point beyond which we are unable, up to the present at least, to carry our scientific scrutiny.

Biology has succeeded in discovering a "natural," i.e., mechanistic, explanation for many processes which in earlier days were attributed to the operation of instincts. Nonetheless many others have remained which cannot be interpreted as mechanical or chemical responses to mechanical or chemical stimuli. Animals display attitudes which cannot be comprehended otherwise than through the assumption that a directing factor was operative.

The aim of behaviorism to study human action from without with the methods of animal psychology is illusory. As far as animal behavior goes beyond mere physiological processes like breathing and metabolism, it can only be investigated with the aid of the meaning-concepts developed by praxeology. The behaviorist approaches the object of his investigations with the human notions of purpose and success. He unwittingly applies to the subject matter of his studies the human concepts of serviceableness and perniciousness. He deceives himself in excluding all verbal reference to consciousness and aiming at ends. In fact his mind searches everywhere for ends and measures every attitude with the yardstick of a garbled notion of serviceableness. The science of human behavior—as far as it is not physiology—cannot abandon reference to meaning and purpose. It cannot learn anything from animal psychology and the observation of the unconscious reactions of newborn infants. It is, on the contrary, animal psychology and infant psychology which cannot renounce the aid afforded by the science of human action. Without praxeological categories we would be at a loss to conceive and to understand the behavior both of animals and of infants.

The observation of the instinctive behavior of animals fills man with astonishment and raises questions which nobody can answer satisfactorily. Yet the fact that animals and even plants react in a quasi-purposeful way is neither more nor less miraculous than that man thinks and acts, that in the inorganic universe those functional correspondences prevail which physics describes, and that in the organic universe biological processes occur. All this is miraculous in the sense that it is an ultimate given for our searching mind.

Such an ultimate given is also what we call animal instinct. Like the concepts of motion, force, life, and consciousness, the concept of instinct too is merely a term to signify an ultimate given. To be sure, it neither "explains" anything nor indicates a cause or an ultimate cause.[10]

The Absolute End

In order to avoid any possible misinterpretation of the praxeological categories it seems expedient to emphasize a truism.

Praxeology, like the historical sciences of human action, deals with purposeful *human action*. If it mentions *ends*, what it has in view is the ends at which acting men aim. If it speaks of *meaning*, it refers to the meaning which acting men attach to their actions.

Praxeology and history are manifestations of the human mind and as such are conditioned by the intellectual abilities of mortal men. Praxeology and history do not pretend to know anything about the intentions of an absolute and objective mind, about an objective meaning inherent in the course of events and of historical evolution, and about the plans which God or Nature or Weltgeist or Manifest

10. "La vie est une cause première qui nous échappe comme toutes les causes premières et dont la science expérimentale n'a pas à se préoccuper." Claude Bernard, *La Science expérimentale* (Paris, 1878), p. 137. [Life is a first cause which eludes us, as all first causes do, and with which experimental science does not have to concern itself.]

Destiny is trying to realize in directing the universe and human affairs. They have nothing in common with what is called philosophy of history. They do not, like the works of Hegel, Comte, Marx, and a host of other writers, claim to reveal information about the true, objective, and absolute meaning of life and history.[11]

Vegetative Man

Some philosophies advise men to seek as the ultimate end of conduct the complete renunciation of any action. They look upon life as an absolute evil full of pain, suffering, and anguish, and apodictically deny that any purposeful human effort can render it tolerable. Happiness can be attained only by complete extinction of consciousness, volition, and life. The only way toward bliss and salvation is to become perfectly passive, indifferent, and inert like the plants. The sovereign good is the abandonment of thinking and acting.

Such is the essence of the teachings of various Indian philosophies, especially of Buddhism, and of Schopenhauer. Praxeology does not comment upon them. It is neutral with regard to all judgments of value and the choice of ultimate ends. Its task is not to approve or to disapprove, but to describe what is.

The subject matter of praxeology is human action. It deals with acting man, not with man transformed into a plant and reduced to a merely vegetative existence.

11. On the philosophy of history, cf. Mises, *Theory and History* (New Haven, 1957), pp. 159 ff.

CHAPTER 2

The Epistemological Problems
of the Sciences of Human Action

1	Praxeology and History

There are two main branches of the sciences of human action: praxeology and
history.

History is the collection and systematic arrangement of all the data of experience concerning human action. It deals with the concrete content of human action. It studies all human endeavors in their infinite multiplicity and
variety and all individual actions with all their accidental, special, and particular implications. It scrutinizes the ideas guiding acting men and the outcome
of the actions performed. It embraces every aspect of human activities. It is on
the one hand general history and on the other hand the history of various narrower fields. There is the history of political and military action, of ideas and
philosophy, of economic activities, of technology, of literature, art, and science, of religion, of mores and customs, and of many other realms of human
life. There is ethnology and anthropology, as far as they are not a part of biology, and there is psychology as far as it is neither physiology nor epistemology
nor philosophy. There is linguistics as far as it is neither logic nor the physiology of speech.[1]

The subject matter of all historical sciences is the past. They cannot
teach us anything which would be valid for all human actions, that
is, for the future too. The study of history makes a man wise

1. Economic history, descriptive economics, and economic statistics are, of course, history. The
term *sociology* is used in two different meanings. Descriptive sociology deals with those historical
phenomena of human action which are not viewed in descriptive economics; it overlaps to some
extent the field claimed by ethnology and anthropology. General sociology, on the other hand, approaches historical experience from a more nearly universal point of view than that of the other
branches of history. History proper, for instance, deals with an individual town or with towns in a
definite period or with an individual people or with a certain geographical area. Max Weber in
his main treatise (*Wirtschaft und Gesellschaft* [Tübingen, 1922], pp. 513–600) deals with the town
in general, i.e., with the whole historical experience concerning towns without any limitation to
historical periods, geographical areas, or individual peoples, nations, races, and civilizations.

and judicious. But it does not by itself provide any knowledge and skill which could be utilized for handling concrete tasks.

The natural sciences too deal with past events. Every experience is an experience of something passed away; there is no experience of future happenings. But the experience to which the natural sciences owe all their success is the experience of the experiment in which the individual elements of change can be observed in isolation. The facts amassed in this way can be used for induction, a peculiar procedure of inference which has given pragmatic evidence of its expediency, although its satisfactory epistemological characterization is still an unsolved problem.

The experience with which the sciences of human action have to deal is always an experience of complex phenomena. No laboratory experiments can be performed with regard to human action. We are never in a position to observe the change in one element only, all other conditions of the event remaining unchanged. Historical experience as an experience of complex phenomena does not provide us with facts in the sense in which the natural sciences employ this term to signify isolated events tested in experiments. The information conveyed by historical experience cannot be used as building material for the construction of theories and the prediction of future events. Every historical experience is open to various interpretations, and is in fact interpreted in different ways.

The postulates of positivism and kindred schools of metaphysics are therefore illusory. It is impossible to reform the sciences of human action according to the pattern of physics and the other natural sciences. There is no means to establish an a posteriori theory of human conduct and social events. History can neither prove nor disprove any general statement in the manner in which the natural sciences accept or reject a hypothesis on the ground of laboratory experiments. Neither experimental verification nor experimental falsification of a general proposition is possible in its field.

Complex phenomena in the production of which various causal chains are interlaced cannot test any theory. Such phenomena, on the contrary, become intelligible only through an interpretation in terms of theories previously developed from other sources. In the case of natural phenomena the interpretation of an event must not be at variance with the theories satisfactorily verified by experiments. In the case of historical events there is no such restriction. Commentators would be free to resort to quite arbitrary explanations. Where there is something to explain, the human mind has never been at a loss to invent ad hoc some imaginary theories, lacking any logical justification.

In the field of human history a limitation similar to that which the experimentally tested theories enjoin upon the attempts to interpret and elucidate individual physical, chemical, and physiological events is provided by praxeology. Praxeology is a theoretical and systematic, not a historical, science. Its scope is human action as such, irrespective of all environmental, accidental, and individual circumstances of the concrete acts. Its cognition is purely formal and general without reference to the material content and the particular features of the actual case. It aims at knowledge valid for all instances in which the conditions exactly correspond to those implied in its assumptions and inferences. Its statements and propositions are not derived from experience. They are, like those of logic and mathematics, a priori. They are not subject to verification or falsification on the ground of experience and facts. They are both logically and temporally antecedent to any comprehension of historical facts. They are a necessary requirement of any intellectual grasp of historical events. Without them we should not be able to see in the course of events anything else than kaleidoscopic change and chaotic muddle.

2   The Formal and Aprioristic Character of Praxeology

A fashionable tendency in contemporary philosophy is to deny the existence of any a priori knowledge. All human knowledge, it is contended, is derived from experience. This attitude can easily be understood as an excessive reaction against the extravagances of theology and a spurious philosophy of history and of nature. Metaphysicians were eager to discover by intuition moral precepts, the meaning of historical evolution, the properties of soul and matter, and the laws governing physical, chemical, and physiological events. Their volatile speculations manifested a blithe disregard for matter-of-fact knowledge. They were convinced that, without reference to experience, reason could explain all things and answer all questions.

The modern natural sciences owe their success to the method of observation and experiment. There is no doubt that empiricism and pragmatism are right as far as they merely describe the procedures of the natural sciences. But it is no less certain that they are entirely wrong in their endeavors to reject any kind of a priori knowledge and to characterize logic, mathematics, and praxeology either as empirical and experimental disciplines or as mere tautologies.

With regard to praxeology the errors of the philosophers are due to their complete ignorance of economics[2] and very often to their shockingly insufficient knowledge of history. In the eyes of the philosopher the treatment of philosophical issues is a sublime and noble vocation which must not be put upon the low level of other gainful employments. The professor resents the fact that he derives an income from philosophizing; he is offended by the thought that he earns money like the artisan and the farmhand. Monetary matters are mean things, and the philosopher investigating the eminent problems of truth and absolute eternal values should not soil his mind by paying attention to problems of economics.

The problem of whether there are or whether there are not a priori elements of thought—i.e., necessary and ineluctable intellectual conditions of thinking, anterior to any actual instance of conception and experience— must not be confused with the genetic problem of how man acquired his characteristically human mental ability. Man is descended from nonhuman ancestors who lacked this ability. These ancestors were endowed with some potentiality which in the course of ages of evolution converted them into reasonable beings. This transformation was achieved by the influence of a changing cosmic environment operating upon succeeding generations. Hence the empiricist concludes that the fundamental principles of reasoning are an outcome of experience and represent an adaptation of man to the conditions of his environment.

This idea leads, when consistently followed, to the further conclusion that there were between our prehuman ancestors and *Homo sapiens* various intermediate stages. There were beings which, although not yet equipped with the human faculty of reason, were endowed with some rudimentary elements of ratiocination. Theirs was not yet a logical mind, but a prelogical (or rather imperfectly logical) mind. Their desultory and defective logical functions evolved step by step from the prelogical state toward the logical state. Reason, intellect, and logic are historical phenomena. There is a history of logic as there is a history of technology. Nothing suggests that logic as we know it is the last and final stage of intellectual evolution. Human logic is a historical phase between prehuman nonlogic on the one

2. Hardly any philosopher had a more universal familiarity with various branches of contemporary knowledge than Bergson. Yet a casual remark in his last great book clearly proves that Bergson was completely ignorant of the fundamental theorem of the modern theory of value and exchange. Speaking of exchange he remarks "l'on ne peut le pratiquer sans s'être demandé si les deux objets échangés sont bien de même valeur, c'est-à-dire échangeables contre un même troisième." (*Les Deux Sources de la morale et de la religion* [Paris, 1932], p. 68.) [One cannot practice it [exchange] without having asked himself whether the two objects exchanged are goods of the same value, that is to say [goods] exchangeable for a third [good] with the very same value.]

hand and superhuman logic on the other hand. Reason and mind, the human beings' most efficacious equipment in their struggle for survival, are embedded in the continuous flow of zoological events. They are neither eternal nor unchangeable. They are transitory.

Furthermore, there is no doubt that every human being repeats in his personal evolution not only the physiological metamorphosis from a simple cell into a highly complicated mammal organism but no less the spiritual metamorphosis from a purely vegetative and animal existence into a reasonable mind. This transformation is not completed in the prenatal life of the embryo, but only later when the newborn child step by step awakens to human consciousness. Thus every man in his early youth, starting from the depths of darkness, proceeds through various states of the mind's logical structure.

Then there is the case of the animals. We are fully aware of the unbridgeable gulf separating our reason from the reactive processes of their brains and nerves. But at the same time we divine that forces are desperately struggling in them toward the light of comprehension. They are like prisoners anxious to break out from the doom of eternal darkness and inescapable automatism. We feel with them because we ourselves are in a similar position: pressing in vain against the limitation of our intellectual apparatus, striving unavailingly after unattainable perfect cognition.

But the problem of the a priori is of a different character. It does not deal with the problem of how consciousness and reason have emerged. It refers to the essential and necessary character of the logical structure of the human mind.

The fundamental logical relations are not subject to proof or disproof. Every attempt to prove them must presuppose their validity. It is impossible to explain them to a being who would not possess them on his own account. Efforts to define them according to the rules of definition must fail. They are primary propositions antecedent to any nominal or real definition. They are ultimate unanalyzable categories. The human mind is utterly incapable of imagining logical categories at variance with them. No matter how they may appear to superhuman beings, they are for man inescapable and absolutely necessary. They are the indispensable prerequisite of perception, apperception, and experience.

They are no less an indispensable prerequisite of memory. There is a tendency in the natural sciences to describe memory as an instance of a more general phenomenon. Every living organism conserves the effects of earlier stimulation, and the present state of inorganic matter is shaped by the effects of all the influences to which it was exposed in the past. The present state of the universe is the product of its past. We may, therefore, in a loose metaphorical sense, say that the geological structure of our globe conserves the memory of all earlier cosmic changes, and that a man's body is the sedimentation of his ancestors' and his own destinies and vicissitudes. But memory is something entirely different from the fact of the structural unity and continuity of cosmic evolution. It is a phenomenon of consciousness and as such conditioned by the logical a priori. Psychologists have been puzzled by the fact that man does not remember anything from the time of his existence as an embryo and as a suckling. Freud tried to explain this absence of recollection as brought about by suppression of undesired reminiscences. The truth is that there is nothing to be remembered of unconscious states. Animal automatism and unconscious response to physiological stimulations are neither for embryos and sucklings nor for adults material for remembrance. Only conscious states can be remembered.

The human mind is not a tabula rasa on which the external events write their own history. It is equipped with a set of tools for grasping reality. Man acquired these tools, i.e., the logical structure of his mind, in the course of his evolution from an amoeba to his present state. But these tools are logically prior to any experience.

Man is not only an animal totally subject to the stimuli unavoidably determining the circumstances of his life. He is also an acting being. And the category of action is logically antecedent to any concrete act.

The fact that man does not have the creative power to imagine categories at variance with the fundamental logical relations and with the principles of causality and teleology enjoins upon us what may be called *methodological apriorism*.

Everybody in his daily behavior again and again bears witness to the immutability and universality of the categories of thought and action. He who addresses fellow men, who wants to inform and convince them, who asks questions and answers other people's questions, can proceed in this way only because he can appeal to something common to all men — namely, the logical structure of human reason. The idea that A could at the same time be *non*-A or that to prefer A to B could at the same time be to prefer B to A is simply inconceivable and absurd to a human mind. We are not in the position to comprehend any kind of prelogical or metalogical thinking. We cannot think of a world without causality and teleology.

It does not matter for man whether or not beyond the sphere accessible to the human mind there are other spheres in which there is something categorially different from human thinking and acting. No knowledge from such spheres penetrates to the human mind. It is idle to ask whether things-in-themselves are different from what they appear to us, and whether there are worlds which we cannot divine and ideas which we cannot comprehend. These are problems beyond the scope of human cognition. Human knowledge is conditioned by the structure of the human mind. If it chooses human action as the subject matter of its inquiries, it cannot mean anything else than the categories of action which are proper to the human mind and are its projection into the external world of becoming and change. All the theorems of praxeology refer only to these categories of action and are valid only in the orbit of their operation. They do not pretend to convey any information about never dreamed of and unimaginable worlds and relations.

Thus praxeology is human in a double sense. It is human because it claims for its theorems, within the sphere precisely defined in the underlying assumptions, universal validity for all human action. It is human moreover because it deals only with human action and does not aspire to know anything about nonhuman—whether subhuman or superhuman—action.

The Alleged Logical Heterogeneity of Primitive Man

It is a general fallacy to believe that the writings of Lucien Lévy-Bruhl give support to the doctrine that the logical structure of mind of primitive man was and is categorially different from that of civilized man. On the contrary, what Lévy-Bruhl, on the basis of a careful scrutiny of the entire ethnological material available, reports about the mental functions of primitive man proves clearly that the fundamental logical relations and the categories of thought and action play in the intellectual activities of savages the same role they play in our own life. The content of primitive man's thoughts differs from the content of our thoughts, but the formal and logical structure is common to both.

It is true that Lévy-Bruhl himself maintains that the mentality of primitive peoples is essentially "mystic and prelogical" in character; primitive man's collective representations are regulated by the "law of participation" and are consequently indifferent to the law of contradiction. However, Lévy-Bruhl's distinction between prelogical and logical thinking refers to the content and not to the form and categorial structure of thinking. For he declares that also among peoples like ourselves ideas and relations between ideas governed by the "law of participation" exist, more or less independently, more or less impaired, but yet ineradicable, side by side, with those subject to the law of reasoning. "The prelogical and the mystic are co-existent with the logical."[3]

Lévy-Bruhl relegates the essential teachings of Christianity to the realm of the prelogical mind.[4] Now, many objections can possibly be raised and have been raised against the Christian doctrines and their interpretation by theology. But nobody ever ventured to contend that the Christian fathers and philosophers — among them St. Augustine and St. Thomas — had minds whose logical structure was categorially different from that of our contemporaries. The dispute between a man who believes in miracles and another who does not refers to the content of thought, not to its logical form. A man who tries to demonstrate the possibility and reality of miracles may err. But to unmask his error is — as the brilliant essays of Hume and Mill show — certainly no less logically intricate than to explode any philosophical or economic fallacy.

Explorers and missionaries report that in Africa and Polynesia primitive man stops short at his earliest perception of things and never reasons if he can in any way avoid it.[5] European and American educators sometimes report the same of their students. With regard to the Mossi on the Niger Lévy-Bruhl quotes a missionary's observation: "Conversation with them turns only upon women, food, and (in the rainy season) the crops."[6] What other subjects did many contemporaries and neighbors of Newton, Kant, and Lévy-Bruhl prefer?

The conclusion to be drawn from Lévy-Bruhl's studies is best expressed in his own words: "The primitive mind, like our own, is anxious to find the reasons for what happens, but it does not seek these in the same direction as we do."[7]

A peasant eager to get a rich crop may — according to the content of his ideas — choose various methods. He may perform some magical rites, he may embark upon a pilgrimage, he may offer a candle to the image of his patron saint, or he may employ more and better fertilizer. But whatever he does, it is always action, i.e., the employment of means for the attainment of ends. Magic is in a broader sense a variety of technology. Exorcism is a deliberate purposeful action based on a world view which most of our contemporaries condemn as superstitious and therefore as inappropriate. But the concept of action does not imply that the action is guided by a correct theory and a technology promising success and that it attains the end aimed at. It only implies that the performer of the action believes that the means applied will produce the desired effect.

3. Lévy-Bruhl, *How Natives Think*, trans. by L. A. Clare (New York, 1932), p. 386.
4. *Ibid.*, p. 377.
5. Lévy-Bruhl, *Primitive Mentality*, trans. by L. A. Clare (New York, 1923), pp. 27–29.
6. *Ibid.*, p. 27.
7. *Ibid.*, p. 437.

No facts provided by ethnology or history contradict the assertion that the logical structure of mind is uniform with all men of all races, ages, and countries.[8]

3　The A Priori and Reality

Aprioristic reasoning is purely conceptual and deductive. It cannot produce anything else but tautologies and analytic judgments. All its implications are logically derived from the premises and were already contained in them. Hence, according to a popular objection, it cannot add anything to our knowledge.

All geometrical theorems are already implied in the axioms. The concept of a rectangular triangle already implies the theorem of Pythagoras. This theorem is a tautology, its deduction results in an analytic judgment. Nonetheless nobody would contend that geometry in general and the theorem of Pythagoras in particular do not enlarge our knowledge. Cognition from purely deductive reasoning is also creative and opens for our mind access to previously barred spheres. The significant task of aprioristic reasoning is on the one hand to bring into relief all that is implied in the categories, concepts, and premises and, on the other hand, to show what they do not imply. It is its vocation to render manifest and obvious what was hidden and unknown before.[9]

In the concept of money all the theorems of monetary theory are already implied. The quantity theory does not add to our knowledge anything which is not virtually contained in the concept of money. It transforms, develops, and unfolds; it only analyzes and is therefore tautological like the theorem of Pythagoras in relation to the concept of the rectangular triangle. However, nobody would deny the cognitive value of the quantity theory. To a mind not enlightened by economic reasoning it remains unknown. A long line of abortive attempts to solve the problems concerned shows that it was certainly not easy to attain the present state of knowledge.

It is not a deficiency of the system of aprioristic science that it does not convey to us full cognition of reality. Its concepts and theorems are mental tools opening the approach to a complete grasp of reality; they are, to be sure, not in themselves already the totality of factual knowledge about all things. Theory and the comprehension

8. Cf. the brilliant statements of Ernst Cassirer, *Philosophie der symbolischen Formen* (Berlin, 1925), II, 78.
9. Science, says Meyerson, is "l'acte per lequel nous ramenons à l'identique ce qui nous a, tout d'abord, paru n'être pas tel." (*De l'Explication dans les sciences* [Paris, 1927], p. 154.) Cf. also Morris R. Cohen, *A Preface to Logic* (New York, 1944), pp. 11–14. [the process by which we are led back to the very thing which, at first, did not seem to us to be so]

of living and changing reality are not in opposition to one another. Without theory, the general aprioristic science of human action, there is no comprehension of the reality of human action.

The relation between reason and experience has long been one of the fundamental philosophical problems. Like all other problems of the critique of knowledge, philosophers have approached it only with reference to the natural sciences. They have ignored the sciences of human action. Their contributions have been useless for praxeology.

It is customary in the treatment of the epistemological problems of economics to adopt one of the solutions suggested for the natural sciences. Some authors recommend Poincaré's conventionalism.[10] They regard the premises of economic reasoning as a matter of linguistic or postulational convention.[11] Others prefer to acquiesce in ideas advanced by Einstein. Einstein raises the question: "How can mathematics, a product of human reason that does not depend on any experience, so exquisitely fit the objects of reality? Is human reason able to discover, unaided by experience through pure reasoning the features of real things?" And his answer is: "As far as the theorems of mathematics refer to reality, they are not certain, and as far as they are certain, they do not refer to reality."[12]

However, the sciences of human action differ radically from the natural sciences. All authors eager to construct an epistemological system of the sciences of human action according to the pattern of the natural sciences err lamentably.

The real thing which is the subject matter of praxeology, human action, stems from the same source as human reasoning. Action and reason are congeneric and homogeneous; they may even be called two different aspects of the same thing. That reason has the power to make clear through pure ratiocination the essential features of action is a consequence of the fact that action is an offshoot of reason. The theorems attained by correct praxeological reasoning are not only perfectly certain and incontestable, like the correct mathematical theorems. They refer, moreover, with the full rigidity of their apodictic certainty and incontestability to the reality of action as it appears in life and history. Praxeology conveys exact and precise knowledge of real things.

The starting point of praxeology is not a choice of axioms and a decision about methods of procedure, but reflection about the essence of action. There is no action in which the praxeological categories

10. Henri Poincaré, *La Science et l'hypothèse* (Paris, 1918), p. 69.
11. Felix Kaufmann, *Methodology of the Social Sciences* (London, 1944), pp. 46–47.
12. Albert Einstein, *Geometrie und Erfahrung* (Berlin, 1923), p. 3.

do not appear fully and perfectly. There is no mode of action thinkable in which means and ends or costs and proceeds cannot be clearly distinguished and precisely separated. There is nothing which only approximately or incompletely fits the economic category of an exchange. There are only exchange and nonexchange; and with regard to any exchange all the general theorems concerning exchanges are valid in their full rigidity and with all their implications. There are no transitions from exchange to nonexchange or from direct exchange to indirect exchange. No experience can ever be had which would contradict these statements.

Such an experience would be impossible in the first place for the reason that all experience concerning human action is conditioned by the praxeological categories and becomes possible only through their application. If we had not in our mind the schemes provided by praxeological reasoning, we should never be in a position to discern and to grasp any action. We would perceive motions, but neither buying nor selling, nor prices, wage rates, interest rates, and so on. It is only through the utilization of the praxeological scheme that we become able to have an experience concerning an act of buying and selling, but then independently of the fact of whether or not our senses concomitantly perceive any motions of men and of nonhuman elements of the external world. Unaided by praxeological knowledge we would never learn anything about media of exchange. If we approach coins without such preexisting knowledge, we would see in them only round plates of metal, nothing more. Experience concerning money requires familiarity with the praxeological category *medium of exchange.*

Experience concerning human action differs from that concerning natural phenomena in that it requires and presupposes praxeological knowledge. This is why the methods of the natural sciences are inappropriate for the study of praxeology, economics, and history.

In asserting the a priori character of praxeology we are not drafting a plan for a future new science different from the traditional sciences of human action. We do not maintain that the theoretical science of human action should be aprioristic, but that it is and always has been so. Every attempt to reflect upon the problems raised by human action is necessarily bound to aprioristic reasoning. It does not make any difference in this regard whether the men discussing a problem are theorists aiming at pure knowledge only or statesmen, politicians, and regular citizens eager to comprehend occurring changes and to discover what kind of public policy or private conduct would best suit their own interests. People may begin arguing about the significance of any concrete experience, but the debate inevitably turns away from the accidental and environmental features of the event concerned to an analysis of fundamental principles, and imperceptibly abandons any reference to the factual happenings which evoked the argument. The history of the natural sciences is a record of theories and hypotheses discarded because they were disproved by experience. Remember for instance the fallacies of older mechanics disproved by Galileo or the fate of the phlogiston theory. No such case is recorded by the history of economics. The champions of logically incompatible theories claim the same events as the proof that their point of view has been tested by experience. The truth is that the experience of a complex phenomenon—and there is no other experience in the realm of human action—can always be interpreted on the ground of various antithetic theories. Whether the interpretation is considered satisfactory or unsatisfactory depends on the appreciation of the theories in question established beforehand on the ground of aprioristic reasoning.[13]

History cannot teach us any general rule, principle, or law. There is no means to abstract from a historical experience a posteriori any theories or theorems concerning human conduct and policies. The data of history would be nothing but a clumsy accumulation of disconnected occurrences, a heap of confusion, if they could not be clarified, arranged, and interpreted by systematic praxeological knowledge.

4   The Principle of Methodological Individualism

Praxeology deals with the actions of individual men. It is only in the further course of its inquiries that cognition of human cooperation is attained and social action is treated as a special case of the more universal category of human action as such.

This methodological individualism has been vehemently attacked by various metaphysical schools and disparaged as a nominalistic fallacy. The notion of an individual, say the critics, is an empty abstraction. Real man is necessarily always a member of a social whole. It is even impossible to imagine the existence of a man separated from the rest of mankind and not connected with society. Man as man is the product of a social evolution. His most eminent feature, reason, could only emerge within the framework of social mutuality. There is no thinking which does not depend on the concepts and notions of

13. Cf. E. P. Cheyney, *Law in History and Other Essays* (New York, 1927), p. 27.

language. But speech is manifestly a social phenomenon. Man is always the member of a collective. As the whole is both logically and temporally prior to its parts or members, the study of the individual is posterior to the study of society. The only adequate method for the scientific treatment of human problems is the method of universalism or collectivism.

Now the controversy whether the whole or its parts are logically prior is vain. Logically the notions of a whole and its parts are correlative. As logical concepts they are both apart from time.

No less inappropriate with regard to our problem is the reference to the antagonism of realism and nominalism, both these terms being understood in the meaning which medieval scholasticism attached to them. It is uncontested that in the sphere of human action social entities have real existence. Nobody ventures to deny that nations, states, municipalities, parties, religious communities, are real factors determining the course of human events. Methodological individualism, far from contesting the significance of such collective wholes, considers it as one of its main tasks to describe and to analyze their becoming and their disappearing, their changing structures, and their operation. And it chooses the only method fitted to solve this problem satisfactorily.

First we must realize that all actions are performed by individuals. A collective operates always through the intermediary of one or several individuals whose actions are related to the collective as the secondary source. It is the meaning which the acting individuals and all those who are touched by their action attribute to an action, that determines its character. It is the meaning that marks one action as the action of an individual and another action as the action of the state or of the municipality. The hangman, not the state, executes a criminal. It is the meaning of those concerned that discerns in the hangman's action an action of the state. A group of armed men occupies a place. It is the meaning of those concerned which imputes this occupation not to the officers and soldiers on the spot, but to their nation. If we scrutinize the meaning of the various actions performed by individuals we must necessarily learn everything about the actions of collective wholes. For a social collective has no existence and reality outside of the individual members' actions. The life of a collective is lived in the actions of the individuals constituting its body. There is no social collective conceivable which is not operative in the actions of some individuals. The reality of a social integer consists in its directing and releasing definite actions on the part of individuals. Thus the way to a cognition of collective wholes is through an analysis of the individuals' actions.

As a thinking and acting being man emerges from his prehuman existence already as a social being. The evolution of reason, language, and cooperation is the outcome of the same process; they were inseparably and necessarily linked together. But this process took place in individuals. It consisted in changes in the behavior of individuals. There is no other substance in which it occurred than the individuals. There is no substratum of society other than the actions of individuals.

That there are nations, states, and churches, that there is social cooperation under the division of labor, becomes discernible only in the actions of certain individuals. Nobody ever perceived a nation without perceiving its members. In this sense one may say that a social collective comes into being through the actions of individuals. That does not mean that the individual is temporally antecedent. It merely means that definite actions of individuals constitute the collective.

There is no need to argue whether a collective is the sum resulting from the addition of its elements or more, whether it is a being *sui generis*, and whether it is reasonable or not to speak of its will, plans, aims, and actions and to attribute to it a distinct "soul." Such pedantic talk is idle. A collective whole is a particular aspect of the actions of various individuals and as such a real thing determining the course of events.

It is illusory to believe that it is possible to visualize collective wholes. They are never visible; their cognition is always the outcome of the understanding of the meaning which acting men attribute to their acts. We can see a crowd, i.e., a multitude of people. Whether this crowd is a mere gathering or a mass (in the sense in which this term is used in contemporary psychology) or an organized body or any other kind of social entity is a question which can only be answered by understanding the meaning which they themselves attach to their presence. And this meaning is always the meaning of individuals. Not our senses, but understanding, a mental process, makes us recognize social entities.

Those who want to start the study of human action from the collective units encounter an insurmountable obstacle in the fact that an individual at the same time can belong and—with the exception of the most primitive tribesmen—really belongs to various collective entities. The problems raised by the multiplicity of coexisting social units and their mutual antagonisms can be solved only by methodological individualism.[14]

14. See below, pp. 145–53, the critique of the collectivist theory of society.

I and *We*

The *Ego* is the unity of the acting being. It is unquestionably given and cannot be dissolved or conjured away by any reasoning or quibbling.

The *We* is always the result of a summing up which puts together two or more *Egos*. If somebody says *I*, no further questioning is necessary in order to establish the meaning. The same is valid with regard to the *Thou* and, provided the person in view is precisely indicated, with regard to the *He*. But if a man says *We*, further information is needed to denote who the Egos are who are comprised in this *We*. It is always single individuals who say *We*; even if they say it in chorus, it yet remains an utterance of single individuals.

The *We* cannot act otherwise than each of them acting on his own behalf. They can either all act together in accord, or one of them may act for them all. In the latter case the cooperation of the others consists in their bringing about the situation which makes one man's action effective for them too. Only in this sense does the officer of a social entity act for the whole; the individual members of the collective body either cause or allow a single man's action to concern them too.

The endeavors of psychology to dissolve the *Ego* and to unmask it as an illusion are idle. The praxeological *Ego* is beyond any doubts. No matter what a man was and what he may become later, in the very act of choosing and acting he is an *Ego*.

From the *pluralis logicus* (and from the merely *ceremonial pluralis majestaticus*) we must distinguish the *pluralis gloriosus*. If a Canadian who never tried skating says, "We are the world's foremost ice hockey players," or if an Italian boor proudly contends, "We are the world's most eminent painters," nobody is fooled. But with reference to political and economic problems the *pluralis gloriosus* evolves into the *pluralis imperialis* and as such plays a significant role in paving the way for the acceptance of doctrines determining international economic policies.

5   The Principle of Methodological Singularism

No less than from the action of an individual praxeology begins its investigations from the individual action. It does not deal in vague terms with human action in general, but with concrete action which a definite man has performed at a definite date and at a definite place. But, of course, it does not concern itself with the accidental and environmental features of this action and with what distinguishes it from all other actions, but only with what is necessary and universal in its performance.

The philosophy of universalism has from time immemorial blocked access to a satisfactory grasp of praxeological problems, and contemporary universalists are utterly incapable of finding an approach to them. Universalism, collectivism, and conceptual realism see only wholes and universals. They speculate about mankind, nations, states, classes, about virtue and vice, right and wrong, about entire classes of wants and of commodities. They ask, for instance: Why is the value of "gold" higher than that of "iron"? Thus they never find solutions, but antinomies and paradoxes only. The best-known instance is the value-paradox which frustrated even the work of the classical economists.

Praxeology asks: What happens in acting? What does it mean to say that an individual then and there, today and here, at any time and at any place, acts? What results if he chooses one thing and rejects another?

The act of choosing is always a decision among various opportunities open to the choosing individual. Man never chooses between virtue and vice, but only between two modes of action which we call from an adopted point of view virtuous or vicious. A man never chooses between "gold" and "iron" in general, but always only between a definite quantity of gold and a definite quantity of iron. Every single action is strictly limited in its immediate consequences. If we want to reach correct conclusions, we must first of all look at these limitations.

Human life is an unceasing sequence of single actions. But the single action is by no means isolated. It is a link in a chain of actions which together form an action on a higher level aiming at a more distant end. Every action has two aspects. It is on the one hand a partial action in the framework of a further-stretching action, the performance of a fraction of the aims set by a more far-reaching action. It is on the other hand itself a whole with regard to the actions aimed at by the performance of its own parts.

It depends upon the scope of the project on which acting man is intent at the instant whether the more far-reaching action or a partial action directed to a more immediate end only is thrown into relief. There is no need for praxeology to raise questions of the type of those raised by *Gestaltpsychologie*. The road to the performance of great things must always lead through the performance of partial tasks. A cathedral is something other than a heap of stones joined together. But the only procedure for constructing a cathedral is to lay one stone upon another. For the architect the whole project is the main thing. For the mason it is the single wall, and for the brick-layer the single stones. What counts for praxeology is the fact that the only method to achieve greater tasks is to build from the foundations step by step, part by part.

6   The Individual and Changing Features of Human Action

The content of human action, i.e., the ends aimed at and the means chosen and applied for the attainment of these ends, is determined by the personal qualities of every acting man. Individual man is the product of a long line of zoological evolution which has shaped his physiological inheritance. He is born the offspring and the heir of his ancestors, and the precipitate and sediment of all that his forefathers experienced are his biological patrimony. When he is born, he does not enter the world in general as such, but a definite environment. The innate and inherited biological qualities and all that life has worked upon him make a man what he is at any instant of his pilgrimage. They are his fate and destiny. His will is not "free" in the metaphysical sense of this term. It is determined by his background and all the influences to which he himself and his ancestors were exposed.

Inheritance and environment direct a man's actions. They suggest to him both the ends and the means. He lives not simply as man *in abstracto*; he lives as a son of his family, his race, his people, and his age; as a citizen of his country; as a member of a definite social group; as a practitioner of a certain vocation; as a follower of definite religious, metaphysical, philosophical, and political ideas; as a partisan in many feuds and controversies. He does not himself create his ideas and standards of value; he borrows them from other people. His ideology is what his environment enjoins upon him. Only very few men have the gift of thinking new and original ideas and of changing the traditional body of creeds and doctrines.

Common man does not speculate about the great problems. With regard to them he relies upon other people's authority, he behaves as "every decent fellow must behave," he is like a sheep in the herd. It is precisely this intellectual inertia that characterizes a man as a common man. Yet the common man does choose. He chooses to adopt traditional patterns or patterns adopted by other people because he is convinced that this procedure is best fitted to achieve his own welfare. And he is ready to change his ideology and consequently his mode of action whenever he becomes convinced that this would better serve his own interests.

Most of a man's daily behavior is simple routine. He performs certain acts without paying special attention to them. He does many things because he was trained in his childhood to do them, because other people behave in the same way, and because it is customary in his environment. He acquires habits, he develops automatic reactions. But he indulges in these habits only because he welcomes their effects. As soon as he discovers that the pursuit of the habitual way may hinder the attainment of ends considered as more desirable, he changes his attitude. A man brought up in an area in which the water is clean acquires the habit of heedlessly drinking, washing, and bathing. When he moves to a place in which the water is polluted by morbific germs, he will devote the most careful attention to procedures about which he never bothered before. He will watch himself permanently in order not to hurt himself by indulging unthinkingly in his traditional routine and his automatic reactions. The fact that an action is in the regular course of affairs performed spontaneously, as it were, does not mean that it is not due to a conscious volition and to a deliberate choice. Indulgence in a routine which possibly could be changed is action.

Praxeology is not concerned with the changing content of acting, but with its pure form and its categorial structure. The study of the accidental and environmental features of human action is the task of history.

7   The Scope and the Specific Method of History

The study of all the data of experience concerning human action is the scope of history. The historian collects and critically sifts all available documents. On the ground of this evidence he approaches his genuine task.

It has been asserted that the task of history is to show how events actually happened, without imposing presuppositions and values (*wertfrei*, i.e., neutral with regard to all value judgments). The historian's report should be a faithful image of the past, an intellectual photograph, as it were, giving a complete and unbiased description of all facts. It should reproduce before our intellectual eye the past with all its features.

Now, a real reproduction of the past would require a duplication not humanly possible. History is not an intellectual reproduction, but a condensed representation of the past in conceptual terms. The historian does not simply let the events speak for themselves. He arranges them from the aspect of the ideas underlying the formation of the general notions he uses in their presentation. He does not report facts as they happened, but only *relevant* facts. He does not approach the documents without presuppositions, but equipped with the whole apparatus of his age's scientific knowledge, that is, with all the teachings of contemporary logic, mathematics, praxeology, and natural science.

It is obvious that the historian must not be biased by any prejudices and party tenets. Those writers who consider historical events as an arsenal of weapons for the conduct of their party feuds are not historians but propagandists and apologists. They are not eager to acquire knowledge but to justify the program of their parties. They are fighting for the dogmas of a metaphysical, religious, national, political or social doctrine. They usurp the name of history for their writings as a blind in order to deceive the credulous. A historian must first of all aim at cognition. He must free himself from any partiality. He must in this sense be neutral with regard to any value judgments.

This postulate of *Wertfreiheit* [(German) neutrality with respect to values] can easily be satisfied in the field of the aprioristic sciences — logic, mathematics, and praxeology — and in the field of the experimental natural sciences. It is logically not difficult to draw a sharp line between a scientific, unbiased treatment of these disciplines and a treatment distorted by superstition, preconceived ideas, and passion. It is much more difficult to comply with the requirement of valuational neutrality in history. For the subject matter of history, the concrete accidental and environmental content of human action, is value judgments and their projection into the reality of change. At every step of his activities the historian is concerned with value judgments. The value judgments of the men whose actions he reports are the substratum of his investigations.

It has been asserted that the historian himself cannot avoid judgments of value. No historian — not even the naïve chronicler or newspaper reporter — registers all facts as they happen. He must discriminate, he must select some events which he deems worthy of being registered and pass over in silence other events. This choice, it is said, implies in itself a value judgment. It is necessarily conditioned by the historian's world view and thus not impartial but an outcome of preconceived ideas. History can never be anything else than distortion of facts; it can never be really scientific, that is neutral with regard to values and intent only upon discovering truth.

There is, of course, no doubt that the discretion which the selection of facts places in the hands of the historian can be abused. It can and does happen that the historian's choice is guided by party bias. However, the problems involved are much more intricate than this popular doctrine would have us believe. Their solution must be sought on the ground of a much more thorough scrutiny of the methods of history.

In dealing with a historical problem the historian makes use of all the knowledge provided by logic, mathematics, the natural sciences, and especially by praxeology. However, the mental tools of these nonhistorical disciplines do not suffice for his task. They are indispensable auxiliaries for him, but in themselves they do not make it possible to answer those questions he has to deal with.

The course of history is determined by the actions of individuals and by the effects of these actions. The actions are determined by the value judgments of the acting individuals, i.e., the ends which they were eager to attain, and by the means which they applied for the attainment of these ends. The choice of the means is an outcome of the whole body of technological knowledge of the acting individuals. It is in many instances possible to appreciate the effects of the means applied from the point of view of praxeology or of the natural sciences. But there remain a great many things for the elucidation of which no such help is available.

The specific task of history for which it uses a specific method is the study of these value judgments and of the effects of the actions as far as they cannot be analyzed by the teachings of all other branches of knowledge. The historian's genuine problem is always to interpret things as they happened. But he cannot solve this problem on the ground of the theorems provided by all other sciences alone. There always remains at the bottom of each of his problems something which resists analysis at the hand of these teachings of other sciences. It is these individual and unique characteristics of each event which are studied by the *understanding*.

The uniqueness or individuality which remains at the bottom of every historical fact, when all the means for its interpretation provided by logic, mathematics, praxeology, and the natural sciences have been exhausted, is an ultimate datum. But whereas the natural sciences cannot say anything about their ultimate data than that they are such, history can try to make its ultimate data intelligible. Although it is impossible to reduce them to their causes — they would not be ultimate data if such a reduction were possible — the historian can understand them because he is himself a human being. In the philosophy of Bergson this understanding is called an intuition, viz., *"la sympathie par laquelle on se transporte a l'intérieur d'un objet pour coïncider avec ce qu'il a d'unique et par conséquent d'inexprimable."*[15] [The sympathy with which one enters inside an object in order to identify thereby what it has that is unique and therefore inexpressible.]" German epistemology calls this act *das spezifische Verstehen der*

15. Henri Bergson, *La Pensée et le mouvant* (4th ed. Paris, 1934), p. 205.

Geisteswissenschaften [the specific understanding of the moral sciences.] or simply *Verstehen* [understanding]. It is the method which all historians and all other people always apply in commenting upon human events of the past and in forecasting future events. The discovery and the delimitation of understanding was one of the most important contributions of modern epistemology. It is, to be sure, neither a project for a new science which does not yet exist and is to be founded nor the recommendation of a new method of procedure for any of the already existing sciences.

The understanding must not be confused with approval, be it only conditional and circumstantial. The historian, the ethnologist, and the psychologist sometimes register actions which are for their feelings simply repulsive and disgusting; they understand them only as actions, i.e., in establishing the underlying aims and the technological and praxeological methods applied for their execution. To understand an individual case does not mean to justify or to excuse it.

Neither must understanding be confused with the act of aesthetic enjoyment of a phenomenon. Empathy (*Einfühlung*) and understanding are two radically different attitudes. It is a different thing, on the one hand, to understand a work of art historically, to determine its place, its meaning, and its importance in the flux of events, and, on the other hand, to appreciate it emotionally as a work of art. One can look at a cathedral with the eyes of a historian. But one can look at the same cathedral either as an enthusiastic admirer or as an unaffected and indifferent sightseer. The same individuals are capable of both modes of reaction, of the aesthetic appreciation and of the scientific grasp of understanding.

The understanding establishes the fact that an individual or a group of individuals have engaged in a definite action emanating from definite value judgments and choices and aiming at definite ends, and that they have applied for the attainment of these ends definite means suggested by definite technological, therapeutical, and praxeological doctrines. It furthermore tries to appreciate the effects and the intensity of the effects brought about by an action; it tries to assign to every action its relevance, i.e., its bearing upon the course of events.

The scope of understanding is the mental grasp of phenomena which cannot be totally elucidated by logic, mathematics, praxeology, and the natural sciences to the extent that they cannot be cleared up by all these sciences. It must never contradict the teachings of these other branches of knowledge.[16] The real corporeal existence of the

16. Cf. Ch. V. Langlois and Ch. Seignobos, *Introduction to the Study of History*, trans. by G. G. Berry (London, 1925), pp. 205–8.

devil is attested by innumerable historical documents which are rather reliable in all other regards. Many tribunals in due process of law have on the basis of the testimony of witnesses and the confessions of defendants established the fact that the devil had carnal intercourse with witches. However, no appeal to understanding could justify a historian's attempt to maintain that the devil really existed and interfered with human events otherwise than in the visions of an excited human brain.

While this is generally admitted with regard to the natural sciences, there are some historians who adopt another attitude with regard to economic theory. They try to oppose to the theorems of economics an appeal to documents allegedly proving things incompatible with these theorems. They do not realize that complex phenomena can neither prove nor disprove any theorem and therefore cannot bear witness against any statement of a theory. Economic history is possible only because there is an economic theory capable of throwing light upon economic actions. If there were no economic theory, reports concerning economic facts would be nothing more than a collection of unconnected data open to any arbitrary interpretation.

8   Conception and Understanding

The task of the sciences of human action is the comprehension of the meaning and relevance of human action. They apply for this purpose two different epistemological procedures: conception and understanding. Conception is the mental tool of praxeology; understanding is the specific mental tool of history.

The cognition of praxeology is conceptual cognition. It refers to what is necessary in human action. It is cognition of universals and categories.

The cognition of history refers to what is unique and individual in each event or class of events. It analyzes first each object of its studies with the aid of the mental tools provided by all other sciences. Having achieved this preliminary work, it faces its own specific problem: the elucidation of the unique and individual features of the case by means of the understanding.

As was mentioned above, it has been asserted that history can never be scientific because historical understanding depends on the historian's subjective value judgments. Understanding, it is maintained, is only a euphemistic term for arbitrariness. The writings of historians are always one-sided and partial; they do not report the facts; they distort them.

It is, of course, a fact that we have historical books written from various points of view. There are histories of the Reformation written from the Catholic point of view and others written from the Protestant point of view. There are "proletarian" histories and "bourgeois" histories, Tory historians and Whig historians; every nation, party, and linguistic group has its own historians and its own ideas about history.

But the problem which these differences of interpretation offer must not be confused with the intentional distortion of facts by propagandists and apologists parading as historians. Those facts which can be established in an unquestionable way on the ground of the source material available must be established as the preliminary work of the historian. This is not a field for understanding. It is a task to be accomplished by the employment of the tools provided by all nonhistorical sciences. The phenomena are gathered by cautious critical observation of the records available. As far as the theories of the nonhistorical sciences on which the historian grounds his critical examination of the sources are reasonably reliable and certain, there cannot be any arbitrary disagreement with regard to the establishment of the phenomena as such. What a historian asserts is either correct or contrary to fact, is either proved or disproved by the documents available, or vague because the sources do not provide us with sufficient information. The experts may disagree, but only on the ground of a reasonable interpretation of the evidence available. The discussion does not allow any arbitrary statements.

However, the historians very often do not agree with regard to the teachings of the nonhistorical sciences. Then, of course, disagreement with regard to the critical examination of the records and to the conclusions to be drawn from them can ensue. An unbridgeable conflict arises. But its cause is not an arbitrariness with regard to the concrete historical phenomenon. It stems from an undecided issue referring to the nonhistorical sciences.

An ancient Chinese historian could report that the emperor's sin brought about a catastrophic drought and that rain fell again when the ruler had atoned for his sin. No modern historian would accept such a report. The underlying meteorological doctrine is contrary to uncontested fundamentals of contemporary natural science. But no such unanimity exists in regard to many theological, biological, and economic issues. Accordingly historians disagree.

A supporter of the racial doctrine of Nordic-Aryanism will disregard as fabulous and simply unbelievable any report concerning intellectual and moral achievements of "inferior" races. He will treat such reports in the same way in which all modern historians deal with the above-mentioned Chinese report. No agreement with regard to any phenomenon of the history of Christianity can be attained between people for whom the gospels are Holy Writ and people in whose eyes they are human documents. Catholic and Protestant historians disagree about many questions of fact because they start from different theological ideas. A Mercantilist or Neo-Mercantilist must necessarily be at variance with an economist. An account of German monetary history in the years 1914 to 1923 is conditioned by the author's monetary doctrines. The facts of the French Revolution are presented in a quite different manner by those who believe in the sacred rights of the anointed king and those who hold other views.

The historians disagree on such issues not in their capacity as historians, but in their application of the nonhistorical sciences to the subject matter of history. They disagree as agnostic doctors disagree, in regard to the miracles of Lourdes, with the members of the medical committee for the collection of evidence concerning these miracles. Only those who believe that facts write their own story into the tabula rasa of the human mind blame the historians for such differences of opinion. They fail to realize that history can never be studied without presuppositions, and that dissension with regard to the presuppositions, i.e., the whole content of the nonhistorical branches of knowledge, must determine the establishment of historical facts.

These presuppositions also determine the historian's decision concerning the choice of facts to be mentioned and those to be omitted as irrelevant. In searching for the causes of a cow's not giving milk a modern veterinarian will disregard entirely all reports concerning a witch's evil eye; his view would have been different three hundred years ago. In the same way the historian selects from the indefinite multitude of events that preceded the fact he is dealing with those which could have contributed to its emergence — or have delayed it — and neglects those which, according to his grasp of the nonhistorical sciences, could not have influenced it.

Changes in the teachings of the nonhistorical sciences consequently must involve a rewriting of history. Every generation must treat anew the same historical problems because they appear to it in a different light. The theological world view of older times led to a treatment of history other than the theorems of modern natural science. Subjective economics produces historical works very different from those based on mercantilist doctrines. As far as divergences in the books of historians stem from these disagreements, they are not an outcome of alleged vagueness and precariousness in historical studies. They are, on the contrary, the result of the lack of unanimity in the realm of those other sciences which are popularly called certain and exact.

To avoid any possible misunderstanding it is expedient to emphasize some further points. The divergences referred to above must not be confused:

1. With purposeful ill-intentioned distortion of facts.
2. With attempts to justify or to condemn any actions from a legal or moral point of view.
3. With the merely incidental insertion of remarks expressing value judgments in a strictly objective representation of the state of affairs. A treatise on bacteriology does not lose its objectivity if the author, accepting the human viewpoint, considers the preservation of human life as an ultimate end and, applying this standard, labels effective methods of fighting germs good and fruitless methods bad. A germ writing such a book would reverse these judgments, but the material content of its book would not differ from that of the human bacteriologist. In the same way a European historian dealing with the Mongol invasions of the thirteenth century may speak of "favorable" and "unfavorable" events because he takes the standpoint of the European defenders of Western civilization. But this approval of one party's standard of value need not necessarily interfere with the material content of his study. It may—from the viewpoint of contemporary knowledge—be absolutely objective. A Mongolian historian could endorse it completely but for such casual remarks.
4. With a representation of one party's action in diplomatic or military antagonisms. The clash of conflicting groups can be dealt with from the point of view of the ideas, motives, and aims which impelled either side's acts. For a full comprehension of what happened it is necessary to take account of what was done on both sides. The outcome was the result of the interaction of both parties. But in order to understand their actions the historian must try to see things as they appeared to the acting men at the critical time, not only as we see them now from the point of view of our present-day knowledge. A history of Lincoln's policy in the weeks and months preceding the outbreak of the Civil War is of course incomplete. But no historical study is complete. Regardless of whether the historian sympathizes with the Unionists or with the Confederates or whether he is

absolutely neutral, he can deal in an objective way with Lincoln's policy in the spring of 1861. Such an investigation is an indispensable preliminary to answering the broader question of how the Civil War broke out.

Now finally, having settled these problems, it is possible to attack the genuine question: Is there any subjective element in historical understanding, and, if so, in what manner does it determine the result of historical studies?

As far as the task of understanding is to establish the facts that people were motivated by definite value judgments and aimed at definite ends, there cannot be any disagreement among true historians, i.e., people intent upon cognition of past events. There may be uncertainty because of the insufficient information provided by the sources available. But this has nothing to do with understanding. It refers to the preliminary work to be achieved by the historian.

But understanding has a second task to fulfill. It must appraise the effects and the intensity of the effects brought about by an action; it must deal with the relevance of each motive and each action.

Here we are faced with one of the main differences between physics and chemistry on the one hand and the sciences of human action on the other. In the realm of physical and chemical events there exist (or, at least, it is generally assumed that there exist) constant relations between magnitudes, and man is capable of discovering these constants with a reasonable degree of precision by means of laboratory experiments. No such constant relations exist in the field of human action outside of physical and chemical technology and therapeutics. For some time economists believed that they had discovered such a constant relation in the effects of changes in the quantity of money upon commodity prices. It was asserted that a rise or fall in the quantity of money in circulation must result in proportional changes of commodity prices. Modern economics has clearly and irrefutably exposed the fallaciousness of this statement.[17] Those economists who want to substitute "quantitative economics" for what they call "qualitative economics" are utterly mistaken. There are, in the field of economics, no constant relations, and consequently no measurement is possible. If a statistician determines that a rise of 10 per cent in the supply of potatoes in Atlantis at a definite time was followed by a fall of 8 per cent in the price, he does not establish anything about what happened or may happen with a change in the supply of potatoes in another country or at another time. He has not "measured"

17. See below, pp. 412–14.

the "elasticity of demand" of potatoes. He has established a unique and individual historical fact. No intelligent man can doubt that the behavior of men
with regard to potatoes and every other commodity is variable. Different individuals value the same things in a different way, and valuations change with
the same individuals with changing conditions.[18]

Outside of the field of economic history nobody every ventured to maintain
that constant relations prevail in human history. It is a fact that in the armed
conflicts fought in the past between Europeans and backward peoples of other
races, one European soldier was usually a match for several native fighters.
But nobody was ever foolish enough to "measure" the magnitude of European
superiority.

The impracticability of measurement is not due to the lack of technical
methods for the establishment of measure. It is due to the absence of constant relations. If it were only caused by technical insufficiency, at least an
approximate estimation would be possible in some cases. But the main fact
is that there are no constant relations. Economics is not, as ignorant positivists repeat again and again, backward because it is not "quantitative." It
is not quantitative and does not measure because there are no constants.
Statistical figures referring to economic events are historical data. They tell
us what happened in a nonrepeatable historical case. Physical events can
be interpreted on the ground of our knowledge concerning constant relations established by experiments. Historical events are not open to such an
interpretation.

The historian can enumerate all the factors which cooperated in bringing
about a known effect and all the factors which worked against them and may
have resulted in delaying and mitigating the final outcome. But he cannot co-
ordinate, except by understanding, the various causative factors in a quantitative way to the effects produced. He cannot, except by understanding, assign
to each of n factors its role in producing the effect P. Understanding is in the
realm of history the equivalent, as it were, of quantitative analysis and measurement.

Technology can tell us how thick a steel plate must be in order
not to be pierced by a bullet fired at a distance of 300 yards from a
Winchester rifle. It can thus answer the question why a man who
took shelter behind a steel plate of a known thickness was hurt or
not hurt by a shot fired. History is at a loss to explain with the same
assurance why there was a rise in the price of milk of 10 per cent or

18. Cf. below, p. 351.

why President Roosevelt defeated Governor Dewey in the election of 1944 or why France was from 1870 to 1940 under a republican constitution. Such problems do not allow any treatment other than that of understanding.

To every historical factor understanding tries to assign its relevance. In the exercise of understanding there is no room for arbitrariness and capriciousness. The freedom of the historian is limited by his endeavor to provide a satisfactory explanation of reality. His guiding star must be the search for truth. But there necessarily enters into understanding an element of subjectivity. The understanding of the historian is always tinged with the marks of his personality. It reflects the mind of its author.

The a priori sciences—logic, mathematics, and praxeology—aim at a knowledge unconditionally valid for all beings endowed with the logical structure of the human mind. The natural sciences aim at a cognition valid for all those beings which are not only endowed with the faculty of human reason but with human senses. The uniformity of human logic and sensation bestows upon these branches of knowledge the character of universal validity. Such at least is the principle guiding the study of the physicists. Only in recent years have they begun to see the limits of their endeavors and, abandoning the excessive pretensions of older physicists, discovered the "uncertainty principle." They realize today that there are unobservables whose unobservability is a matter of epistemological principle.[19]

Historical understanding can never produce results which must be accepted by all men. Two historians who fully agree with regard to the teachings of the nonhistorical sciences and with regard to the establishment of the facts as far as they can be established without recourse to the understanding of relevance, may disagree in their understanding of the relevance of these facts. They may fully agree in establishing that the factors a, b, and c worked together in producing the effect P; nonetheless they can widely disagree with regard to the relevance of the respective contributions of a, b, and c to the final outcome. As far as understanding aims at assigning its relevance to each factor, it is open to the influence of subjective judgments. Of course, these are not judgments of value, they do not express preferences of the historian. They are judgments of relevance.[20]

19. Cf. A. Eddington, *The Philosophy of Physical Science* (New York, 1939), pp. 28–48.
20. As this is not a dissertation on general epistemology, but the indispensable foundation of a treatise of economics, there is no need to stress the analogies between the understanding of historical relevance and the tasks to be accomplished by a diagnosing physician. The epistemology of biology is outside of the scope of our inquiries.

Historians may disagree for various reasons. They may hold different views with regard to the teachings of the nonhistorical sciences; they may base their reasoning on a more or less complete familiarity with the records; they may differ in the understanding of the motives and aims of the acting men and of the means applied by them. All these differences are open to a settlement by "objective" reasoning; it is possible to reach a universal agreement with regard to them. But as far as historians disagree with regard to judgments of relevance it is impossible to find a solution which all sane men must accept.

The intellectual methods of science do not differ in kind from those applied by the common man in his daily mundane reasoning. The scientist uses the same tools which the layman uses; he merely uses them more skillfully and cautiously. Understanding is not a privilege of the historians. It is everybody's business. In observing the conditions of his environment everybody is a historian. Everybody uses understanding in dealing with the uncertainty of future events to which he must adjust his own actions. The distinctive reasoning of the speculator is an understanding of the relevance of the various factors determining future events. And—let us emphasize it even at this early point of our investigations—action necessarily always aims at future and therefore uncertain conditions and thus is always speculation. Acting man looks, as it were, with the eyes of a historian into the future.

Natural History and Human History

Cosmogony, geology, and the history of biological changes are historical disciplines as they deal with unique events of the past. However, they operate exclusively with the epistemological methods of the natural sciences and have no need for understanding. They must sometimes take recourse to only approximate estimates of magnitudes. But such estimates are not judgments of relevance. They are a less perfect method of determining quantitative relations than is "exact" measurement. They must not be confused with the state of affairs in the field of human action which is characterized by the absence of constant relations.

If we speak of history, what we have in mind is only the history of human action, whose specific mental tool is understanding.

The assertion that modern natural science owes all its achievements to the experimental method is sometimes assailed by referring to astronomy. Now, modern astronomy is essentially an application of the physical laws, experimentally discovered on the earth, to the celestial bodies. In earlier days astronomy was mainly based on the assumption that the movements of the celestial bodies would not change their course. Copernicus and Kepler simply tried to guess in what kind of curve the earth moves around the sun. As the circle was considered the "most perfect" curve, Copernicus chose it for his theory. Later, by similar guesswork, Kepler substituted the ellipse for the circle. Only since Newton's discoveries has astronomy become a natural science in the strict sense.

9   On Ideal Types

History deals with unique and unrepeatable events, with the irreversible flux of human affairs. A historical event cannot be described without reference to the persons involved and to the place and date of its occurrence. As far as a happening can be narrated without such a reference, it is not a historical event but a fact of the natural sciences. The report that Professor X on February 20, 1945, performed a certain experiment in his laboratory is an account of a historical event. The physicist believes that he is right in abstracting from the person of the experimenter and the date and place of the experiment. He relates only those circumstances which, in his opinion, are relevant for the production of the result achieved and, when repeated, will produce the same result again. He transforms the historical event into a *fact* of the empirical natural sciences. He disregards the active interference of the experimenter and tries to imagine him as an indifferent observer and relater of unadulterated reality. It is not the task of praxeology to deal with the epistemological issues of this philosophy.

Although unique and unrepeatable, historical events have one common feature: they are human action. History comprehends them as human actions; it conceives their meaning by the instrumentality of praxeological cognition and understands their meaning in looking at their individual and unique features. What counts for history is always the meaning of the men concerned: the meaning that they attach to the state of affairs they want to alter, the meaning they attach to their actions, and the meaning they attach to the effects produced by the actions.

The aspect from which history arranges and assorts the infinite multiplicity of events is their meaning. The only principle which it applies for the systemization of its objects — men, ideas, institutions, social entities, and artifacts — is meaning affinity. According to meaning affinity it arranges the elements into ideal types.

Ideal types are specific notions employed in historical research and in the representation of its results. They are concepts of understanding. As such they are entirely different from praxeological categories and concepts and from the concepts of the natural sciences. An ideal type is not a class concept, because its description does not indicate the marks whose presence definitely and unambiguously determines class membership. An ideal type cannot be defined; it must be characterized by an enumeration of those features whose presence by and large decides whether in a concrete instance we are or are not faced with a specimen belonging to the ideal type in question. It is peculiar to the ideal type that not all its characteristics need to be present in any one example. Whether or not the absence of some characteristics prevents the inclusion of a concrete specimen in the ideal type in question, depends on a relevance judgment by understanding. The ideal type itself is an outcome of an understanding of the motives, ideas, and aims of the acting individuals and of the means they apply.

An ideal type has nothing at all to do with statistical means and averages. Most of the characteristics concerned are not open to a numerical determination, and for this reason alone they could not enter into a calculation of averages. But the main reason is to be seen in something else. Statistical averages denote the behavior of the members of a class or a type, already constituted by means of a definition or characterization referring to other marks, with regard to features not referred to in the definition or characterization. The membership of the class or type must be known before the statistician can start investigating special features and use the result of this investigation for the establishment of an average. We can establish the average age of the United States Senators or we can reckon averages concerning the behavior of an age class of the population with regard to a special problem. But it is logically impossible to make the membership of a class or type depend upon an average.

No historical problem can be treated without the aid of ideal types. Even when the historian deals with an individual person or with a single event, he cannot avoid referring to ideal types. If he speaks of Napoleon, he must refer to such ideal types as commander, dictator, revolutionary leader; and if he deals with the French Revolution he must refer to ideal types such as revolution, disintegration of an established regime, anarchy. It may be that the reference to an ideal type consists merely in rejecting its applicability to the case in question. But all historical events are described and interpreted by means of ideal types. The layman too, in dealing with events of the past or of the future, must always make use of ideal types and unwittingly always does so.

Whether or not the employment of a definite ideal type is expedient and conducive to an adequate grasp of phenomena can only be decided by un-derstanding. It is not the ideal type that determines the mode of understand-ing; it is the mode of understanding that requires the construction and use of corresponding ideal types.

The ideal types are constructed with the use of ideas and concepts devel-oped by all nonhistorical branches of knowledge. Every cognition of history is, of course, conditioned by the findings of the other sciences, depends upon them, and must never contradict them. But historical knowledge has another subject matter and another method than these other sciences, and they in turn have no use for understanding. Thus the ideal types must not be confused with concepts of the nonhistorical sciences. This is valid also with regard to the praxeological categories and concepts. They provide, to be sure, the indis-pensable mental tools for the study of history. However, they do not refer to the understanding of the unique and individual events which are the subject mat-ter of history. An ideal type can therefore never be a simple adoption of a prax-eological concept.

It happens in many instances that a term used by praxeology to signify a praxeological concept serves to signify an ideal type for the historian. Then the historian uses *one* word for the expression of two different things. He applies the term sometimes to signify its praxeological connotation, but more often to signify an ideal type. In the latter case the historian attaches to the word a meaning different from its praxeological meaning; he trans-forms it by transferring it to a different field of inquiry. The economic con-cept "entrepreneur" belongs to a stratum other than the ideal type "entre-preneur" as used by economic history and descriptive economics. (On a third stratum lies the legal term "entrepreneur.") The economic term "en-trepreneur" is a precisely defined concept which in the framework of a the-ory of market economy signifies a clearly integrated function.[21] The histori-cal ideal type "entrepreneur" does not include the same members. Nobody in using it thinks of shoeshine boys, cab drivers who own their cars, small businessmen, and small farmers. What economics establishes with regard to entrepreneurs is rigidly valid for all members of the class without any re-gard to temporal and geographical conditions and to the various branches of business. What economic history establishes for its ideal types can differ according to the particular circumstances of various ages, countries, branches of business, and many other conditions. History has little use for a general ideal type of entrepreneur. It is more concerned with such types as: the American entrepreneur of the time of Jefferson, Ger-

21. See below, pp. 251–55.

man heavy industries in the age of William II, New England textile manufacturing in the last decades preceding the first World War, the Protestant *haute finance* of Paris, self-made entrepreneurs, and so on.

Whether the use of a definite ideal type is to be recommended or not depends entirely on the mode of understanding. It is quite common nowadays to employ two ideal types: Left-Wing Parties (Progressives) and Right-Wing Parties (Fascists). The former includes the Western democracies, some Latin American dictatorships, and Russian Bolshevism; the latter Italian Fascism and German Nazism. This typification is the outcome of a definite mode of understanding. Another mode would contrast Democracy and Dictatorship. Then Russian Bolshevism, Italian Fascism, and German Nazism belong to the ideal type of dictatorial government, and the Western systems to the ideal type of democratic government.

It was a fundamental mistake of the Historical School of *Wirtschaftliche Staatswissenschaften* in Germany and of Institutionalism in America to interpret economics as the characterization of the behavior of an ideal type, the *Homo oeconomicus*. According to this doctrine traditional or orthodox economics does not deal with the behavior of man as he really is and acts, but with a fictitious or hypothetical image. It pictures a being driven exclusively by "economic" motives, i.e., solely by the intention of making the greatest possible material or monetary profit. Such a being, say these critics, does not have and never did have a counterpart in reality; it is a phantom of a spurious armchair philosophy. No man is exclusively motivated by the desire to become as rich as possible; many are not at all influenced by this mean craving. It is vain to refer to such an illusory homunculus in dealing with life and history.

Even if this really were the meaning of classical economics, the *Homo oeconomicus* would certainly not be an ideal type. The ideal type is not an embodiment of one side or aspect of man's various aims and desires. It is always the representation of complex phenomena of reality, either of men, of institutions, or of ideologies.

The classical economists sought to explain the formation of prices. They were fully aware of the fact that prices are not a product of the activities of a special group of people, but the result of an interplay of all members of the market society. This was the meaning of their statement that demand and supply determine the formation of prices. However, the classical economists failed in their endeavors to provide a satisfactory theory of value. They were at a loss to find a solution for the apparent paradox of value. They were puzzled by

THE EPISTEMOLOGICAL PROBLEMS OF HUMAN ACTION ～ 63

the alleged paradox that "gold" is more highly valued than "iron," although the latter is more "useful" than the former. Thus they could not construct a general theory of value and could not trace back the phenomena of market exchange and of production to their ultimate sources, the behavior of the consumers. This shortcoming forced them to abandon their ambitious plan to develop a general theory of human action. They had to satisfy themselves with a theory explaining only the activities of the businessman without going back to the choices of everybody as the ultimate determinants. They dealt only with the actions of businessmen eager to buy in the cheapest market and to sell in the dearest. The consumer was left outside the field of their theorizing. Later the epigones of classical economics explained and justified this insufficiency as an intentional and methodologically necessary procedure. It was, they asserted, the deliberate design of economists to restrict their investigations to only one aspect of human endeavor—namely, to the "economic" aspect. It was their intention to use the fictitious image of a man driven solely by "economic" motives and to neglect all others although they were fully aware of the fact that real men are driven by many other, "noneconomic" motives. To deal with these other motives, one group of these interpreters maintained, is not the task of economics but of other branches of knowledge. Another group admitted that the treatment of these "noneconomic" motives and their influence on the formation of prices was a task of economics also, but they believed that it must be left to later generations. It will be shown at a later stage of our investigations that this distinction between "economic" and "noneconomic" motives of human action is untenable.[22] At this point it is only important to realize that this doctrine of the "economic" side of human action utterly misrepresents the teachings of the classical economists. They never intended to do what this doctrine ascribes to them. They wanted to conceive the real formation of prices—not fictitious prices as they would be determined if men were acting under the sway of hypothetical conditions different from those really influencing them. The prices they try to explain and do explain—although without tracing them back to the choices of the consumers—are real market prices. The demand and supply of which they speak are real factors determined by all motives instigating men to buy or to sell. What was wrong with their theory was that they did not trace demand back to the choices of the consumers; they lacked a satisfactory theory of demand. But it was not their idea that demand as they used this concept in their dissertations was exclusively

22. See below, pp. 232–34 and 239–44.

determined by "economic" motives as distinguished from "noneconomic" motives. As they restricted their theorizing to the actions of businessmen, they did not deal with the motives of the ultimate consumers. Nonetheless their theory of prices was intended as an explanation of real prices irrespective of the motives and ideas instigating the consumers.

Modern subjective economics starts with the solution of the apparent paradox of value. It neither limits its theorems to the actions of businessmen alone nor deals with a fictitious *Homo oeconomicus*. It treats the inexorable categories of everybody's action. Its theorems concerning commodity prices, wage rates, and interest rates refer to all these phenomena without any regard to the motives causing people to buy or to sell or to abstain from buying or selling. It is time to discard entirely any reference to the abortive attempt to justify the shortcoming of older economists through the appeal to the *Homo oeconomicus* phantom.

10   The Procedure of Economics

The scope of praxeology is the explication of the category of human action. All that is needed for the deduction of all praxeological theorems is knowledge of the essence of human action. It is a knowledge that is our own because we are men; no being of human descent that pathological conditions have not reduced to a merely vegetative existence lacks it. No special experience is needed in order to comprehend these theorems, and no experience, however rich, could disclose them to a being who did not know *a priori* what human action is. The only way to a cognition of these theorems is logical analysis of our inherent knowledge of the category of action. We must bethink ourselves and reflect upon the structure of human action. Like logic and mathematics, praxeological knowledge is in us; it does not come from without.

All the concepts and theorems of praxeology are implied in the category of human action. The first task is to extract and to deduce them, to expound their implications and to define the universal conditions of acting as such. Having shown what conditions are required by any action, one must go further and define — of course, in a categorial and formal sense — the less general conditions required for special modes of acting. It would be possible to deal with this second task by delineating all thinkable conditions and deducing from them all inferences logically permissible. Such an all-comprehensive system would provide a theory referring not only to human action as it is under the conditions and circumstances given in the real world in which man lives and acts. It would deal no less with hypothetical acting such as would take place under the unrealizable conditions of imaginary worlds.

But the end of science is to know reality. It is not mental gymnastics or a logical pastime. Therefore praxeology restricts its inquiries to the study of acting under those conditions and presuppositions which are given in reality. It studies acting under unrealized and unrealizable conditions only from two points of view. It deals with states of affairs which, although not real in the present and past world, could possibly become real at some future date. And it examines unreal and unrealizable conditions if such an inquiry is needed for a satisfactory grasp of what is going on under the conditions present in reality.

However, this reference to experience does not impair the aprioristic character of praxeology and economics. Experience merely directs our curiosity toward certain problems and diverts it from other problems. It tells us what we should explore, but it does not tell us how we could proceed in our search for knowledge. Moreover, it is not experience but thinking alone which teaches us that, and in what instances, it is necessary to investigate unrealizable hypothetical conditions in order to conceive what is going on in the real world.

The disutility of labor is not of a categorial and aprioristic character. We can without contradiction think of a world in which labor does not cause uneasiness, and we can depict the state of affairs prevailing in such a world.[23] But the real world is conditioned by the disutility of labor. Only theorems based on the assumption that labor is a source of uneasiness are applicable for the comprehension of what is going on in this world.

Experience teaches that there is disutility of labor. But it does not teach it directly. There is no phenomenon that introduces itself as disutility of labor. There are only data of experience which are interpreted, on the ground of aprioristic knowledge, to mean that men consider leisure — i.e., the absence of labor — other things being equal, as a more desirable condition than the expenditure of labor. We see that men renounce advantages which they could get by working more — that is, that they are ready to make sacrifices for the attainment of leisure. We infer from this fact that leisure is valued as a good and that labor is regarded as a burden. But for previous praxeological insight, we would never be in a position to reach this conclusion.

A theory of indirect exchange and all further theories built upon it — as the theory of circulation credit — are applicable only to the interpretation of events within a world in which indirect exchange

___

23. See below, pp. 131–33.

is practiced. In a world of barter trade only it would be mere intellectual play. It is unlikely that the economists of such a world, if economic science could have emerged at all in it, would have given any thought to the problems of indirect exchange, money, and all the rest. In our actual world, however, such studies are an essential part of economic theory.

The fact that praxeology, in fixing its eye on the comprehension of reality, concentrates upon the investigation of those problems which are useful for this purpose, does not alter the aprioristic character of its reasoning. But it marks the way in which economics, up to now the only elaborated part of praxeology, presents the results of its endeavors.

Economics does not follow the procedure of logic and mathematics. It does not present an integrated system of pure aprioristic ratiocination severed from any reference to reality. In introducing assumptions into its reasoning, it satisfies itself that the treatment of the assumptions concerned can render useful services for the comprehension of reality. It does not strictly separate in its treatises and monographs pure science from the application of its theorems to the solution of concrete historical and political problems. It adopts for the organized presentation of its results a form in which aprioristic theory and the interpretation of historical phenomena are intertwined.

It is obvious that this mode of procedure is enjoined upon economics by the very nature and essence of its subject matter. It has given proof of its expediency. However, one must not overlook the fact that the manipulation of this singular and logically somewhat strange procedure requires caution and subtlety, and that uncritical and superficial minds have again and again been led astray by careless confusion of the two epistemologically different methods implied.

There are no such things as a historical method of economics or a discipline of institutional economics. There is economics and there is economic history. The two must never be confused. All theorems of economics are necessarily valid in every instance in which all the assumptions presupposed are given. Of course, they have no practical significance in situations where these conditions are not present. The theorems referring to indirect exchange are not applicable to conditions where there is no indirect exchange. But this does not impair their validity.[24]

The issue has been obfuscated by the endeavors of governments

24. Cf. F. H. Knight, *The Ethics of Competition and Other Essays* (New York, 1935), p. 139.

and powerful pressure groups to disparage economics and to defame the economists. Despots and democratic majorities are drunk with power. They must reluctantly admit that they are subject to the laws of nature. But they reject the very notion of economic law. Are they not the supreme legislators? Don't they have the power to crush every opponent? No war lord is prone to acknowledge any limits other than those imposed on him by a superior armed force. Servile scribblers are always ready to foster such complacency by expounding the appropriate doctrines. They call their garbled presumptions "historical economics." In fact, economic history is a long record of government policies that failed because they were designed with a bold disregard for the laws of economics.

It is impossible to understand the history of economic thought if one does not pay attention to the fact that economics as such is a challenge to the conceit of those in power. An economist can never be a favorite of autocrats and demagogues. With them he is always the mischief-maker, and the more they are inwardly convinced that his objections are well founded, the more they hate him.

In the face of all this frenzied agitation it is expedient to establish the fact that the starting point of all praxeological and economic reasoning, the category of human action, is proof against any criticisms and objections. No appeal to any historical or empirical considerations whatever can discover any fault in the proposition that men purposefully aim at certain chosen ends. No talk about irrationality, the unfathomable depths of the human soul, the spontaneity of the phenomena of life, automatisms, reflexes, and tropisms, can invalidate the statement that man makes use of his reason for the realization of wishes and desires. From the unshakable foundation of the category of human action praxeology and economics proceed step by step by means of discursive reasoning. Precisely defining assumptions and conditions, they construct a system of concepts and draw all the inferences implied by logically unassailable ratiocination. With regard to the results thus obtained only two attitudes are possible: either one can unmask logical errors in the chain of the deductions which produced these results, or one must acknowledge their correctness and validity.

It is vain to object that life and reality are not logical. Life and reality are neither logical nor illogical; they are simply given. But logic is the only tool available to man for the comprehension of both. It is vain to object that life and history are inscrutable and ineffable and that human reason can never penetrate to their inner core. The critics contradict themselves in uttering words about the ineffable and expounding theories — of course, spurious theories — about the unfathomable. There are many things beyond the reach of the human mind. But as far as man is able to attain any knowledge, however limited, he can use only one avenue of approach, that opened by reason.

No less illusory are the endeavors to play off understanding against the theorems of economics. The domain of historical understanding is exclusively the elucidation of those problems which cannot be entirely elucidated by the nonhistorical sciences. Understanding must never contradict the theories developed by the nonhistorical sciences. Understanding can never do anything but, on the one hand, establish the fact that people were motivated by certain ideas, aimed at certain ends, and applied certain means for the attainment of these ends, and, on the other hand, assign to the various historical factors their relevance so far as this cannot be achieved by the nonhistorical sciences. Understanding does not entitle the modern historian to assert that exorcism ever was an appropriate means to cure sick cows. Neither does it permit him to maintain that an economic law was not valid in ancient Rome or in the empire of the Incas.

Man is not infallible. He searches for truth — that is, for the most adequate comprehension of reality as far as the structure of his mind and reason makes it accessible to him. Man can never become omniscient. He can never be absolutely certain that his inquiries were not misled and that what he considers as certain truth is not error. All that man can do is to submit all his theories again and again to the most critical reexamination. This means for the economist to trace back all theorems to their unquestionable and certain ultimate basis, the category of human action, and to test by the most careful scrutiny all assumptions and inferences leading from this basis to the theorem under examination. It cannot be contended that this procedure is a guarantee against error. But it is undoubtedly the most effective method of avoiding error.

Praxeology — and consequently economics too — is a deductive system. It draws its strength from the starting point of its deductions, from the category of action. No economic theorem can be considered sound that is not solidly fastened upon this foundation by an irrefutable chain of reasoning. A statement proclaimed without such a connection is arbitrary and floats in midair. It is impossible to deal with a special segment of economics if one does not encase it in a complete system of action.

The empirical sciences start from singular events and proceed from the unique and individual to the more universal. Their treatment is subject to specialization. They can deal with segments without paying attention to the whole field. The economist must never be a specialist. In dealing with any problem he must always fix his glance upon the whole system.

Historians often sin in this respect. They are ready to invent theorems ad hoc. They sometimes fail to recognize that it is impossible to abstract any causal relations from the study of complex phenomena. Their pretension to investigate reality without any reference to what they disparage as preconceived ideas is vain. In fact they unwittingly apply popular doctrines long since unmasked as fallacious and contradictory.

11   The Limitations on Praxeological Concepts

The praxeological categories and concepts are devised for the comprehension of human action. They become self-contradictory and nonsensical if one tries to apply them in dealing with conditions different from those of human life. The naïve anthropomorphism of primitive religions is unpalatable to the philosophic mind. However, the endeavors of philosophers to define, by the use of praxeological concepts, the attributes of an absolute being, free from all the limitations and frailties of human existence, are no less questionable.

Scholastic philosophers and theologians and likewise Theists and Deists of the Age of Reason conceived an absolute and perfect being, unchangeable, omnipotent, and omniscient, and yet planning and acting, aiming at ends and employing means for the attainment of these ends. But action can only be imputed to a discontented being, and repeated action only to a being who lacks the power to remove his uneasiness once and for all at one stroke. An acting being is discontented and therefore not almighty. If he were contented, he would not act, and if he were almighty, he would have long since radically removed his discontent. For an all-powerful being there is no pressure to choose between various states of uneasiness; he is not under the necessity of acquiescing in the lesser evil. Omnipotence would mean the power to achieve everything and to enjoy full satisfaction without being restrained by any limitations. But this is incompatible with the very concept of action. For an almighty being the categories of ends and means do not exist. He is above all human comprehension, concepts, and understanding. For the almighty being every "means" renders unlimited services, he can apply every "means" for the attainment of any ends, he can achieve every end without the employment of any means. It is beyond the faculties of the human mind to think the concept of almightiness consistently to its ultimate logical consequences. The paradoxes are insoluble. Has the almighty being the power to achieve something which is immune to his later interference? If he has this power, then there are limits to his might and he is no longer almighty; if he lacks this power, he is by virtue of this fact alone not almighty.

Are omnipotence and omniscience compatible? Omniscience presupposes that all future happenings are already unalterably determined. If there is omniscience, omnipotence is inconceivable. Impotence to change anything in the predetermined course of events would restrict the power of any agent.

Action is a display of potency and control that are limited. It is a manifestation of man who is restrained by the circumscribed powers of his mind, the physiological nature of his body, the vicissitudes of his environment, and the scarcity of the external factors on which his welfare depends. It is vain to refer to the imperfections and weaknesses of human life if one aims at depicting something absolutely perfect. The very idea of absolute perfection is in every way self-contradictory. The state of absolute perfection must be conceived as complete, final, and not exposed to any change. Change could only impair its perfection and transform it into a less perfect state; the mere possibility that a change can occur is incompatible with the concept of absolute perfection. But the absence of change—i.e., perfect immutability, rigidity and immobility—is tantamount to the absence of life. Life and perfection are incompatible, but so are death and perfection.

The living is not perfect because it is liable to change; the dead is not perfect because it does not live.

The language of living and acting men can form comparatives and superlatives in comparing degrees. But absoluteness is not a degree; it is a limiting notion. The absolute is indeterminable, unthinkable and ineffable. It is a chimerical conception. There are no such things as perfect happiness, perfect men, eternal bliss. Every attempt to describe the conditions of a land of Cockaigne, or the life of the Angels, results in paradoxes. Where there are conditions, there are limitations and not perfection; there are endeavors to conquer obstacles, there are frustration and discontent.

After the philosophers had abandoned the search for the absolute, the utopians took it up. They weave dreams about the perfect state. They do not realize that the state, the social apparatus of compulsion and coercion, is an institution to cope with human imperfection and that its essential function is to inflict punishment upon minorities in order to protect majorities against the detrimental consequences of certain actions. With "perfect" men there would not be any need for compulsion and coercion. But utopians do not pay heed to human nature and the inalterable conditions of human life. Godwin thought that man might become immortal after the abolition of private property.[25] Charles Fourier babbled about the ocean containing lemonade instead of salt water.[26] Marx's economic system blithely ignored the fact of the scarcity of material factors of production. Trotsky revealed that in the proletarian paradise "the average human type will rise to the heights of an Aristotle, a Goethe, or a Marx. And above this ridge new peaks will rise."[27]

Nowadays the most popular chimeras are stabilization and security. We will test these catchwords later.

25. William Godwin, *An Enquiry Concerning Political Justice and Its Influence on General Virtue and Happiness* (Dublin, 1793), II, 393–403.
26. Charles Fourier, *Théorie des quatre mouvements* (Oeuvres complètes, 3d ed., Paris, 1846), I, 43.
27. Leon Trotsky, *Literature and Revolution*, trans. by R. Strunsky (London, 1925), p. 256.

CHAPTER 3

Economics and the Revolt Against Reason

1   The Revolt Against Reason

It is true that some philosophers were ready to overrate the power of human reason. They believed that man can discover by ratiocination the final causes of cosmic events, the inherent ends the prime mover aims at in creating the universe and determining the course of its evolution. They expatiated on the "Absolute" as if it were their pocket watch. They did not shrink from announcing eternal absolute values and from establishing moral codes unconditionally binding on all men.

Then there was the long line of utopian authors. They drafted schemes for an earthly paradise in which pure reason alone should rule. They failed to realize that what they called absolute reason and manifest truth was the fancy of their own minds. They blithely arrogated to themselves infallibility and often advocated intolerance, the violent oppression of all dissenters and heretics. They aimed at dictatorship either for themselves or for men who would accurately put their plans into execution. There was, in their opinion, no other salvation for suffering mankind.

There was Hegel. He was a profound thinker and his writings are a treasury of stimulating ideas. But he was laboring under the delusion that *Geist*, the Absolute, revealed itself through his words. There was nothing in the universe that was hidden to Hegel. It was a pity that his language was so ambiguous that it could be interpreted in various ways. The right-wing Hegelians interpreted it as an endorsement of the Prussian system of autocratic government and of the dogmas of the Prussian Church. The left-wing Hegelians read out of it atheism, intransigent revolutionary radicalism, and anarchistic doctrines.

There was Auguste Comte. He knew precisely what the future had in store for mankind. And, of course, he considered himself as the supreme legislator. For example, he regarded certain astronomical studies as useless and wanted to prohibit them. He planned to substitute a new religion for Christianity, and selected a lady who in this new church was destined to replace the Virgin. Comte can be exculpated, as he was insane in the full sense which pathology attaches to this term. But what about his followers?

Many more facts of this kind could be mentioned. But they are no argument against reason, rationalism, and rationality. These dreams have nothing at all to do with the question of whether or not reason is the right and only instrument available for man in his endeavors to attain as much knowledge as is accessible to him. The honest and conscientious truth-seekers have never pretended that reason and scientific research can answer all questions. They were fully aware of the limitations imposed upon the human mind. They cannot be taxed with responsibility for the crudities of the philosophy of Haeckel and the simplism of the various materialist schools.

The rationalist philosophers themselves were always intent upon showing the boundaries both of aprioristic theory and of empirical research.[1] The first representative of British political economy, David Hume, the Utilitarians, and the American Pragmatists are certainly not guilty of having exaggerated the power of man to attain truth. It would be more justifiable to blame the philosophy of the last two hundred years for too much agnosticism and skepticism than for overconfidence in what could be achieved by the human mind.

The revolt against reason, the characteristic mental attitude of our age, was not caused by a lack of modesty, caution, and self-examination on the part of the philosophers. Neither was it due to failures in the evolution of modern natural science. The amazing achievements of technology and therapeutics speak a language which nobody can ignore. It is hopeless to attack modern science, whether from the angle of intuitionism and mysticism, or from any other point of view. The revolt against reason was directed against another target. It did not aim at the natural sciences, but at economics. The attack against the natural sciences was only the logically necessary outcome of the attack against economics. It was impermissible to dethrone reason in one field only and not to question it in other branches of knowledge also.

The great upheaval was born out of the historical situation existing in the middle of the nineteenth century. The economists had entirely demolished the fantastic delusions of the socialist utopians. The deficiencies of the classical system prevented them from comprehending why every socialist plan must be unrealizable; but they knew enough to demonstrate the futility of all socialist schemes produced up to their time. The communist ideas were done for. The socialists

1. Cf., for instance, Louis Rougier, *Les Paralogismes du rationalisme* (Paris, 1920).

were absolutely unable to raise any objection to the devastating criticism of their schemes and to advance any argument in their favor. It seemed as if socialism was dead forever.

Only one way could lead the socialists out of this impasse. They could attack logic and reason and substitute mystical intuition for ratiocination. It was the historical role of Karl Marx to propose this solution. On the basis of Hegel's dialectic mysticism, he blithely arrogated to himself the ability to predict the future. Hegel pretended to know that Geist, in creating the universe, wanted to bring about the Prussian monarchy of Frederick William III. But Marx was better informed about Geist's plans. He knew that the final cause of historical evolution was the establishment of the socialist millennium. Socialism is bound to come "with the inexorability of a law of nature." And as, according to Hegel, every later stage of history is a higher and better stage, there cannot be any doubt that socialism, the final and ultimate stage of mankind's evolution, will be perfect from any point of view. It is consequently useless to discuss the details of the operation of a socialist commonwealth. History, in due time, will arrange everything for the best. It does not need the advice of mortal men.

There was still the main obstacle to overcome: the devastating criticism of the economists. Marx had a solution at hand. Human reason, he asserted, is constitutionally unfitted to find truth. The logical structure of mind is different with various social classes. There is no such thing as a universally valid logic. What mind produces can never be anything but "ideology," that is, in the Marxian terminology, a set of ideas disguising the selfish interests of the thinker's own social class. Hence, the "bourgeois" mind of the economists is utterly incapable of producing more than an apology for capitalism. The teachings of "bourgeois" science, an offshoot of "bourgeois" logic, are of no avail for the proletarians, the rising class destined to abolish all classes and to convert the earth into a Garden of Eden.

But, of course, the logic of the proletarians is not merely a class logic. "The ideas of proletarian logic are not party ideas, but emanations of logic pure and simple."[2] Moreover, by virtue of a special privilege, the logic of certain elect bourgeois is not tainted with the original sin of being bourgeois. Karl Marx, the son of a well-to-do lawyer, married to the daughter of a Prussian noble, and his collaborator Frederick Engels, a wealthy textile manufacturer, never doubted that they themselves were above the law and, notwithstanding their bourgeois background, were endowed with the power to discover absolute truth.

---

2. Cf. Joseph Dietzgen, *Briefe über Logik, speziell demokratisch-proletarische Logik* (2d ed. Stuttgart, 1903), p. 112.

It is the task of history to describe the historical conditions which made such a crude doctrine popular. Economics has another task. It must analyze both Marxian polylogism and the other brands of polylogism formed after its pattern, and expose their fallacies and contradictions.

2 The Logical Aspect of Polylogism

Marxian polylogism asserts that the logical structure of the mind is different with the members of various social classes. Racial polylogism differs from Marxian polylogism only in so far as it ascribes to each race a peculiar logical structure of mind and maintains that all members of a definite race, no matter what their class affiliation may be, are endowed with this peculiar logical structure.

There is no need to enter here into a critique of the concepts *social class* and *race* as applied by these doctrines. It is not necessary to ask the Marxians when and how a proletarian who succeeds in joining the ranks of the bourgeoisie changes his proletarian mind into a bourgeois mind. It is superfluous to ask the racists to explain what kind of logic is peculiar to people who are not of pure racial stock. There are much more serious objections to be raised.

Neither the Marxians nor the racists nor the supporters of any other brand of polylogism ever went further than to declare that the logical structure of mind is different with various classes, races, or nations. They never ventured to demonstrate precisely in what the logic of the proletarians differs from the logic of the bourgeois, or in what the logic of the Aryans differs from the logic of the non-Aryans, or the logic of the Germans from the logic of the French or the British. In the eyes of the Marxians the Ricardian theory of comparative cost is spurious because Ricardo was a bourgeois. The German racists condemn the same theory because Ricardo was a Jew, and the German nationalists because he was an Englishman. Some German professors advanced all these three arguments together against the validity of Ricardo's teachings. However, it is not enough to reject a theory wholesale by unmasking the background of its author. What is wanted is first to expound a system of logic different from that applied by the criticized author. Then it would be necessary to examine the contested theory point by point and to show where in its reasoning inferences are made which — although correct from the point of view of its author's logic — are invalid from the point of view of the proletarian, Aryan, or German logic. And finally, it should be explained what kind of conclusions the replacement of the author's vicious inferences by the correct inferences of the critic's own logic must lead to. As everybody knows, this never has been and never can be attempted by anybody.

Then there is the fact that there is disagreement concerning essential problems among people belonging to the same class, race, or nation. Unfortunately there are, say the Nazis, Germans who do not think in a correct German way. But if a German does not always necessarily think as he should, but may think in the manner of a man equipped with a non-German logic, who is to decide which German's ideas are truly German and which un-German? Says the late Professor Franz Oppenheimer: "The individual errs often in looking after his interests; a class never errs in the long run."[3] This would suggest the infallibility of a majority vote. However, the Nazis rejected decision by majority vote as manifestly un-German. The Marxians pay lip service to the democratic principle of majority vote.[4] But whenever it comes to a test they favor minority rule, provided it is the rule of their own party. Let us remember how Lenin dispersed by force the Constituent Assembly elected, under the auspices of his own government, by adult franchise, because only about one-fifth of its members were Bolshevik.

A consistent supporter of polylogism would have to maintain that ideas are correct because their author is a member of the right class, nation, or race. But consistency is not one of their virtues. Thus the Marxians are prepared to assign the epithet "proletarian thinker" to everybody whose doctrines they approve. All the others they disparage either as foes of their class or as social traitors. Hitler was even frank enough to admit that the only method available for him to sift the true Germans from the mongrels and the aliens was to enunciate a genuinely German program and to see who were ready to support it.[5] A dark-haired man whose bodily features by no means fitted the prototype of the fair-haired Aryan master race, arrogated to himself the gift of discovering the only doctrine adequate to the German mind and of expelling from the ranks of the Germans all those who did not accept this doctrine whatever their bodily characteristics might be. No further proof is needed of the insincerity of the whole doctrine.

3   The Praxeological Aspect of Polylogism

An ideology in the Marxian sense of this term is a doctrine which,

---

3. Cf. Franz Oppenheimer, *System der Soziologie* (Jena, 1926), II, 559.
4. It must be emphasized that the case for democracy is not based on the assumption that majorities are always right, still less that they are infallible. Cf. below, pp. 149–51.
5. Cf. his speech on the Party Convention in Nuremberg, September 3, 1933 (*Frankfurter Zeitung*, September 4, 1933, p. 2).

although erroneous from the point of view of the correct logic of the proletarians, is beneficial to the selfish interests of the class which has developed
it. An ideology is objectively vicious, but it furthers the interests of the
thinker's class precisely on account of its viciousness. Many Marxians believe
that they have proved this tenet by stressing the point that people do not thirst
for knowledge only for its own sake. The aim of the scientist is to pave the
way for successful action. Theories are always developed with a view to practical application. There are no such things as pure science and the disinterested search for truth.

For the sake of argument we may admit that every effort to attain truth is
motivated by considerations of its practical utilization for the attainment
of some end. But this does not answer the question why an "ideological"—i.e.,
a false—theory should render better service than a correct one. The fact that
the practical application of a theory results in the outcome predicted on the
basis of this theory is universally considered a confirmation of its correctness.
It is paradoxical to assert that a vicious theory is from any point of view more
useful than a correct one.

Men use firearms. In order to improve these weapons they developed the
science of ballistics. But, of course, precisely because they were eager to hunt
game and to kill one another, a correct ballistics. A merely "ideological" ballistics would not have been of any use.

For the Marxians the view that scientists labor for knowledge alone is nothing but an "arrogant pretense" of the scientists. Thus they declare that
Maxwell was led to his theory of electromagnetic waves by the craving of
business for wireless telegraphs.[6] It is of no relevance for the problem of ideology whether this is true or not. The question is whether the alleged fact
that nineteenth-century industrialism considered telegraphy without wires
"the philosopher's stone and the elixir of youth"[7] impelled Maxwell to formulate a correct theory or an ideological superstructure of the selfish class
interests of the bourgeoisie. There is no doubt that bacteriological research
was instigated not only by the desire to fight contagious diseases, but also by
the desire of the producers of wine and of cheese to improve their methods
of production. But the result obtained was certainly not "ideological" in the
Marxian sense.

What induced Marx to invent his ideology-doctrine was the wish to
sap the prestige of economics. He was fully aware of his impotence to
refute the objections raised by the economists to the practicability

6. Cf. Lancelot Hogben, *Science for the Citizen* (New York, 1938), pp. 726–28.
7. *Ibid.*, p. 726.

of the socialist schemes. In fact he was so fascinated by the theoretical system of British classical economics that he firmly believed in its impregnability. He either never learned about the doubts that the classical theory of value raised in the minds of judicious scholars, or, if he ever heard of them, he did not comprehend their weight. His own economic ideas are hardly more than a garbled version of Ricardianism. When Jevons and Menger inaugurated a new era of economic thought, his career as an author of economic writings had already come to an end; the first volume of *Das Kapital* had already been published several years previously. Marx's only reaction to the marginal theory of value was that he postponed the publication of the later volumes of his main treatise. They were made accessible to the public only after his death.

In developing the ideology-doctrine Marx exclusively aims at economics and the social philosophy of Utilitarianism. His only intention was to destroy the reputation of economic teachings which he was unable to refute by means of logic and ratiocination. He gave to his doctrine the form of a universal law valid for the whole historical age of social classes because a statement which is applicable only to one individual historical event could not be considered as a law. For the same reasons he did not restrict its validity to economic thought only, but included every branch of knowledge.

The service which bourgeois economics rendered to the bourgeoisie was in Marx's eyes twofold. It aided them first in their fight against feudalism and royal despotism and then later again in their fight against the rising proletarian class. It provided a rational and moral justification for capitalist exploitation. It was, if we want to use a notion developed after Marx's death, a rationalization of the claims of the capitalists.[8] The capitalists, in their subconsciousness ashamed of the mean greed motivating their own conduct and anxious to avoid social disapproval, encouraged their sycophants, the economists, to proclaim doctrines which could rehabilitate them in public opinion.

Now, recourse to the notion of rationalization provides a psychological description of the incentives which impelled a man or a group of men to formulate a theorem or a whole theory. But it does not predicate anything about the validity or invalidity of the theory

8. Although the term *rationalization* is new, the thing itself was known long ago. Cf., for instance, the words of Benjamin Franklin: "So convenient a thing it is to be a *reasonable creature*, since it enables one to find or make a reason for every thing one has a mind to do." (*Autobiography*, ed. New York, 1944, p. 41.)

advanced. If it is proved that the theory concerned is untenable, the notion of rationalization is a psychological interpretation of the causes which made its authors liable to error. But if we are not in a position to find any fault in the theory advanced, no appeal to the concept of rationalization can possibly explode its validity. If it were true that the economists had in their subconsciousness no design other than that of justifying the unfair claims of the capitalists, their theories could nevertheless be quite correct. There is no means to expose a faulty theory other than to refute it by discursive reasoning and to substitute a better theory for it. In dealing with the theorem of Pythagoras or with the theory of comparative cost, we are not interested in the psychological factors that impelled Pythagoras and Ricardo to construct these theorems, although these things may be important for the historian and the biographer. For science the only relevant question is whether or not these theorems can stand the test of rational examination. The social or racial background of their authors is beside the point.

It is a fact that people in the pursuit of their selfish interests try to use doctrines more or less universally accepted by public opinion. Moreover, they are eager to invent and to propagate doctrines which they could possibly use for furthering their own interests. But this does not explain why such doctrines, favoring the interests of a minority and contrary to the interests of the rest of the people, are endorsed by public opinion. No matter whether such "ideological" doctrines are the product of a "false consciousness," forcing a man to think unwittingly in a manner that serves the interests of his class, or whether they are the product of a purposeful distortion of truth, they must encounter the ideologies of other classes and try to supplant them. Then a rivalry between antagonistic ideologies emerges. The Marxians explain victory and defeat in such conflicts as an outcome of the interference of historical providence. *Geist*, the mythical prime mover, operates according to a definite plan. He leads mankind through various preliminary stages to the final bliss of socialism. Every stage is the product of a certain state of technology; all its other characteristics are the necessary ideological superstructure of this technological state. *Geist* causes man to bring about in due time the technological ideas adequate to the stage in which he lives, and to realize them. All the rest is an outgrowth of the state of technology. The hand-mill made feudal society; the steam-mill made capitalism.[9]

9. "Le moulin à bras vous donnera la société avec le souzerain; le moulin à vapeur, la société avec le capitaliste industriel." Marx, *Misère de la philosophie* (Paris and Brussels, 1847), p. 100.

Human will and reason play only an ancillary role in these changes. The inexorable law of historical development forces men — independently of their wills — to think and to behave according to the patterns corresponding to the material basis of their age. Men fool themselves in believing that they are free to choose between various ideas and between what they call truth and error. They themselves do not think; it is historical providence that manifests itself in their thoughts.

This is a purely mystical doctrine. The only proof given in its support is the recourse of Hegelian dialectics. Capitalistic private property is the first negation of individual private property. It begets, with the inexorability of a law of nature, its own negation, namely common ownership of the means of production.[10] However, a mystical doctrine based on intuition does not lose its mysticism by referring to another no less mystical doctrine. This makeshift by no means answers the question why a thinker must necessarily develop an ideology in accordance with the interests of his class. For the sake of argument we may admit that man's thoughts must result in doctrines beneficial to his interests. But are a man's interests necessarily identical with those of his whole class? Marx himself had to admit that the organization of the proletarians into a class, and consequently into a political party, is continually being upset again by the competition between the workers themselves.[11] It is an undeniable fact that there prevails an irreconcilable conflict of interests between those workers who are employed at union wage rates and those who remain unemployed because the enforcement of union rates prevents the demand for and the supply of labor from finding the appropriate price for meeting. It is no less true that the interests of the workers of the comparatively overpopulated countries and those of the comparatively underpopulated countries are antagonistic with regard to migration barriers. The statement that the interests of all proletarians uniformly require the substitution of socialism for capitalism is an arbitrary postulate of Marx and the other socialists. It cannot be proved by the mere assertion that the socialist idea is the emanation of proletarian thought and therefore certainly beneficial to the interests of the proletariat as such.

A popular interpretation of the vicissitudes of British foreign trade policies, based on the ideas of Sismondi, Frederick List, Marx, and the German Historical School, runs this way: In the second part of the eighteenth century and in the greater part of the nineteenth century the class interests of the British bourgeoisie required a free-

10. Marx, *Das Kapital* (7th ed. Hamburg, 1914), I, 728–29.
11. *The Communist Manifesto*, I. [*Capital, The Communist Manifesto and Other Writings* by Karl Marx, edited, with an introduction by Max Eastman. New York: Modern Library/Random House, 1932/59); the Manifesto appears there on pp. 321–34.]

trade policy. Therefore British political economy elaborated a free trade doctrine, and the British manufacturers organized a popular movement which finally succeeded in abolishing protective tariffs. Then later conditions changed. The British bourgeoisie could no longer stand the competition of foreign manufacturing and badly needed protective tariffs. Consequently the economists substituted a theory of protection for the antiquated free trade ideology, and Great Britain returned to protectionism.

The first error in this interpretation is that it considers the "bourgeoisie" as a homogeneous class composed of members whose interests are identical. A businessman is always under the necessity of adjusting the conduct of his business to the institutional conditions of his country. In the long run he is, in his capacity as entrepreneur and capitalist, neither favored nor injured by tariffs or the absence of tariffs. He will turn to the production of those commodities which under the given state of affairs he can most profitably produce. What may hurt or further his short-run interests are only *changes* in the institutional setting. But such changes do not affect the various branches of business and the various enterprises in the same way and to the same extent. A measure that benefits one branch or enterprise may be detrimental to other branches or enterprises. What counts for a businessman is only a limited number of customs items. And with regard to these items the interests of various branches and firms are mostly antagonistic.

The interests of every branch or firm can be favored by all kinds of privileges granted to it by the government. But if privileges are granted to the same extent also to the other branches and firms, every businessman loses — not only in his capacity as consumer, but also in his capacity as buyer of raw materials, half-finished products, machines and other equipment — on the one hand as much as he profits on the other. Selfish group interests may impel a man to ask for protection for his own branch or firm. They can never motivate him to ask for universal protection for all branches or firms if he is not sure to be protected to a greater extent than the other industries or enterprises.

Neither were the British manufacturers from the point of view of their class concerns more interested in the abolition of the Corn Laws than other British citizens. The landowners were opposed to the repeal of these laws because a lowering of the prices for agricultural products reduced the rent of land. A special class interest of the manufacturers can only be construed on the basis of the long since discarded iron law of wages and the no less untenable doctrine that profits are an outcome of the exploitation of the workers.

Within a world organized on the basis of the division of labor, every change must in one way or another affect the short-run interests of many groups. It is therefore always easy to expose every doctrine supporting an alteration of existing conditions as an "ideological" disguise of the selfish interests of a special group of people. The main occupation of many present-day authors is such unmasking. Marx did not invent this procedure. It was known long before him. Its most curious manifestation was the attempts of some eighteenth-century writers to explain religious creeds as a fraudulent deception on the part of the priests eager to gain power and wealth both for themselves and for their allies, the exploiters. The Marxians endorsed this statement in labeling religion "opium for the masses."[12] It never occurred to the supporters of such teachings that where there are selfish interests pro there must necessarily be selfish interests contra too. It is by no means a satisfactory explanation of any event that it favored a special class. The question to be answered is why the rest of the population whose interests it injured did not succeed in frustrating the endeavors of those favored by it.

Every firm and every branch of business is in the short run interested in increased sales of its products. In the long run, however, there prevails a tendency toward an equalization of returns in the various branches of production. If demand for the products of a branch increases and raises profits, more capital flows into it and the competition of the new enterprises cuts down the profits. Returns are by no means higher in the sale of socially detrimental articles than in the sale of socially beneficial articles. If a certain branch of business is outlawed and those engaged in it risk prosecution, penalties, and imprisonment, gross profits must be high enough to compensate for the risks involved. But this does not interfere with the height of net returns.

The rich, the owners of the already operating plants, have no particular class interest in the maintenance of free competition. They are opposed to confiscation and expropriation of their fortunes, but their vested interests are rather in favor of measures preventing newcomers from challenging their position. Those fighting for free enterprise and free competition do not defend the interests of those rich

---

12. The meaning that contemporary Marxism attaches to this phrase, viz., that the religious drug has been purposely administered to the people, may have been the meaning of Marx too. But it was not implied in the passage in which — in 1843 — Marx coined this phrase. Cf. R. P. Casey, *Religion in Russia* (New York, 1946), pp. 67–69.

today. They want a free hand left to unknown men who will be the entrepreneurs of tomorrow and whose ingenuity will make the life of coming generations more agreeable. They want the way left open to further economic improvements. They are the spokesmen of material progress.

The nineteenth-century success of free trade ideas was effected by the theories of classical economics. The prestige of these ideas was so great that those whose selfish class interests they hurt could not hinder their endorsements by public opinion and their realization by legislative measures. It is ideas that make history, and not history that makes ideas.

It is useless to argue with mystics and seers. They base their assertions on intuition and are not prepared to submit them to rational examination. The Marxians pretend that what their inner voice proclaims is history's self-revelation. If other people do not hear this voice, it is only a proof that they are not chosen. It is insolence that those groping in darkness dare to contradict the inspired ones. Decency should impel them to creep into a corner and keep silent.

However, science cannot abstain from thinking although it is obvious that it will never succeed in convincing those who dispute the supremacy of reason. Science must emphasize that the appeal to intuition cannot settle the question which of several antagonistic doctrines is the right one and which are wrong. It is an undeniable fact that Marxism is not the only doctrine advanced in our time. There are other "ideologies" besides Marxism. The Marxians assert that the application of these other doctrines would hurt the interests of the many. But the supporters of these doctrines say precisely the same with regard to Marxism.

Of course, the Marxians consider a doctrine vicious if its author's background is not proletarian. But who is proletarian? Doctor Marx, the manufacturer and "exploiter" Engels, and Lenin, the scion of the Russian gentry, were certainly not of proletarian background. But Hitler and Mussolini were genuine proletarians and spent their youth in poverty. The conflict of the Bolsheviks and the Mensheviks or that between Stalin and Trotsky cannot be presented as class conflicts. They were conflicts between various sects of fanatics who called one another traitors.

The essence of Marxian philosophy is this: We are right because we are the spokesmen of the rising proletarian class. Discursive reasoning cannot invalidate our teachings, for they are inspired by the supreme power that determines the destiny of mankind. Our adversaries are wrong because they lack the intuition that guides our minds. It is, of course, not their fault that on account of their class affiliation they are not equipped with the genuine proletarian logic and are blinded by ideologies. The unfathomable decrees of history that have elected us have doomed them. The future is ours.

4 Racial Polylogism

Marxian polylogism is an abortive makeshift to salvage the untenable doctrines of socialism. Its attempt to substitute intuition for ratiocination appeals to popular superstitions. But it is precisely this attitude that places Marxian polylogism and its offshoot, the so-called "sociology of knowledge," in irreconcilable antagonism to science and reason.

It is different with the polylogism of the racists. This brand of polylogism is in agreement with fashionable, although mistaken, tendencies in present-day empiricism. It is an established fact that mankind is divided into various races. The races differ in bodily features. Materialist philosophers assert that thoughts are a secretion of the brain as bile is a secretion of the gallbladder. It would be inconsistent for them to reject beforehand the hypothesis that the thought-secretion of the various races may differ in essential qualities. The fact that anatomy has not succeeded up to now in discovering anatomical differences in the brain cells of various races cannot invalidate the doctrine that the logical structure of mind is different with different races. It does not exclude the assumption that later research may discover such anatomical peculiarities.

Some ethnologists tell us that it is a mistake to speak of higher and lower civilizations and of an alleged backwardness of alien races. The civilizations of various races are different from the Western civilization of the peoples of Caucasian stock, but they are not inferior. Every race has its peculiar mentality. It is faulty to apply to the civilization of any of them yardsticks abstracted from the achievements of other races. Westerners call the civilization of China an arrested civilization and that of the inhabitants of New Guinea primitive barbarism. But the Chinese and the natives of New Guinea despise our civilization no less than we despise theirs. Such estimates are judgments of value and hence arbitrary. Those other races have a different structure of mind. Their civilizations are adequate to their mind as our civilization is adequate to our mind. We are incapable of comprehending that what we call backwardness does not appear such to them. It is, from the point of view of their logic, a better method of coming to a satisfactory arrangement with given natural conditions of life than is our progressivism.

These ethnologists are right in emphasizing that it is not the task of a historian—and the ethnologist too is a historian—to express value judgments. But they are utterly mistaken in contending that these other races have been guided in their activities by motives other than those which have actuated the white race. The Asiatics and the Africans no less than the peoples of European descent have been eager to struggle successfully for survival and to use reason as the foremost weapon in these endeavors. They have sought to get rid of the beasts of prey and of disease, to prevent famines and to raise the productivity of labor. There can be no doubt that in the pursuit of these aims they have been less successful than the whites. The proof is that they are eager to profit from all achievements of the West. Those ethnologists would be right, if Mongols or Africans, tormented by a painful disease, were to renounce the aid of a European doctor because their mentality or their world view led them to believe that it is better to suffer than to be relieved of pain. Mahatma Gandhi disavowed his whole philosophy when he entered a modern hospital to be treated for appendicitis.

The North American Indians lacked the ingenuity to invent the wheel. The inhabitants of the Alps were not keen enough to construct skis which would have rendered their hard life much more agreeable. Such shortcomings were not due to a mentality different from those of the races which had long since used wheels and skis; they were failures, even when judged from the point of view of the Indians and the Alpine mountaineers.

However, these considerations refer only to the motives determining concrete actions, not to the only relevant problem of whether or not there exists between various races a difference in the logical structure of mind. It is precisely this that the racists assert.[13]

We may refer to what has been said in the preceding chapters about the fundamental issues of the logical structure of mind and the categorial principles of thought and action. Some additional observations will suffice to give the finishing stroke to racial polylogism and to any other brand of polylogism.

The categories of human thought and action are neither arbitrary products of the human mind nor conventions. They are not outside of the universe and of the course of cosmic events. They are biological facts and have a definite function in life and reality. They are instruments in man's struggle for existence and in his endeavors to adjust himself as much as possible to the real state of the universe and to remove uneasiness as much as it is in his power to do so. They are

13. Cf. L. G. Tirala, *Rasse, Geist und Seele* (Munich, 1935), pp. 190 ff.

therefore appropriate to the structure of the external world and reflect properties of the world and of reality. They work, and are in this sense true and valid.

It is consequently incorrect to assert that aprioristic insight and pure reasoning do not convey any information about reality and the structure of the
universe. The fundamental logical relations and the categories of thought
and action are the ultimate source of all human knowledge. They are adequate to the structure of reality, they reveal this structure to the human mind
and, in this sense, they are for man basic ontological facts.[14] We do not know
what a superhuman intellect may think and comprehend. For man every
cognition is conditioned by the logical structure of his mind and implied in
this structure. It is precisely the satisfactory results of the empirical sciences
and their practical application that evidence this truth. Within the orbit in
which human action is able to attain ends aimed at there is no room left for
agnosticism.

If there had been races which had developed a different logical structure of
the mind, they would have failed in the use of reason as an aid in the struggle
for existence. The only means for survival that could have protected them
against extermination would have been their instinctive reactions. Natural selection would have eliminated those specimens of such races that tried to employ reasoning for the direction of their behavior. Those individuals alone
would have survived that relied upon instincts only. This means that only
those would have had a chance to survive that did not rise above the mental
level of animals.

The scholars of the West have amassed an enormous amount of material
concerning the high civilizations of China and India and the primitive civilizations of the Asiatic, American, Australian, and African aborigines. It is safe
to say that all that is worth knowing about the ideas of these races is known.
But never has any supporter of polylogism tried to use these data for a description of the allegedly different logic of these peoples and civilizations.

5   Polylogism and Understanding

Some supporters of the tenets of Marxism and racism interpret the
epistemological teachings of their parties in a peculiar way. They are
ready to admit that the logical structure of mind is uniform for all
races, nations, and classes. Marxism or racism, they assert, never intended to deny this undeniable fact. What they really wanted to say

14. Cf. Morris R. Cohen, *Reason and Nature* (New York, 1931), pp. 202–5; *A Preface to Logic* (New
York, 1944), pp. 42–44, 54–56, 92, 180–87.

was that historical understanding, aesthetic empathy, and value judgments are conditioned by a man's background. It is obvious that this interpretation cannot be supported on the basis of the writings of the champions of polylogism. However, it must be analyzed as a doctrine of its own.

There is no need to emphasize again that a man's value judgments and his choice of ends reflect his inborn bodily features and all the vicissitudes of his life.[15] But it is a far cry from the acknowledgment of this fact to the belief that racial inheritance or class affiliation ultimately determines judgments of value and the choice of ends. The fundamental discrepancies in world view and patterns of behavior do not correspond to differences in race, nationality, or class affiliation.

There is hardly any greater divergence in value judgments than that between ascetics and those eager to enjoy life lightheartedly. An unbridgeable gulf separates devout monks and nuns from the rest of mankind. But there have been people dedicated to the monkish ideals among all races, nations, classes, and castes. Some of them were sons and daughters of kings and wealthy noblemen, others were beggars. St. Francis, Santa Clara, and their ardent followers were natives of Italy, whose other inhabitants cannot be described as weary of temporal things. Puritanism was Anglo-Saxon, but so was the lasciviousness of the British under the Tudors, the Stuarts, and the Hanoverians. The nineteenth century's outstanding champion of asceticism was Count Leo Tolstoy, a wealthy member of the profligate Russian aristocracy. Tolstoy saw the pith of the philosophy he attacked embodied in Beethoven's Kreutzer Sonata, a masterpiece of the son of extremely poor parents.

It is the same with aesthetic values. All races and nations have had both classic and romantic art. With all their ardent propaganda the Marxians have not succeeded in bringing about a specifically proletarian art or literature. The "proletarian" writers, painters, and musicians have not created new styles and have not established new aesthetic values. What characterizes them is solely their tendency to call everything they detest "bourgeois" and everything they like "proletarian."

Historical understanding both of the historian and of the acting man always reflects the personality of its author.[16] But if the historian and the politician are imbued with the desire for truth, they will never let themselves be deluded by party bias, provided they are

15. Cf. above, pp. 46–47.
16. Cf. above, pp. 57–58.

efficient and not inept. It is immaterial whether a historian or a politician considers the interference of a certain factor beneficial or detrimental. He cannot derive any advantage from underrating or overrating the relevance of one of the operating factors. Only clumsy would-be historians believe that they can serve their cause by distortion.

This is no less true of the statesman's understanding. What use could a champion of Protestantism derive from misunderstanding the tremendous power and prestige of Catholicism, or a liberal from misunderstanding the relevance of socialist ideas? In order to succeed a politician must see things as they are; whoever indulges in wishful thinking will certainly fail. Judgments of relevance differ from judgments of value in that they aim at the appraisal of a state of affairs not dependent on the author's arbitrariness. They are colored by their author's personality and can therefore never be unanimously agreed upon by all people. But here again we must raise the question: What advantage could a race or class derive from an "ideological" distortion of understanding?

As has already been pointed out, the serious discrepancies to be found in historical studies are an outcome of differences in the field of the nonhistorical sciences and not in various modes of understanding.

Today many historians and writers are imbued with the Marxian dogma that the realization of the socialist plans is both unavoidable and the supreme good, and that the labor movement is entrusted with the historical mission of accomplishing this task by a violent overthrow of the capitalistic system. Starting from this tenet, they take it as a matter of course that the parties of the "Left," the elect, in the pursuit of their policies, should resort to acts of violence and to murder. A revolution cannot be consummated by peaceful methods. It is not worthwhile to dwell upon such trifles as the butchering of the four daughters of the last Tsar, of Leon Trotsky, of tens of thousands of Russian bourgeois and so on. "You can't make an omelet without breaking eggs"; why explicitly mention the eggs broken? But, of course, it is different if one of those assailed ventures to defend himself or even to strike back. Few only mention the acts of sabotage, destruction, and violence committed by strikers. But all authors enlarge upon the attempts of the companies to protect their property and the lives of their employees and their customers against such onslaughts.

Such discrepancies are due neither to judgments of value nor to differences in understanding. They are the outcome of antagonistic theories of economic and historical evolution. If the coming of socialism is un-avoidable and can be achieved only by revolutionary methods, murders committed by the "progressives" are minor incidents of no significance. But the self-defense and counterattacks of the "reactionaries" which can possibly delay the final victory of socialism are of the greatest importance. They are remarkable events, while the revolutionary acts are simply routine.

6   The Case for Reason

Judicious rationalists do not pretend that human reason can ever make man omniscient. They are fully aware of the fact that, however knowledge may increase, there will always remain things ultimately given and not liable to any further elucidation. But, they say, as far as man is able to attain cognition, he must rely upon reason. The ultimate given is the irrational. The knowable is, as far as it is known already, necessarily rational. There is neither an irrational mode of cognition nor a science of irrationality.

With regard to unsolved problems, various hypotheses are permissible provided they do not contradict logic and the uncontested data of experience. But these are hypotheses only.

We do not know what causes the inborn differences in human abilities. Science is at a loss to explain why Newton and Mozart were full of creative genius and why most people are not. But it is by all means an unsatisfactory answer to say that a genius owes his greatness to his ancestry or to his race. The question is precisely why such a man differs from his brothers and from the other members of his race.

It is a little bit less faulty to attribute the great achievements of the white race to racial superiority. Yet this is no more than vague hypothesis which is at variance with the fact that the early foundations of civilization were laid by peoples of other races. We cannot know whether or not at a later date other races will supplant Western civilization.

However, such a hypothesis must be appraised on its own merits. It must not be condemned beforehand because the racists base on it their postulate that there is an irreconcilable conflict between various racial groups and that the superior races must enslave the inferior ones. Ricardo's law of association has long since discarded this mistaken interpretation of the inequality of men.[17] It is nonsensical to fight the racial hypothesis by negating obvious facts. It is vain to deny that up to now certain races have contributed nothing or very

17. See below, pp. 159–64.

little to the development of civilization and can, in this sense, be called inferior.

If somebody were eager to distill at any cost a grain of truth out of the Marxian teachings, he could say that emotions influence a man's reasoning very much. Nobody ever ventured to deny this obvious fact, and Marxism cannot be credited with its discovery. But it is without any significance for epistemology. There are many sources both of success and of error. It is the task of psychology to enumerate and to classify them.

Envy is a widespread frailty. It is certain that many intellectuals envy the higher income of prosperous businessmen and that these feelings drive them toward socialism. They believe that the authorities of a socialist commonwealth would pay them higher salaries than those that they earn under capitalism. But to prove the existence of this envy does not relieve science of the duty of making the most careful examination of the socialist doctrines. Scientists are bound to deal with every doctrine as if its supporters were inspired by nothing else than the thirst for knowledge. The various brands of polylogism substitute for a purely theoretical examination of opposite doctrines the unmasking of the background and the motives of their authors. Such a procedure is incompatible with the first principles of ratiocination.

It is a poor makeshift to dispose of a theory by referring to its historical background, to the "spirit" of its time, to the material conditions of the country of its origin, and to any personal qualities of its authors. A theory is subject to the tribunal of reason only. The yardstick to be applied is always the yardstick of reason. A theory is either correct or incorrect. It may happen that the present state of our knowledge does not allow a decision with regard to its correctness or incorrectness. But a theory can never be valid for a bourgeois or an American if it is invalid for a proletarian or a Chinese.

If the Marxians and the racists were right, it would be impossible to explain why those in power are anxious to suppress dissenting theories and to persecute their supporters. The very fact that there are intolerant governments and political parties intent upon outlawing and exterminating dissenters, is a proof of the excellence of reason. It is not a conclusive proof of a doctrine's correctness that its adversaries use the police, the hangman, and violent mobs to fight it. But it is a proof of the fact that those taking recourse to violent oppression are in their subconsciousness convinced of the untenability of their own doctrines.

It is impossible to demonstrate the validity of the *a priori* foundations of logic and praxeology without referring to these foundations themselves. Reason is an ultimate given and cannot be analyzed or questioned by itself. The very existence of human reason is a nonrational fact. The only statement that can be predicated with regard to reason is that it is the mark that distinguishes man from animals and has brought about everything that is specifically human.

To those pretending that man would be happier if he were to renounce the use of reason and try to let himself be guided by intuition and instincts only, no other answer can be given than an analysis of the achievements of human society. In describing the genesis and working of social cooperation, economics provides all the information required for an ultimate decision between reason and unreason. If man reconsiders freeing himself from the supremacy of reason, he must know what he will have to forsake.

CHAPTER 4

A First Analysis of the Category of Action

1 Ends and Means

The result sought by an action is called its end, goal, or aim. One uses these terms in ordinary speech also to signify intermediate ends, goals, or aims; these are points which acting man wants to attain only because he believes that he will reach his ultimate end, goal, or aim in passing beyond them. Strictly speaking the end, goal, or aim of any action is always the relief from a felt uneasiness.

A means is what serves to the attainment of any end, goal, or aim. Means are not in the given universe; in this universe there exist only things. A thing becomes a means when human reason plans to employ it for the attainment of some end and human action really employs it for this purpose. Thinking man sees the serviceableness of things, i.e., their ability to minister to his ends, and acting man makes them means. It is of primary importance to realize that parts of the external world become means only through the operation of the human mind and its offshoot, human action. External objects are as such only phenomena of the physical universe and the subject matter of the natural sciences. It is human meaning and action which transform them into means. Praxeology does not deal with the external world, but with man's conduct with regard to it. Praxeological reality is not the physical universe, but man's conscious reaction to the given state of this universe. Economics is not about things and tangible material objects; it is about men, their meanings and actions. Goods, commodities, and wealth and all the other notions of conduct are not elements of nature; they are elements of human meaning and conduct. He who wants to deal with them must not look at the external world; he must search for them in the meaning of acting men.

Praxeology and economics do not deal with human meaning and action as they should be or would be if all men were inspired by an absolutely valid philosophy and equipped with a perfect knowledge of technology. For such notions as absolute validity and omniscience there is no room in the frame of a science whose subject matter is erring man. An end is everything which men aim at. A means is everything which acting men consider as such.

It is the task of scientific technology and therapeutics to explode errors in their respective fields. It is the task of economics to expose erroneous doctrines in the field of social action. But if men do not follow the advice of science, but cling to their fallacious prejudices, these errors are reality and must be dealt with as such. Economists consider foreign exchange control as inappropriate to attain the ends aimed at by those who take recourse to it. However, if public opinion does not abandon its delusions and governments consequently resort to foreign exchange control, the course of events is determined by this attitude. Present-day medicine considers the doctrine of the therapeutic effects of mandrake as a fable. But as long as people took this fable as truth, mandrake was an economic good and prices were paid for its acquisition. In dealing with prices economics does not ask what things are in the eyes of other people, but only what they are in the meaning of those intent upon getting them. For it deals with real prices, paid and received in real transactions, not with prices as they would be if men were different from what they really are.

Means are necessarily always limited, i.e., scarce with regard to the services for which man wants to use them. If this were not the case, there would not be any action with regard to them. Where man is not restrained by the insufficient quantity of things available, there is no need for any action.

It is customary to call the end the ultimate good and the means goods. In applying this terminology economists mainly used to think as technologists and not as praxeologists. They differentiated between *free goods* and *economic goods*. They called free goods those things which, being available in superfluous abundance, do not need to be economized. Such goods are, however, not the object of any action. They are general conditions of human welfare; they are parts of the natural environment in which man lives and acts. Only the economic goods are the substratum of action. They alone are dealt with in economics.

Economic goods which in themselves are fitted to satisfy human wants directly and whose serviceableness does not depend on the cooperation of other economic goods, are called consumers' goods or goods of the first order. Means which can satisfy wants only indirectly when complemented by cooperation of other goods are called producers' goods or factors of production or goods of a remoter or higher order. The services rendered by a producers' good consist in bringing about, by the cooperation of complementary producers' goods, a product. This product may be a consumers' good; it may be a producers' good which when combined with other producers' goods will finally bring about a consumers' good. It is possible to think of the producers' goods as arranged in orders according to their proximity to the consumers' good for whose production they can be used. Those producers' goods which are nearest to the production of a consumers' good are ranged in the second order, and accordingly those which are used for the production of goods of the second order in the third order and so on.

The purpose of such an arrangement of goods in orders is to provide a basis for the theory of value and prices of the factors of production. It will be shown later how the valuation and the prices of the goods of higher orders are dependent on the valuation and the prices of the goods of lower orders produced by their expenditure. The first and ultimate valuation of external things refers only to consumers' goods. All other things are valued according to the part they play in the production of consumers' goods.

It is therefore not necessary actually to arrange producers' goods in various orders from the second to the nth. It is no less superfluous to enter into pedantic discussions of whether a concrete good has to be called a good of the lowest order or should rather be attributed to one of the higher orders. Whether raw coffee beans or roast coffee beans or ground coffee or coffee prepared for drinking or only coffee prepared and mixed with cream and sugar are to to called a consumers' good ready for consumption is of no importance. It is immaterial which manner of speech we adopt. For with regard to the problem of valuation, all that we say about a consumers' good can be applied to any good of a higher order (except those of the highest order) if we consider it as a product.

An economic good does not necessarily have to be embodied in a tangible thing. Nonmaterial economic goods are called services.

2   The Scale of Value

Acting man chooses between various opportunities offered for choice. He prefers one alternative to others.

It is customary to say that acting man has a scale of wants or values in his mind when he arranges his actions. On the basis of such a scale he satisfies what is of higher value, i.e., his more urgent wants, and leaves unsatisfied what is of lower value, i.e., what is a less urgent want. There is no objection to such a presentation of the state of affairs. However, one must not forget that the scale of values or wants manifests itself only in the reality of action. These scales have no independent existence apart from the actual behavior of individuals. The only source from which our knowledge concerning these scales is derived is the observation of a man's actions. Every action is always in perfect agreement with the scale of values or wants because these scales are nothing but an instrument for the interpretation of a man's acting.

Ethical doctrines are intent upon establishing scales of value according to which man should act but does not necessarily always act. They claim for themselves the vocation of telling right from wrong and of advising man concerning what he should aim at as the supreme good. They are normative disciplines aiming at the cognition of what ought to be. They are not neutral with regard to facts; they judge them from the point of view of freely adopted standards.

This is not the attitude of praxeology and economics. They are fully aware of the fact that the ultimate ends of human action are not open to examination from any absolute standard. Ultimate ends are ultimately given, they are purely subjective, they differ with various people and with the same people at various moments in their lives. Praxeology and economics deal with the means for the attainment of ends chosen by the acting individuals. They do not express any opinion with regard to such problems as whether or not sybaritism is better than asceticism. They apply to the means only one yardstick, viz., whether or not they are suitable to attain the ends at which the acting individuals aim.

The notions of abnormality and perversity therefore have no place in economics. It does not say that a man is perverse because he prefers the disagreeable, the detrimental, and the painful to the agreeable, the beneficial, and the pleasant. It says only that he is different from other people; that he likes what others detest; that he considers useful what others want to avoid; that he takes pleasure in enduring pain which others avoid because it hurts them. The polar notions normal and perverse can be used anthropologically for the distinction between those who behave as most people do and outsiders and atypical exceptions; they can be applied biologically for the distinction between those whose behavior preserves the vital forces and those whose behavior is self-destructive; they can be applied in an ethical sense for the distinction between those who behave correctly and those who act otherwise than they should. However, in the frame of a theoretical science of human action, there is no room for such a distinction.

Any examination of ultimate ends turns out to be purely subjective and therefore arbitrary.

Value is the importance that acting man attaches to ultimate ends. Only to ultimate ends is primary and original value assigned. Means are valued derivatively according to their serviceableness in contributing to the attainment of ultimate ends. Their valuation is derived from the valuation of the respective ends. They are important for man only as far as they make it possible for him to attain some ends.

Value is not intrinsic, it is not in things. It is within us; it is the way in which man reacts to the conditions of his environment.

Neither is value in words and doctrines. It is reflected in human conduct. It is not what a man or groups of men say about value that counts, but how they act. The oratory of moralists and the pompousness of party programs are significant as such. But they influence the course of human events only as far as they really determine the actions of men.

3   The Scale of Needs

Notwithstanding all declarations to the contrary, the immense majority of men aim first of all at an improvement of the material conditions of well-being. They want more and better food, better homes and clothes, and a thousand other amenities. They strive after abundance and health. Taking these goals as given, applied physiology tries to determine what means are best suited to provide as much satisfaction as possible. It distinguishes, from this point of view, between man's "real" needs and imaginary and spurious appetites. It teaches people how they should act and what they should aim at as a means.

The importance of such doctrines is obvious. From his point of view the physiologist is right in distinguishing between sensible action and action contrary to purpose. He is right in contrasting judicious methods of nourishment from unwise methods. He may condemn certain modes of behavior as absurd and opposed to "real" needs. However, such judgments are beside the point for a science dealing with the reality of human action. Not what a man should do, but what he does, counts for praxeology and economics. Hygiene may be right or wrong in calling alcohol and nicotine poisons. But economics must explain the prices of tobacco and liquor as they are, not as they would be under different conditions.

There is no room left in the field of economics for a scale of needs different from the scale of values as reflected in man's actual behavior. Economics deals with real man, weak and subject to error as he is, not with ideal beings, omniscient and perfect as only gods could be.

4   Action as an Exchange

Action is an attempt to substitute a more satisfactory state of affairs for a less satisfactory one. We call such a willfully induced alteration an exchange. A less desirable condition is bartered for a more desirable. What gratifies less is abandoned in order to attain something that pleases more. That which is abandoned is called the price paid for the attainment of the end sought. The value of the price paid is called cost. Cost is equal to the value attached to the satisfaction which one must forego in order to attain the end aimed at.

The difference between the value of the price paid (the costs incurred) and that of the goal attained is called gain or profit or net yield. Profit in this primary sense is purely subjective, it is an increase in the acting man's happiness, it is a psychical phenomenon that can be neither measured nor weighed. There is a more and a less in the removal of uneasiness felt; but how much one satisfaction surpasses another one can only be felt; it cannot be established and determined in an objective way. A judgment of value does not measure, it arranges in a scale of degrees, it grades. It is expressive of an order of preference and sequence, but not expressive of measure and weight. Only the ordinal numbers can be applied to it, but not the cardinal numbers.

It is vain to speak of any calculation of values. Calculation is possible only with cardinal numbers. The difference between the valuation of two states of affairs is entirely psychical and personal. It is not open to any projection into the external world. It can be sensed only by the individual. It cannot be communicated or imparted to any fellow man. It is an intensive magnitude.

Physiology and psychology have developed various methods by means of which they pretend to have attained a substitute for the unfeasible measurement of intensive magnitudes. There is no need for economics to enter into an examination of these rather questionable makeshifts. Their supporters themselves realize that they are not applicable to value judgments. But even if they were, they would not have any bearing on economic problems. For economics deals with action as such, and not with the psychical facts that result in definite actions.

It happens again and again that an action does not attain the end sought. Sometimes the result, although inferior to the end aimed at, is still an improvement when compared with the previous state of affairs; then there is still a profit, although a smaller one than that expected. But it can happen that the action produces a state of affairs less desirable than the previous state it was intended to alter. Then the difference between the valuation of the result and the costs incurred is called loss.

CHAPTER 5

Time

1   Time as a Praxeological Factor

The notion of change implies the notion of temporal sequence. A rigid, eternally immutable universe would be out of time, but it would be dead. The concepts of change and of time are inseparably linked together. Action aims at change and is therefore in the temporal order. Human reason is even incapable of conceiving the ideas of timeless existence and of timeless action.

He who acts distinguishes between the time before the action, the time absorbed by the action, and the time after the action has been finished. He cannot be neutral with regard to the lapse of time.

Logic and mathematics deal with an ideal system of thought. The relations and implications of their system are coexistent and interdependent. We may say as well that they are synchronous or that they are out of time. A perfect mind could grasp them all in one thought. Man's inability to accomplish this makes thinking itself an action, proceeding step by step from the less satisfactory state of insufficient cognition to the more satisfactory state of better insight. But the temporal order in which knowledge is acquired must not be confused with the logical simultaneity of all parts of an aprioristic deductive system. Within such a system the notions of anteriority and consequence are metaphorical only. They do not refer to the system, but to our action in grasping it. The system itself implies neither the category of time nor that of causality. There is functional correspondence between elements, but there is neither cause nor effect.

What distinguishes epistemologically the praxeological system from the logical system is precisely that it implies the categories both of time and of causality. The praxeological system too is aprioristic and deductive. As a system it is out of time. But change is one of its elements. The notions of sooner and later and of cause and effect are among its constituents. Anteriority and consequence are essential concepts of praxeological reasoning. So is the irreversibility of events. In the frame of the praxeological system any reference to functional correspondence is no less metaphorical and misleading than is the reference to anteriority and consequence in the frame of the logical system.[1]

2   Past, Present, and Future

It is acting that provides man with the notion of time and makes him aware of the flux of time. The idea of time is a praxeological category.

Action is always directed toward the future; it is essentially and necessarily always a planning and acting for a better future. Its aim is always to render future conditions more satisfactory than they would be without the interference of action. The uneasiness that impels a man to act is caused by a dissatisfaction with expected future conditions as they would probably develop if nothing were done to alter them. In any case action can influence only the future, never the present that with every infinitesimal fraction of a second sinks down into the past. Man becomes conscious of time when he plans to convert a less satisfactory present state into a more satisfactory future state.

For contemplative meditation time is merely duration, "la durée pure, dont l'écoulement est continu, et où l'on passe, par gradations insensibles, d'un état à l'autre: Continuité réellement vécue." [2] [(French) "Pure duration, in which the flow is continuous and one passes by imperceptible degrees from one state to another. Continuity really lived (or experienced)."] The "now" of the present is continually shifted to the past and is retained in the memory only. Reflecting about the past, say the philosophers, man becomes aware of time.[3] However, it is not recollection that conveys to man the categories of change and of time, but the will to improve the conditions of his life.

Time as we measure it by various mechanical devices is always past, and time as the philosophers use this concept is always either past or future. The present is, from these aspects, nothing but an ideal boundary line separating the past from the future. But from the praxeological aspect there is between the past and the future a real extended present. Action is as such in the real present because it utilizes the instant and thus embodies its reality.[4] Later retrospective

---

1. In a treatise on economics there is no need to enter into a discussion of the endeavors to construct mechanics as an axiomatic system in which the concept of function is substituted for that of cause and effect. It will be shown later that axiomatic mechanics cannot serve as a model for the treatment of the economic system. Cf. below, pp. 353–57.

2. Henri Bergson, Matière et mémoire (7th ed. Paris, 1911), p. 205.

3. Edmund Husserl, "Vorlesungen zur Phänomenologie des inneren Zeitbewusstseins," Jahrbuch für Philosophie und Phänomenologische Forschung, IX (1928), 391 ff.; A. Schütz, loc. cit., pp. 45 ff.

4. "Ce que j'appelle mon présent, c'est mon attitude vis-à-vis de l'avenir immédiat, c'est mon action imminente." Bergson, op. cit., p. 152. [(French) "What I call my present is my mental attitude toward the immediate future, my imminent action."]

reflection discerns in the instant passed away first of all the action and the conditions which it offered to action. That which can no longer be done or consumed because the opportunity for it has passed away, contrasts the past with the present. That which cannot yet be done or consumed, because the conditions for undertaking it or the time for its ripening have not yet come, contrasts the future with the past. The present offers to acting opportunities and tasks for which it was hitherto too early and for which it will be hereafter too late.

The present *qua* [as] duration is the continuation of the conditions and opportunities given for acting. Every kind of action requires special conditions to which it must be adjusted with regard to the aims sought. The concept of the present is therefore different for various fields of action. It has no reference whatever to the various methods of measuring the passing of time by spatial movements. The present encloses as much of the time passed away as still is actual, i.e., of importance for acting. The present contrasts itself, according to the various actions one has in view, with the Middle Ages, with the nineteenth century, with the past year, month, or day, but no less with the hour, minute, or second just passed away. If a man says: Nowadays Zeus is no longer worshipped, he has a present in mind other than that the motorcar driver who thinks: *Now* it is still too early to turn.

As the future is uncertain it always remains undecided and vague how much of it we can consider as *now* and present. If a man had said in 1913: At present — now — in Europe freedom of thought is undisputed, he would have not foreseen that this present would very soon be a past.

3   The Economization of Time

Man is subject to the passing of time. He comes into existence, grows, becomes old, and passes away. His time is scarce. He must economize it as he economizes other scarce factors.

The economization of time has a peculiar character because of the uniqueness and irreversibility of the temporal order. The importance of these facts manifests itself in every part of the theory of action.

Only one fact must be stressed at this point. The economization of time is independent of the economization of economic goods and services. Even in the land of Cockaigne man would be forced to economize time, provided he were not immortal and not endowed with eternal youth and indestructible health and vigor. Although all his appetites could be satisfied immediately without any expenditure of labor, he would have to arrange his time schedule, as there are states of satisfaction which are incompatible and cannot be consummated at the same time. For this man, too, time would be scarce and subject to the aspect of *sooner* and *later.*

4   The Temporal Relation Between Actions

Two actions of an individual are never synchronous; their temporal relation is that of sooner and later. Actions of various individuals can be considered as synchronous only in the light of the physical methods for the measurement of time. Synchronism is a praxeological notion only with regard to the concerted efforts of various acting men.[5]

A man's individual actions succeed one another. They can never be effected at the same instant; they can only follow one another in more or less rapid succession. There are actions which serve several purposes at one blow. It would be misleading to refer to them as a coincidence of various actions.

People have often failed to recognize the meaning of the term "scale of value" and have disregarded the obstacles preventing the assumption of synchronism in the various actions of an individual. They have interpreted a man's various acts as the outcome of a scale of value, independent of these acts and preceding them, and of a previously devised plan whose realization they aim at. The scale of value and the plan to which duration and immutability for a certain period of time were attributed, were hypostasized into the cause and motive of the various individual actions. Synchronism which could not be asserted with regard to various acts was then easily discovered in the scale of value and in the plan. But this overlooks the fact that the scale of value is nothing but a constructed tool of thought. The scale of value manifests itself only in real acting; it can be discerned only from the observation of real acting. It is therefore impermissible to contrast it with real acting and to use it as a yardstick for the appraisal of real actions.

It is no less impermissible to differentiate between rational and allegedly irrational acting on the basis of a comparison of real acting with earlier drafts and plans for future actions. It may be very inter-

5. In order to avoid any possible misunderstanding it may be expedient to emphasize that this theorem has nothing at all to do with Einstein's theorem concerning the temporal relation of spatially distant events.

esting that yesterday goals were set for today's acting other than those really aimed at today. But yesterday's plans do not provide us with any more objective and nonarbitrary standard for the appraisal of today's real acting than any other ideas and norms.

The attempt has been made to attain the notion of a nonrational action by this reasoning: If a is preferred to b and b to c, logically a should be preferred to c. But if actually c is preferred to a, we are faced with a mode of acting to which we cannot ascribe consistency and rationality.[6] This reasoning disregards the fact that two acts of an individual can never be synchronous. If in one action a is preferred to b and in another action b to c, it is, however short the interval between the two actions may be, not permissible to construct a uniform scale of value in which a precedes b and b precedes c. Nor is it permissible to consider a later third action as coincident with the two previous actions. All that the example proves is that value judgments are not immutable and that therefore a scale of value, which is abstracted from various, necessarily nonsynchronous actions of an individual, may be self-contradictory.[7]

One must not confuse the logical concept of consistency (viz., absence of contradiction) and the praxeological concept of consistency (viz., constancy or clinging to the same principles). Logical consistency has its place only in thinking, constancy has its place only in acting.

Constancy and rationality are entirely different notions. If one's valuations have changed, unremitting faithfulness to the once espoused principles of action merely for the sake of constancy would not be rational but simply stubborn. Only in one respect can acting be constant: in preferring the more valuable to the less valuable. If the valuations change, acting must change also. Faithfulness, under changed conditions, to an old plan would be nonsensical. A logical system must be consistent and free of contradictions because it implies the coexistence of all its parts and theorems. In acting, which is necessarily in the temporal order, there cannot be any question of such consistency. Acting must be suited to purpose, and purposefulness requires adjustment to changing conditions.

Presence of mind is considered a virtue in acting man. A man has presence of mind if he has the ability to think and to adjust his acting

6. Cf. Felix Kaufmann, "On the Subject-Matter of Economic Science," *Economica*, XIII, 390.
7. Cf. P. H. Wicksteed, *The Common Sense of Political Economy*, ed. Robbins (London, 1933), I, 32 ff.; L. Robbins, *An Essay on the Nature and Significance of Economic Science* (2d ed. London, 1935), pp. 91 ff.

so quickly that the interval between the emergence of new conditions and the adaptation of his actions to them becomes as short as possible. If constancy is viewed as faithfulness to a plan once designed without regard to changes in conditions, then presence of mind and quick reaction are the very opposite of constancy.

When the speculator goes to the stock exchange, he may sketch a definite plan for his operations. Whether or not he clings to this plan, his actions are rational also in the sense which those eager to distinguish rational acting from irrational attribute to the term "rational." This speculator in the course of the day may embark upon transactions which an observer, not taking into account the changes occurring in market conditions, will not be able to interpret as the outcome of constant behavior. But the speculator is firm in his intention to make profits and to avoid losses. Accordingly he must adjust his conduct to the change in market conditions and in his own judgment concerning the future development of prices.[8]

However one twists things, one will never succeed in formulating the notion of "irrational" action whose "irrationality" is not founded upon an arbitrary judgment of value. Let us suppose that somebody has chosen to act inconstantly for no other purpose than for the sake of refuting the praxeological assertion that there is no irrational action. What happens here is that a man aims at a peculiar goal, viz., the refutation of a praxeological theorem, and that he accordingly acts differently from what he would have done otherwise. He has chosen an unsuitable means for the refutation of praxeology, that is all.

---

8. Plans too, of course, may be self-contradictory. Sometimes their contradictions may be the effect of mistaken judgment. But sometimes such contradictions may be intentional and serve a definite purpose. If, for instance, a publicized program of a government or a political party promises high prices to the producers and at the same time low prices to the consumers, the purpose of such an espousal of incompatible goals may be demagogic. Then the program, the publicized plan, is self-contradictory; but the plan of its authors who wanted to attain a definite end through the endorsement of incompatible aims and their public announcement is free of any contradiction.

CHAPTER 6

Uncertainty

1   Uncertainty and Acting

The uncertainty of the future is already implied in the very notion of action. That man acts and that the future is uncertain are by no means two independent matters. They are only two different modes of establishing one thing.

We may assume that the outcome of all events and changes is uniquely determined by eternal unchangeable laws governing becoming and development in the whole universe. We may consider the necessary connection and interdependence of all phenomena, i.e., their causal concatenation, as the fundamental and ultimate fact. We may entirely discard the notion of undetermined chance. But however that may be, or appear to the mind of a perfect intelligence, the fact remains that to acting man the future is hidden. If man knew the future, he would not have to choose and would not act. He would be like an automaton, reacting to stimuli without any will of his own.

Some philosophers are prepared to explode the notion of man's will as an illusion and self-deception because man must unwittingly behave according to the inevitable laws of causality. They may be right or wrong from the point of view of the prime mover or the cause of itself. However, from the human point of view action is the ultimate thing. We do not assert that man is "free" in choosing and acting. We merely establish the fact that he chooses and acts and that we are at a loss to use the methods of the natural sciences for answering the question why he acts this way and not otherwise.

Natural science does not render the future predictable. It makes it possible to foretell the results to be obtained by definite actions. But it leaves unpredictable two spheres: that of insufficiently known natural phenomena and that of human acts of choice. Our ignorance with regard to these two spheres taints all human actions with uncertainty. Apodictic certainty is only within the orbit of the deductive system of aprioristic theory. The most that can be attained with regard to reality is probability.

It is not the task of praxeology to investigate whether or not it is permissible to consider as certain some of the theorems of the empirical natural sciences. This problem is without practical importance for praxeological considerations. At any rate, the theorems of physics and chemistry have such a high degree of probability that we are entitled to call them certain for all practical purposes. We can practically forecast the working of a machine constructed according to the rules of scientific technology. But the construction of a machine is only a part in a broader program that aims at supplying the consumers with the machine's products. Whether this was or was not the most appropriate plan depends on the development of future conditions which at the time of the plan's execution cannot be forecast with certainty. Thus the degree of certainty with regard to the technological outcome of the machine's construction, whatever it may be, does not remove the uncertainty inherent in the whole action. Future needs and valuations, the reaction of men to changes in conditions, future scientific and technological knowledge, future ideologies and policies can never be foretold with more than a greater or smaller degree of probability. Every action refers to an unknown future. It is in this sense always a risky speculation.

The problems of truth and certainty concern the general theory of human knowledge. The problem of probability, on the other hand, is a primary concern of praxeology.

2   The Meaning of Probability

The treatment of probability has been confused by the mathematicians. From the beginning there was an ambiguity in dealing with the calculus of probability. When the Chevalier de Méré consulted Pascal on the problems involved in the games of dice, the great mathematician should have frankly told his friend the truth, namely, that mathematics cannot be of any use to the gambler in a game of pure chance. Instead he wrapped his answer in the symbolic language of mathematics. What could easily be explained in a few sentences of mundane speech was expressed in a terminology which is unfamiliar to the immense majority and therefore regarded with reverential awe. People suspected that the puzzling formulas contain some important revelations, hidden to the uninitiated; they got the impression that a scientific method of gambling exists and that the esoteric teachings of mathematics provide a key for winning. The heavenly mystic Pascal unintentionally became the patron saint of gambling. The textbooks of the calculus of probability gratuitously propagandize for the gambling casinos precisely because they are sealed books to the layman.

No less havoc was spread by the equivocations of the calculus of probability in the field of scientific research. The history of every branch of knowledge records instances of the misapplication of the calculus of probability which, as John Stuart Mill observed, made it "the real opprobrium of mathematics."[1]

The problem of probable inference is much bigger than those problems which constitute the field of the calculus of probability. Only preoccupation with the mathematical treatment could result in the prejudice that probability always means frequency.

A further error confused the problem of probability with the problem of inductive reasoning as applied by the natural sciences. The attempt to substitute a universal theory of probability for the category of causality characterizes an abortive mode of philosophizing, very fashionable only a few years ago.

A statement is probable if our knowledge concerning its content is deficient. We do not know everything which would be required for a definite decision between true and not true. But, on the other hand, we do know something about it; we are in a position to say more than simply *non liquet* [(Latin) not clear or proven] or *ignoramus* [we do not know].

There are two entirely different instances of probability; we may call them class probability (or frequency probability) and case probability (or the specific understanding of the sciences of human action). The field for the application of the former is the field of the natural sciences, entirely ruled by causality; the field for the application of the latter is the field of the sciences of human action, entirely ruled by teleology.

3   Class Probability

Class probability means: We know or assume to know, with regard to the problem concerned, everything about the behavior of a whole class of events or phenomena; but about the actual singular events or phenomena we know nothing but that they are elements of this class.

We know, for instance, that there are ninety tickets in a lottery and that five of them will be drawn. Thus we know all about the behavior of the whole class of tickets. But with regard to the singular tickets we do not know anything but that they are elements of this class of tickets.

We have a complete table of mortality for a definite period of the past in a definite area. If we assume that with regard to mortality no changes will occur, we may say that we know everything about the mortality of the whole population in question. But with regard to the

1. John Stuart Mill, A *System of Logic Ratiocinative and Inductive* (new impression, London, 1936), p. 353.

life expectancy of the individuals we do not know anything but that they are members of this class of people.

For this defective knowledge the calculus of probability provides a presentation in symbols of the mathematical terminology. It neither expands nor deepens nor complements our knowledge. It translates it into mathematical language. Its calculations repeat in algebraic formulas what we knew beforehand. They do not lead to results that would tell us anything about the actual singular events. And, of course, they do not add anything to our knowledge concerning the behavior of the whole class, as this knowledge was already perfect — or was considered perfect — at the very outset of our consideration of the matter.

It is a serious mistake to believe that the calculus of probability provides the gambler with any information which could remove or lessen the risk of gambling. It is, contrary to popular fallacies, quite useless for the gambler, as is any other mode of logical or mathematical reasoning. It is the characteristic mark of gambling that it deals with the unknown, with pure chance. The gambler's hopes for success are not based on substantial considerations. The nonsuperstitious gambler thinks: "There is a slight chance [or, in other words: 'it is not impossible'] that I may win; I am ready to put up the stake required. I know very well that in putting it up I am behaving like a fool. But the biggest fools have the most luck. Anyway!"

Cool reasoning must show the gambler that he does not improve his chances by buying two tickets instead of one of a lottery in which the total amount of the winnings is smaller than the proceeds from the sale of all tickets. If he were to buy all the tickets, he would certainly lose a part of his outlay. Yet every lottery customer is firmly convinced that it is better to buy more tickets than less. The habitués of the casinos and slot machines never stop. They do not give a thought to the fact that, because the ruling odds favor the banker over the player, the outcome will the more certainly result in a loss for them the longer they continue to play. The lure of gambling consists precisely in its unpredictability and its adventurous vicissitudes.

Let us assume that ten tickets, each bearing the name of a different man, are put into a box. One ticket will be drawn, and the man whose name it bears will be liable to pay 100 dollars. Then an insurer can promise to the loser full indemnification if he is in a position to insure each of the ten for a premium of ten dollars. He will collect 100 dollars and will have to pay the same amount to one of the ten. But if he were to insure one only of them at a rate fixed by the calculus, he would embark not upon an insurance business, but upon gambling. He would substitute himself for the insured. He would collect ten dollars and would get the chance either of keeping it or of losing that ten dollars and ninety dollars more.

If a man promises to pay at the death of another man a definite sum and charges for this promise the amount adequate to the life expectancy as determined by the calculus of probability, he is not an insurer but a gambler. Insurance, whether conducted according to business principles or according to the principle of mutuality, requires the insurance of a whole class or what can reasonably be considered as such. Its basic idea is pooling and distribution of risks, not the calculus of probability. The mathematical operation that it requires are the four elementary operations of arithmetic. The calculus of probability is mere by-play.

This is clearly evidenced by the fact that the elimination of hazardous risk by pooling can also be effected without any recourse to actuarial methods. Everybody practices it in his daily life. Every businessman includes in his normal cost accounting the compensation for losses which regularly occur in the conduct of affairs. "Regularly" means in this context: The amount of these losses is known as far as the whole class of the various items is concerned. The fruit dealer may know, for instance, that one of every fifty apples will rot in this stock; but he does not know to which individual apple this will happen. He deals with such losses as with any other item in the bill of costs.

The definition of the essence of class probability as given above is the only logically satisfactory one. It avoids the crude circularity implied in all definitions referring to the equiprobability of possible events. In stating that we know nothing about actual singular events except that they are elements of a class the behavior of which is fully known, this vicious circle is disposed of. Moreover, it is superfluous to add a further condition called the absence of any regularity in the sequence of the singular events.

The characteristic mark of insurance is that it deals with the whole class of events. As we pretend to know everything about the behavior of the whole class, there seems to be no specific risk involved in the conduct of the business.

Neither is there any specific risk in the business of the keeper of a gambling bank or in the enterprise of a lottery. From the point of view of the lottery enterprise the outcome is predictable, provided that all tickets have been sold. If some tickets remain unsold, the enterpriser is in the same position with regard to them as every buyer of a ticket is with regard to the tickets he bought.

4   Case Probability

Case probability means: We know, with regard to a particular event, some of the factors which determine its outcome; but there are other determining factors about which we know nothing.

Case probability has nothing in common with class probability but the incompleteness of our knowledge. In every other regard the two are entirely different.

There are, of course, many instances in which men try to forecast a particular future event on the basis of their knowledge about the behavior of the class. A doctor may determine the chances for the full recovery of his patient if he knows that 70 per cent of those afflicted with the same disease recover. If he expresses his judgment correctly, he will not say more than that the probability of recovery is 0.7, that is, that out of ten patients not more than three on the average die. All such predictions about external events, i.e., events in the field of the natural sciences, are of this character. They are in fact not forecasts about the issue of the case in question, but statements about the frequency of the various possible outcomes. They are based either on statistical information or simply on the rough estimate of the frequency derived from nonstatistical experience.

So far as such types of probable statements are concerned, we are not faced with case probability. In fact we do not know anything about the case in question except that it is an instance of a class the behavior of which we know or think we know.

A surgeon tells a patient who considers submitting himself to an operation that thirty out of every hundred undergoing such an operation die. If the patient asks whether this number of deaths is already full, he has misunderstood the sense of the doctor's statement. He has fallen prey to the error known as the "gambler's fallacy." Like the roulette player who concludes from a run of ten red in succession that the probability of the next turn being black is now greater than it was before the run, he confuses case probability with class probability.

All medical prognoses, when based only on general physiological knowledge, deal with class probability. A doctor who hears that a man he does not know has been seized by a definite illness will, on the basis of his general medical experience, say: His chances for recovery are 7 to 3. If the doctor himself treats the patient, he may have a different opinion. The patient is a young, vigorous man; he was in good health before he was taken with the illness. In such cases, the doctor may think, the mortality figures are lower; the chances for this patient are not 7:3, but 9:1. The logical approach remains the same, although it may be based not on a collection of statistical data, but simply on a more or less exact résumé of the doctor's own experience with previous cases. What the doctor knows is always only the behavior of classes. In our instance the class is the class of young, vigorous men seized by the illness in question.

Case probability is a particular feature of our dealing with problems of human action. Here any reference to frequency is inappropriate, as our statements always deal with unique events which as such — i.e., with regard to the problem in question — are not members of any class. We can form a class "American presidential elections." This class concept may prove useful or even necessary for various kinds of reasoning, as, for instance, for a treatment of the matter from the viewpoint of constitutional law. But if we are dealing with the election of 1944 — either, before the election, with its future outcome or, after the election, with an analysis of the factors which determined the outcome — we are grappling with an individual, unique, and nonrepeatable case. The case is characterized by its unique merits, it is a class by itself. All the marks which make it permissible to subsume it under any class are irrelevant for the problem in question.

Two football teams, the Blues and the Yellows, will play tomorrow. In the past the Blues have always defeated the Yellows. This knowledge is not knowledge about a class of events. If we were to consider it as such, we would have to conclude that the Blues are always victorious and that the Yellows are always defeated. We would not be uncertain with regard to the outcome of the game. We would know for certain that the Blues will win again. The mere fact that we consider our forecast about tomorrow's game as only probable shows that we do not argue this way.

On the other hand, we believe that the fact that the Blues were victorious in the past is not immaterial with regard to the outcome of tomorrow's game. We consider it as a favorable prognosis for the repeated success of the Blues. If we were to argue correctly according to the reasoning appropriate to class probability, we would not attach any importance to this fact. If we were not to resist the erroneous conclusion of the "gambler's fallacy," we would, on the contrary, argue that tomorrow's game will result in the success of the Yellows.

If we risk some money on the chance of one team's victory, the lawyers would qualify our action as a bet. They would call it gambling if class probability were involved.

Everything that outside the field of class probability is commonly implied in the term probability refers to the peculiar mode of reasoning involved in dealing with historical uniqueness or individuality, the specific understanding of the historical sciences.

Understanding is always based on incomplete knowledge. We may believe we know the motives of the acting men, the ends they are aiming at, and the means they plan to apply for the attainment of these ends. We have a definite opinion with regard to the effects to be expected from the operation of these factors. But this knowledge is defective. We cannot exclude beforehand the possibility that we have erred in the appraisal of their influence or have failed to take into consideration some factors whose interference we did not foresee at all, or not in a correct way.

Gambling, engineering, and speculating are three different modes of dealing with the future.

The gambler knows nothing about the event on which the outcome of his gambling depends. All that he knows is the frequency of a favorable outcome of a series of such events, knowledge which is useless for his undertaking. He trusts to good luck, that is his only plan.

Life itself is exposed to many risks. At any moment it is endangered by disastrous accidents which cannot be controlled, or at least not sufficiently. Every man banks on good luck. He counts upon not being struck by lightning and not being bitten by a viper. There is an element of gambling in human life. Man can remove some of the chrematistic consequences of such disasters and accidents by taking out insurance policies. In doing so he banks upon the opposite chances. On the part of the insured the insurance is gambling. His premiums were spent in vain if the disaster does not occur.[2] With regard to noncontrollable natural events man is always in the position of a gambler.

The engineer, on the other hand, knows everything that is needed for a technologically satisfactory solution of his problem, the construction of a machine. As far as some fringes of uncertainty are left in his power to control, he tries to eliminate them by taking safety

---

2. In life insurance the insured's stake spent in vain consists only in the difference between the amount collected and the amount he could have accumulated by saving.

margins. The engineer knows only soluble problems and problems which cannot be solved under the present state of knowledge. He may sometimes discover from adverse experience that his knowledge was less complete than he had assumed and that he failed to recognize the indeterminateness of some issues which he thought he was able to control. Then he will try to render his knowledge more complete. Of course he can never eliminate altogether the element of gambling present in human life. But it is his principle to operate only within an orbit of certainty. He aims at full control of the elements of his action.

It is customary nowadays to speak of "social engineering." Like planning, this term is a synonym for dictatorship and totalitarian tyranny. The idea is to treat human beings in the same way in which the engineer treats the stuff out of which he builds bridges, roads, and machines. The social engineer's will is to be substituted for the will of the various people he plans to use for the construction of his utopia. Mankind is to be divided into two classes: the almighty dictator, on the one hand, and the underlings who are to be reduced to the status of mere pawns in his plans and cogs in his machinery, on the other. If this were feasible, then of course the social engineer would not have to bother about understanding other people's actions. He would be free to deal with them as technology deals with lumber and iron.

In the real world acting man is faced with the fact that there are fellow men acting on their own behalf as he himself acts. The necessity to adjust his actions to other people's actions makes him a speculator for whom success and failure depend on his greater or lesser ability to understand the future. Every action is speculation. There is in the course of human events no stability and consequently no safety.

5   Numerical Evaluation of Case Probability

Case probability is not open to any kind of numerical evaluation. What is commonly considered as such exhibits, when more closely scrutinized, a different character.

On the eve of the 1944 presidential election people could have said:
(a) I am ready to bet three dollars against one that Roosevelt will be elected.
(b) I guess that out of the total amount of electors 45 millions will exercise their franchise, 25 millions of whom will vote for Roosevelt.
(c) I estimate Roosevelt's chances as 9 to 1.
(d) I am certain that Roosevelt will be elected.

Statement (d) is obviously inexact. If asked under oath on the witness stand whether he is as certain about Roosevelt's future victory as about the fact that a block of ice will melt when exposed to a temperature of 150 degrees, our man would have answered no. He would have rectified his statement and would have declared: I am personally fully convinced that Roosevelt will carry on. That is my opinion. But, of course, this is not certainty, only the way I understand the conditions involved.

The case of statement (a) is similar. This man believed that he risked very little when laying such a wager. The relation 3:1 is the outcome of the interplay of two factors: the opinion that Roosevelt will be elected and the man's propensity for betting.

Statement (b) is an evaluation of the outcome of the impending event. Its figures refer not to a greater or smaller degree of probability, but to the expected result of the voting. Such a statement may be based on a systematic investigation like the Gallup poll or simply on estimates.

It is different with statement (c). This is a proposition about the expected outcome couched in arithmetical terms. It certainly does not mean that out of ten cases of the same type nine are favorable for Roosevelt and one unfavorable. It cannot have any reference to class probability. But what else can it mean?

It is a metaphorical expression. Most of the metaphors used in daily speech imaginatively identify an abstract object with another object that can be apprehended directly by the senses. Yet this is not a necessary feature of metaphorical language, but merely a consequence of the fact that the concrete is as a rule more familiar to us than the abstract. As metaphors aim at an explanation of something which is less well known by comparing it with something better known, they consist for the most part in identifying something abstract with a better-known concrete. The specific mark of our case is that it is an attempt to elucidate a complicated state of affairs by resorting to an analogy borrowed from a branch of higher mathematics, the calculus of probability. As it happens, this mathematical discipline is more popular than the analysis of the epistemological nature of understanding.

There is no use in applying the yardstick of logic to a critique of metaphorical language. Analogies and metaphors are always defective and logically unsatisfactory. It is usual to search for the underlying *tertium comparationis* [(Latin) a basis for comparison]. But even this is not permissible with regard to the metaphor we are dealing with. For the comparison is based on a conception which is in itself faulty in the very frame of the calculus of probability, namely the gambler's fallacy. In asserting that Roosevelt's chances are 9:1, the idea is that Roosevelt is in regard to the impending election in the position of a man who owns 90 per cent of all tickets of a lottery in regard to the first prize. It is implied that this ratio 9:1 tells us something substantial about the outcome of the unique case in which we are interested. There is no need to repeat that this is a mistaken idea.

No less impermissible is the recourse to the calculus of probability in dealing with hypotheses in the field of the natural sciences. Hypotheses are tentative explanations consciously based on logically insufficient arguments. With regard to them all that can be asserted is: The hypothesis does or does not contradict either logical principles or the facts as experimentally established and considered as true. In the first case it is untenable, in the second case it is — under the present state of our experimental knowledge — not untenable. (The intensity of personal conviction is purely subjective.) Neither frequency probability nor historical understanding enters into the matter.

The term hypothesis, applied to definite modes of understanding historical events, is a misnomer. If a historian asserts that in the fall of the Romanoff dynasty the fact that this house was of German background played a relevant role, he does not advance a hypothesis. The facts on which his understanding is founded are beyond question. There was a widespread animosity against Germans in Russia, and the ruling line of the Romanoffs, having for 200 years intermarried exclusively with scions of families of German descent, was viewed by many Russians as a germanized family, even by those who assumed that Tsar Paul was not the son of Peter III. But the question remains what the relevance of these facts was in the chain of events which brought about the dethronement of this dynasty. Such problems are not open to any elucidation other than that provided by understanding.

6   Betting, Gambling, and Playing Games

A bet is the engagement to risk money or other things against another man on the result of an event about the outcome of which we know only so much as can be known on the ground of understanding. Thus people may bet on the result of an impending election or a tennis match. Or they may bet on whose opinion concerning the content of a factual assertion is right and whose is wrong.

Gambling is the engagement to risk money or other things against another man on the result of an event about which we do not know anything more than is known on the ground of knowledge concerning the behavior of the whole class.

Sometimes betting and gambling are combined. The outcome of horse racing depends both on human action — on the part of the owner of the horse, the trainer, and the jockey — and on nonhuman factors — the qualities of the horse. Most of those risking money on the turf are simply gamblers. But the experts believe they know something by understanding the people involved; as far as this factor influences their decision they are bettors. Furthermore they pretend to know the horses; they make a prognosis on the ground of their knowledge about the behavior of the classes of horses to which they assign the various competing horses. So far they are gamblers.

Later chapters of this book deal with the methods business applies in handling the problem of the uncertainty of the future. On this point of our reasoning only one more observation must be made.

Embarking upon games can be either an end or a means. It is an end for people who yearn for the stimulation and excitement with which the vicissitudes of a game provide them, or whose vanity is flattered by the display of their skill and superiority in playing a game which requires cunning and expertness. It is a means for professionals who want to make money by winning.

Playing a game can therefore be called an action. But it is not permissible to reverse this statement and to call every action a game or to deal with all actions as if they were games. The immediate aim in playing a game is to defeat the partner according to the rules of the game. This is a peculiar and special case of acting. Most actions do not aim at anybody's defeat or loss. They aim at an improvement in conditions. It can happen that this improvement is attained at some other men's expense. But this is certainly not always the case. It is, to put it mildly, certainly not the case within the regular operation of a social system based on the division of labor.

There is not the slightest analogy between playing games and the conduct of business within a market society. The card player wins money by outsmarting his antagonist. The businessman makes money by supplying customers with goods they want to acquire. There may exist an analogy between the strategy of a card player and that of a bluffer. There is no need to investigate this problem. He who interprets the conduct of business as trickery is on the wrong path.

The characteristic feature of games is the antagonism of two or more players or groups of players.[3] The characteristic feature of business

---

3. "Patience" or "Solitaire" is not a one-person game, but a pastime, a means of escaping boredom. It certainly does not represent a pattern for what is going on in a communistic society, as John von Neumann and Oscar Morgenstern (*Theory of Games and Economic Behavior* [Princeton, 1944], p. 86) assert.

within a society, i.e., within an order based on the division of labor, is concord in the endeavors of its members. As soon as they begin to antagonize one another, a tendency toward social disintegration emerges.

Within the frame of a market economy competition does not involve antagonism in the sense in which this term is applied to the hostile clash of incompatible interests. Competition, it is true, may sometimes or even often evoke in the competitors those passions of hatred and malice which usually accompany the intention of inflicting evil on other people. Psychologists are therefore prone to confuse combat and competition. But praxeology must beware of such artificial and misleading equivocations. From its point of view there exists a fundamental difference between catallactic competition and combat. Competitors aim at excellence and preeminence in accomplishments within a system of mutual cooperation. The function of competition is to assign to every member of a social system that position in which he can best serve the whole of society and all its members. It is a method of selecting the most able man for each performance. Where there is social cooperation, there some variety of selection must be applied. Only where the assignment of various individuals to various tasks is effected by the dictator's decisions alone and the individuals concerned do not aid the dictator by endeavors to represent their own virtues and abilities in the most favorable light, is there no competition.

We will have to deal at a later stage of our investigations with the function of competition.[4] At this point we must only emphasize that it is misleading to apply the terminology of mutual extermination to the problems of mutual cooperation as it works within a society. Military terms are inappropriate for the description of business operations. It is, e.g., a bad metaphor to speak of the conquest of a market. There is no conquest in the fact that one firm offers better or cheaper products than its competitors. Only in a metaphorical sense is there strategy in business operations.

7   Praxeological Prediction

Praxeological knowledge makes it possible to predict with apodictic certainty the outcome of various modes of action. But, of course, such prediction can never imply anything regarding quantitative matters. Quantitative problems are in the field of human action open

---

4. See below, pp. 273–77.

to no other elucidation than that by understanding.

We can predict, as will be shown later, that—other things being equal—a fall in the demand for a will result in a drop in the price of a. But we cannot predict the extent of this drop. This question can be answered only by understanding.

The fundamental deficiency implied in every quantitative approach to economic problems consists in the neglect of the fact that there are no constant relations between what are called economic dimensions. There is neither constancy nor continuity in the valuations and in the formation of exchange ratios between various commodities. Every new datum brings about a reshuffling of the whole price structure. Understanding, by trying to grasp what is going on in the minds of the men concerned, can approach the problem of forecasting future conditions. We may call its methods unsatisfactory and the positivists may arrogantly scorn it. But such arbitrary judgments must not and cannot obscure the fact that understanding is the only appropriate method of dealing with the uncertainty of future conditions.

CHAPTER 7

Action Within the World

1   The Law of Marginal Utility

Action sorts and grades; originally it knows only ordinal numbers, not cardinal numbers. But the external world to which acting man must adjust his conduct is a world of quantitative determinateness. In this world there exist quantitative relations between cause and effect. If it were otherwise, if definite things could render unlimited services, such things would never be scarce and could not be dealt with as means.

Acting man values things as means for the removal of his uneasiness. From the point of view of the natural sciences the various events which result in satisfying human needs appear as very different. Acting man sees in these events only a more or a less of the same kind. In valuing very different states of satisfaction and the means for their attainment, man arranges all things in *one* scale and sees in them only their relevance for an increase in his own satisfaction. The satisfaction derived from food and that derived from the enjoyment of a work of art are, in acting man's judgment, a more urgent or a less urgent need; valuation and action place them in one scale of what is more intensively desired and what is less. For acting man there exists primarily nothing but various degrees of relevance and urgency with regard to his own well-being.

Quantity and quality are categories of the external world. Only indirectly do they acquire importance and meaning for action. Because every thing can only produce a limited effect, some things are considered scarce and treated as means. Because the effects which things are able to produce are different, acting man distinguishes various classes of things. Because means of the same quantity and quality are apt always to produce the same quantity of an effect of the same quality, action does not differentiate between concrete definite quantities of homogeneous means. But this does not imply that it attaches the same value to the various portions of a supply of homogeneous means. Each portion is valued separately. To each portion its own rank in the scale of value is assigned. But these orders of rank can be *ad libitum* [(Latin) freely] interchanged among the various portions of the same magnitude.

If acting man has to decide between two or more means of different classes, he grades the individual portions of each of them. He assigns to each portion its special rank. In doing so he need not assign to the various portions of the same means orders of rank which immediately succeed one another.

The assignment of orders of rank through valuation is done only in acting and through acting. How great the portions are to which a single order of rank is assigned depends on the individual and unique conditions under which man acts in every case. Action does not deal with physical or metaphysical units which it values in an abstract academic way; it is always faced with alternatives between which it chooses. The choice must always be made between definite quantities of means. It is permissible to call the smallest quantity which can be the object of such a decision a unit. But one must guard oneself against the error of assuming that the valuation of the sum of such units is derived from the valuation of the units, or that it represents the sum of the valuations attached to these units.

A man owns five units of commodity *a* and three units of commodity *b*. He attaches to the units of *a* the rank-orders 1, 2, 4, 7, and 8, to the units of *b* the rank-orders 3, 5, and 6. This means: If he must choose between two units of *a* and two units of *b*, he will prefer to lose two units of *a* rather than two units of *b*. But if he must choose between three units of *a* and two units of *b*, he will prefer to lose two units of *b* rather than three units of *a*. What counts always and alone in valuing a compound of several units is the utility of this compound as a whole — i.e., the increment in well-being dependent upon it or, what is the same, the impairment of well-being which its loss must bring about. There are no arithmetical processes involved, neither adding nor multiplying; there is a valuation of the utility dependent upon the having of the portion, compound, or supply in question.

Utility means in this context simply: causal relevance for the removal of felt uneasiness. Acting man believes that the services a thing can render are apt to improve his own well-being, and calls this the utility of the thing concerned. For praxeology the term utility is tantamount to importance attached to a thing on account of the belief that it can remove uneasiness. The praxeological notion of utility (*subjective use-value* in the terminology of the earlier Austrian economists) must be sharply distinguished from the technological notion of utility (*objective use-value* in the terminology of the same economists). Use-value in the objective sense is the relation between a thing and the effect it has the capacity to bring about. It is to objective use-value that people refer in employing such terms as the "heating value" or "heating power" of coal. Subjective use-value is not always based on true objective use-value. There are things to which subjective use-value is attached because people erroneously believe that they have the power to bring about a desired effect. On the other hand there are things able to produce a desired effect to which no use-value is attached because people are ignorant of this fact.

Let us look at the state of economic thought which prevailed on the eve of the elaboration of the modern theory of value by Carl Menger, William Stanley Jevons, and Léon Walras. Whoever wants to construct an elementary theory of value and prices must first think of utility. Nothing indeed is more plausible than to assume that things are valued according to their utility. But then a difficulty appears which presented to the older economists a problem they failed to solve. They observed that things whose "utility" is greater are valued less than other things of smaller utility. *Iron* is less appreciated than *gold*. This fact seems to be incompatible with a theory of value and prices based on the concepts of utility and use-value. The economists believed that they had to abandon such a theory and tried to explain the phenomena of value and market exchange by other theories.

Only late did the economists discover that the apparent paradox was the outcome of a vicious formulation of the problem involved. The valuations and choices that result in the exchange ratios of the market do not decide between *gold* and *iron*. Acting man is not in a position in which he must choose between *all* the gold and *all* the iron. He chooses at a definite time and place under definite conditions between a strictly limited quantity of gold and a strictly limited quantity of iron. His decision in choosing between 100 ounces of gold and 100 tons of iron does not depend at all on the decision he would make if he were in the highly improbable situation of choosing between all the gold and all the iron. What counts alone for his actual choice is whether under existing conditions he considers the direct or indirect satisfaction which 100 ounces of gold could give him as greater or smaller than the direct or indirect satisfaction he could derive from 100 tons of iron. He does not express an academic or philosophical judgment concerning the "absolute" value of gold and of iron; he does not determine whether gold or iron is more important for mankind; he does not perorate as an author of books on the philosophy of history or on ethical principles. He simply chooses between two satisfactions both of which he cannot have together.

To prefer and to set aside and the choices and decisions in which they result are not acts of measurement. Action does not measure utility or value; it chooses between alternatives. There is no abstract problem of total utility or total value.[1] There is no ratiocinative operation which could lead from the valuation of a definite quantity or number of things to the determination of the value of a greater or smaller quantity or number. There is no means of calculating the total value of a supply if only the values of its parts are known. There is no means of establishing the value of a part of a supply if only the value of the total supply is known. There are in the sphere of values and valuations no arithmetical operations; there is no such thing as a calculation of values. The valuation of the total stock of two things can differ from the valuation of parts of these stocks. An isolated man owning seven cows and seven horses may value one horse higher than one cow and may, when faced with the alternative, prefer to give up one cow rather than one horse. But at the same time the same man, when faced with the alternative of choosing between his whole supply of horses and his whole supply of cows, may prefer to keep the cows and to give up the horses. The concepts of total utility and total value are meaningless if not applied to a situation in which people must choose between total supplies. The question whether *gold* as such and *iron* as such is more useful and valuable is reasonable only with regard to a situation in which mankind or an isolated part of mankind must choose between *all* the gold and *all* the iron available.

The judgment of value refers only to the supply with which the concrete act of choice is concerned. A supply is *ex definitione* [(Latin) by definition] always composed of homogeneous parts each of which is capable of rendering the same services as, and of being substituted for, any other part. It is therefore immaterial for the act of choosing which particular part forms its object. All parts—units—of the available stock are considered as equally useful and valuable if the problem of giving up *one* of them is raised. If the supply decreased by the loss of one unit, acting man must decide anew how to use the various units of the remaining stock. It is obvious that the smaller stock cannot render all the services the greater stock could. That employment of the various units which under this new disposition is no longer provided for, was in the eyes of acting man the least urgent employment among

1. It is important to note that this chapter does not deal with prices or market values, but with subjective use-value. Prices are a derivative of subjective use-value. Cf. below, Chapter 16.

all those for which he had previously assigned the various units of the greater stock. The satisfaction which he derived from the use of one unit for this employment was the smallest among the satisfactions which the units of the greater stock had rendered to him. It is only the value of this marginal satisfaction on which he must decide if the question of renouncing one unit of the total stock comes up. When faced with the problem of the value to be attached to one unit of a homogeneous supply, man decides on the basis of the value of the least important use he makes of the units of the whole supply; he decides on the basis of marginal utility.

If a man is faced with the alternative of giving up either one unit of his supply of *a* or one unit of his supply of *b*, he does not compare the total value of his total stock of *a* with the total value of his stock of *b*. He compares the marginal values both of *a* and of *b*. Although he may value the total supply of *a* higher than the total supply of *b*, the marginal value of *b* may be higher than the marginal value of *a*.

The same reasoning holds good for the question of increasing the available supply of any commodity by the acquisition of an additional definite number of units.

For the description of these facts economics does not need to employ the terminology of psychology. Neither does it need to resort to psychological reasoning and arguments for proving them. If we say that the acts of choice do not depend on the value attached to a whole class of wants, but on that attached to the concrete wants in question irrespective of the class in which they may be reckoned, we do not add anything to our knowledge and do not trace it back to some better-known or more general knowledge. This mode of speaking in terms of classes of wants becomes intelligible only if we remember the role played in the history of economic thought by the alleged paradox of value. Carl Menger and Böhm-Bawerk had to make use of the term "class of wants" in order to refute the objections raised by those who considered *bread* as such more valuable than *silk* because the class "want of nourishment" is more important than the class "want of luxurious clothing."[2] Today the concept "class of wants" is entirely superfluous. It has no meaning for action and therefore none for the theory of value; it is, moreover, liable to bring about error and confusion. Construction of concepts and classification are mental tools; they acquire meaning and sense only in the con-

2. Cf. Carl Menger, *Grundsätze der Volkswirtschaftslehre* (Vienna, 1871), pp. 88 ff. [It should be noted that it was translated into English by James Dingwall and Bert F. Hoselitz as *Principles of Economics*, Free Press of Glencoe, Ill., 1950; later merged with Crowell-Collier, then Macmillan; reprinted by the Institute of Humane Studies and New York University Press, 1981; and by Libertarian Press (Grove City, Pa.), 1994. The pages cited in the German 1871 edition (pp. 88 ff.) are pp. 123 ff. in the English.]; Böhm-Bawerk, *Kapital und Kapitalzins* (3d ed. Innsbruck, 1909), Pt. II, pp. 237 ff. [It should be noted that *Kapital und Kapitalzins* was translated into English by Hans F. Sennholz as *Capital and Interest* (South Holland, Ill.: Libertarian Press, 1959). The pages cited in the German (Pt. II, pp. 237 ff.) are pp. 137 ff. in Volume II of the English translation.]

text of theories which utilize them.[3] It is nonsensical to arrange various wants into "classes of wants" in order to establish that such a classification is of no avail whatever for the theory of value.

The law of marginal utility and decreasing marginal value is independent of Gossen's law of the saturation of wants (first law of Gossen). In treating marginal utility we deal neither with sensuous enjoyment nor with saturation and satiety. We do not transcend the sphere of praxeological reasoning in establishing the following definition: We call that employment of a unit of a homogeneous supply which a man makes if his supply is n units, but would not make if, other things being equal, his supply were only $n - 1$ units, the least urgent employment or the marginal employment, and the utility derived from it marginal utility. In order to attain this knowledge we do not need any physiological or psychological experience, knowledge, or reasoning. It follows necessarily from our assumptions that people act (choose) and that in the first case acting man has n units of a homogeneous supply and in the second case $n - 1$ units. Under these conditions no other result is thinkable. Our statement is formal and aprioristic and does not depend on any experience.

There are only two alternatives. Either there are or there are not intermediate stages between the felt uneasiness which impels a man to act and the state in which there can no longer be any action (be it because the state of perfect satisfaction is reached or because man is incapable of any further improvement in his conditions). In the second case there could be only one action; as soon as this action is consummated, a state would be reached in which no further action is possible. This is manifestly incompatible with our assumption that there is action; this case no longer implies the general conditions presupposed in the category of action. Only the first case remains. But then there are various degrees in the asymptotic approach to the state in which there can no longer be any action. Thus the law of marginal utility is already implied in the category of action. It is nothing else than the reverse of the statement that what satisfies more is preferred to what gives smaller satisfaction. If the supply available increases from $n - 1$ units to n units, the increment can be employed only for the removal of a want which is less urgent or less painful than the least urgent or least painful among all those wants which could be removed by means of the supply $n - 1$.

3. Classes are not in the world. It is our mind that classifies the phenomena in order to organize our knowledge. The question of whether a certain mode of classifying phenomena is conducive to this end or not is different from the question of whether it is logically permissible or not.

The law of marginal utility does not refer to objective use-value, but to subjective use-value. It does not deal with the physical or chemical capacity of things to bring about a definite effect in general, but with their relevance for the well-being of a man as he himself sees it under the prevailing momentary state of his affairs. It does not deal primarily with the value of things, but with the value of the services a man expects to get from them.

If we were to believe that marginal utility is about things and their objective use-value, we would be forced to assume that marginal utility can as well increase as decrease with an increase in the quantity of units available. It can happen that the employment of a certain minimum quantity — n units — of a good a can provide a satisfaction which is deemed more valuable than the services expected from one unit of a good b. But if the supply of a available is smaller than n, a can only be employed for another service which is considered less valuable than that of b. Then an increase in the quantity of a from $n - 1$ units to n units results in an increase of the value attached to one unit of a. The owner of 100 logs may build a cabin which protects him against rain better than a raincoat. But if fewer than 100 logs are available, he can only use them for a berth that protects him against the dampness of the soil. As the owner of 95 logs he would be prepared to forsake the raincoat in order to get 5 logs more. As the owner of 10 logs he would not abandon the raincoat even for 10 logs. A man whose savings amount to $100 may not be willing to carry out some work for a remuneration of $200. But if his savings were $2,000 and he were extremely anxious to acquire an indivisible good which cannot be bought for less than $2,100, he would be ready to perform this work for $100. All this is in perfect agreement with the rightly formulated law of marginal utility according to which value depends on the utility of the services expected. There is no question of any such thing as a law of increasing marginal utility.

The law of marginal utility must be confused neither with Bernoulli's doctrine *de mensura sortis* [(Latin) of measurement] nor with the Weber-Fechner law. At the bottom of Bernoulli's contribution were the generally known and never disputed facts that people are eager to satisfy the more urgent wants before they satisfy the less urgent, and that a rich man is in a position to provide better for his wants than a poor man. But the inferences Bernoulli drew from these truisms are all wrong. He developed a mathematical theory that the increment in gratification diminishes with the increase in a man's total wealth. His statement that as a rule it is highly probable that for a man whose income is 5,000 ducats one ducat means not more than half a ducat for a man with an income of 2,500 ducats is merely fanciful. Let us set aside the objection that there is no means of drawing comparisons other than entirely arbitrary ones between the valuations of various people. Bernoulli's method is no less inadequate for the valuations of the same individual with various amounts of income. He did not see that all that can be said about the case in question is that with increasing income every new increment is used for the satisfaction of a want less urgently felt than the least urgently felt want already satisfied before this increment took place. He did not see that in valuing, choosing, and acting there is no measurement and no establishment of equivalence, but grading, i.e., preferring and putting aside.[4] Thus neither Bernoulli nor the mathematicians and economists who adopted his mode of reasoning could succeed in solving the paradox of value.

The mistakes inherent in the confusion of the Weber-Fechner law of psychophysics and the subjective theory of value have already been attacked by Max Weber. Max Weber, it is true, was not sufficiently familiar with economics and was too much under the sway of historicism to get a correct insight into the fundamentals of economic thought. But ingenious intuition provided him with a suggestion of a way toward the correct solution. The theory of marginal utility, he asserts, is "not psychologically substantiated, but rather — if an epistemological term is to be applied — pragmatically, i.e., on the employment of the categories: ends and means."[5]

If a man wants to remove a pathological condition by taking a definite quantity of a remedy, the intake of a multiple will not bring about a better effect. The surplus will have either no effect other than the appropriate dose, the optimum, or it will have detrimental effects. The same is true of all kinds of satisfactions, although the optimum is often reached only by the application of a large dose, and the point at which further increments produce detrimental effects is often far away. This is so because our world is a world of causality and of quantitative relations between cause and effect. He who wants to remove the uneasiness caused by living in a room with a temperature of 35 degrees will aim at heating the room to a temperature of 65 or 70 degrees. It has nothing to do with the Weber-Fechner law that he does not aim at a temperature of 180 or 300 degrees. Neither has it

4. Cf. Daniel Bernoulli, *Versuch einer neuen Theorie zur Bestimmung von Glücksfällen*, trans. by Pringsheim (Leipzig, 1896), pp. 27 ff.
5. Cf. Max Weber, *Gesammelte Aufsätze zur Wissenschaftslehre* (Tübingen, 1922), p. 372; also p. 149. The term "pragmatical" as used by Weber is of course liable to bring about confusion. It is inexpedient to employ it for anything other than the philosophy of Pragmatism. If Weber had known the term "praxeology," he probably would have preferred it.

anything to do with psychology. All that psychology can do for the explanation of this fact is to establish as an ultimate given that man as a rule prefers the preservation of life and health to death and sickness. What counts for praxeology is only the fact that acting man chooses between alternatives. That man is placed at crossroads, that he must and does choose, is — apart from other conditions — due to the fact that he lives in a quantitative world and not in a world without quantity, which is even unimaginable for the human mind.

The confusion of marginal utility and the Weber-Fechner law originated from the mistake of looking only at the means for the attainment of satisfaction and not at the satisfaction itself. If the satisfaction had been thought of, the absurd idea would not have been adopted of explaining the configuration of the desire for warmth by referring to the decreasing intensity of the sensation of successive increments in the intensity of the stimuli. That the average man does not want to raise the temperature of his bedroom to 120 degrees has no reference whatever to the intensity of the sensation for warmth. That a man does not heat his room to the same degree as other normal people do and as he himself would probably do, if he were not more intent upon buying a new suit or attending the performance of a Beethoven symphony, cannot be explained by the methods of the natural sciences. Objective and open to a treatment by the methods of the natural sciences are only the problems of objective use-value; the valuation of objective use-value on the part of acting man is another thing.

2   The Law of Returns

Quantitative definiteness in the effects brought about by an economic good means with regard to the goods of the first order (consumers' goods): a quantity a of cause brings about — either once and for all or piecemeal over a definite period of time — a quantity α of effect. With regard to the goods of the higher orders (producers' goods) it means: a quantity b of cause brings about a quantity β of effect, provided the complementary cause c contributes the quantity γ of effect; only the concerted effects β and γ bring about the quantity p of the good of the first order D. There are in this case three quantities: b and c of the two complementary goods B and C, and p of the product D.

With b remaining unchanged, we call that value of c which results in the highest value of p/c the optimum. If several values of c result in this highest value of p/c, then we call that the optimum which results also in the highest value of p. If the two complementary goods are employed in the optimal ratio, they both render the highest output; their power to produce, their objective use-value, is fully utilized; no fraction of them is wasted. If we deviate from this optimal combination by increasing the quantity of C without changing the quantity of B, the return will as a rule increase further, but not in proportion to the increase in the quantity of C. If it is at all possible to increase the return from p to p_1 by increasing the quantity of *one* of the complementary factors only, namely by substituting cx for c, x being greater than 1, we have at any rate: $p_1 > p$ and $p_1c < pcx$. For if it were possible to compensate any decrease in b by a corresponding increase in c in such a way that p remains unchanged, the physical power of production proper to B would be unlimited and B would not be considered as scarce and as an economic good. It would be of no importance for acting man whether the supply of B available were greater or smaller. Even an infinitesimal quantity of B would be sufficient for the production of any quantity of D, provided the supply of C is large enough. On the other hand, an increase in the quantity of B available could not increase the output of D if the supply of C does not increase. The total return of the process would be imputed to C; B could not be an economic good. A thing rendering such unlimited services is, for instance, the knowledge of the causal relation implied. The formula, the recipe that teaches us how to prepare coffee, provided it is known, renders unlimited services. It does not lose anything from its capacity to produce however often it is used; its productive power is inexhaustible; it is therefore not an economic good. Acting man is never faced with a situation in which he must choose between the use-value of a known formula and any other useful thing.

The law of returns asserts that for the combination of economic goods of the higher orders (factors of production) there exists an optimum. If one deviates from this optimum by increasing the input of only one of the factors, the physical output either does not increase at all or at least not in the ratio of the increased input. This law, as has been demonstrated above, is implied in the fact that the quantitative definiteness of the effects brought about by any economic good is a necessary condition of its being an economic good.

That there is such an optimum of combination is all that the law of returns, popularly called the law of diminishing returns, teaches. There are many other questions which it does not answer at all and which can only be solved *a posteriori* by experience.

If the effect brought about by one of the complementary factors is indivisible, the optimum is the only combination which results in the outcome aimed at. In order to dye a piece of wool to a definite shade, a definite quantity of dye is required. A greater or smaller quantity would frustrate the aim sought. He who has more coloring matter must leave the surplus unused. He who has a smaller quantity can dye only a part of the piece. The diminishing return results in this instance in the complete uselessness of the additional quantity which must not even be employed because it would thwart the design.

In other instances a certain minimum is required for the production of the minimum effect. Between this minimum effect and the optimal effect there is a margin in which increased doses result either in a proportional increase in effect or in a more than proportional increase in effect. In order to make a machine turn, a certain minimum of lubricant is needed. Whether an increase of lubricant above this minimum increases the machine's performance in proportion to the increase in the amount applied, or to a greater extent, can only be ascertained by technological experience.

The law of returns does not answer the following questions: (1) Whether or not the optimum dose is the only one that is capable of producing the effect sought. (2) Whether or not there is a rigid limit above which any increase in the amount of the variable factor is quite useless. (3) Whether the decrease in output brought about by progressive deviation from the optimum and the increase in output brought about by progressive approach to the optimum result in proportional or nonproportional changes in output per unit of the variable factor. All this must be discerned by experience. But the law of returns itself, i.e., the fact that there must exist such an optimum combination, is valid *a priori*.

The Malthusian law of population and the concepts of absolute overpopulation and underpopulation and optimum population derived from it are the application of the law of returns to a special problem. They deal with changes in the supply of human labor, other factors being equal. Because people, for political considerations, wanted to reject the Malthusian law, they fought with passion but with faulty arguments against the law of returns—which, incidentally, they knew only as the law of diminishing returns of the use of capital and labor on land. Today we no longer need to pay any attention to these idle remonstrances. The law of returns is not limited to the use of complementary factors of production on land. The endeavors to refute or to demonstrate its validity by historical and experimental investigations of agricultural production are as needless as they are vain. He who wants to reject the law would have to explain why people are ready to pay prices for land. If the law were not valid, a farmer would never consider expanding the size of his farm. He would be in a position to multiply indefinitely the return of any piece of soil by multiplying his input of capital and labor.

People have sometimes believed that, while the law of diminishing returns is valid in agricultural production, with regard to the processing industries a law of increasing returns prevails. It took a long time before they realized that the law of returns refers to all branches of production equally. It is faulty to contrast agriculture and the processing industries with regard to this law. What is called—in a very inexpedient, even misleading terminology—the law of increasing returns is nothing but a reversal of the law of diminishing returns, an unsatisfactory formulation of the law of returns. If one approaches the optimum combination by increasing the quantity of one factor only, the quantity of other factors remaining unchanged, then the returns per unit of the variable factor increase either in proportion to the increase or even to a greater extent. A machine may, when operated by 2 workers, produce p; when operated by 3 workers, 3 p; when operated by 4 workers, 6 p; when operated by 5 workers, 7 p; when operated by 6 workers, also not more than 7 p. Then the employment of 4 workers renders the optimum return per head of the worker, namely $6/4\ p$, while under the other combinations the returns per head are respectively $1/2\ p$, p, $7/5\ p$ and $7/6\ p$. If, instead of 2 workers, 3 or 4 workers are employed, then the returns increase more than in relation to the increase in the number of workers; they do not increase in the proportion 2:3:4, but in the proportion 1:3:6. We are faced with increasing returns per head of the worker. But this is nothing else than the reverse of the law of diminishing returns.

If a plant or enterprise deviates from the optimum combination of the factors employed, it is less efficient than a plant or enterprise for which the deviation from the optimum is smaller. Both in agriculture and in the processing industries many factors of production are not perfectly divisible. It is, especially in the processing industries, for the most part easier to attain the optimum combination by expanding the size of the plant or enterprise than by restricting it. If the smallest unit of one or of several factors is too large to allow for its optimal exploitation in a small or medium-size plant or enterprise, the only way to attain the optimum is by increasing the outfit's size. It is these facts that bring about the superiority of big-scale production. The full importance of this problem will be shown later in discussing the issues of cost accounting.

3   Human Labor as a Means

The employment of the physiological functions and manifestations of human life as a means is called labor. The display of the potentialities of human energy and vital processes which the man whose life they manifest does not use for the attainment of external ends different from the mere running of these processes and from the physiological role they play in the biological consummation of his own vital economy, is not labor; it is simply life. Man works in using his forces and abilities as a means for the removal of uneasiness and in substituting purposeful exploitation of his vital energy for the spontaneous and carefree discharge of his faculties and nerve tensions. Labor is a means, not an end in itself.

Every individual has only a limited quantity of energy to expend, and every unit of labor can only bring about a limited effect. Otherwise human labor would be available in abundance; it would not be scarce and it would not be considered as a means for the removal of uneasiness and economized as such.

In a world in which labor is economized only on account of its being available in a quantity insufficient to attain all ends for which it can be used as a means, the supply of labor available would be equal to the whole quantity of labor which all men together are able to expend. In such a world everybody would be eager to work until he had completely exhausted his momentary capacity to work. The time which is not required for recreation and restoration of the capacity to work, used up by previous working, would be entirely devoted to work. Every nonutilization of the full capacity to work would be deemed a loss. Through the performance of more work one would have increased one's well-being. That a part of the available potential remained unused would be appraised as a forfeiture of well-being not compensated by any corresponding increase in well-being. The very idea of laziness would be unknown. Nobody would think: I could possibly do this or that; but it is not worthwhile; it does not pay; I prefer my leisure. Everybody would consider his whole capacity to work as a supply of factors of production which he would be anxious to utilize completely. Even a chance of the smallest increase in well-being would be considered a sufficient incentive to work more if it happened that at the instant no more profitable use could be made of the quantity of labor concerned.

In our actual world things are different. The expenditure of labor is deemed painful. Not to work is considered a state of affairs more satisfactory than working. Leisure is, other things being equal, preferred to travail. People work only when they value the return of labor higher than the decrease in satisfaction brought about by the curtailment of leisure. To work involves disutility.

Psychology and physiology may try to explain this fact. There is no need for praxeology to investigate whether or not they can succeed in such endeavors. For praxeology it is a datum that men are eager to enjoy leisure and therefore look upon their own capacity to bring about effects with feelings different from those with which they look upon the capacity of material factors of production. Man in considering an expenditure of his own labor investigates not only whether there is no more desirable end for the employment of the quantity of labor in question, but no less whether it would not be more desirable to abstain from any further expenditure of labor. We can express this fact also in calling the attainment of leisure an end of purposeful activity, or an economic good of the first order. In employing this somewhat sophisticated terminology, we must view leisure as any other economic good from the aspect of marginal utility. We must conclude that the first unit of leisure satisfies a desire more urgently felt than the second one, the second one a more urgent desire than the third one, and so on. Reversing this proposition, we get the statement that the disutility of labor felt by the worker increases in a greater proportion than the amount of labor expended.

However, it is needless for praxeology to study the question of whether or not the disutility of labor increases in proportion to the increase in the quantity of labor performed or to a greater extent. (Whether this problem is of any importance for physiology and psychology, and whether or not these sciences can elucidate it, can be left undecided.) At any rate the worker knocks off work at the point at which he no longer considers the utility of continuing work as a sufficient compensation for the disutility of the additional expenditure of labor. In forming this judgment he contrasts, if we disregard the decrease in yield brought about by increasing fatigue, each portion of working time with the same quantity of product as the preceding portions. But the utility of the units of yield decreases with the progress of the labor performed and the increase in the total amount of yield produced. The products of the prior units of working time have provided for the satisfaction of more important needs than the products of the work performed later. The satisfaction of these less important needs may not be considered as a sufficient reward for the further continuation of work, although they are compared with the same quantities of physical output.

It is therefore irrelevant for the praxeological treatment of the matter whether the disutility of labor is proportional to the total expenditure of labor or whether it increases to a greater extent than the time spent in working. At any rate, the propensity to expend the still unused portions of the total potential for work decreases, other things being equal, with the increase in the portions already expended. Whether this decrease in the readiness to work more proceeds with a more rapid or a less rapid acceleration, is always a question of economic data, not a question of categorial principles.

The disutility attached to labor explains why in the course of human history, concomitantly with the progressive increase in the physical productivity of labor brought about by technological improvement and a more abundant supply of capital, by and large a tendency toward shortening the hours of work developed. Among the amenities which civilized man can enjoy in a more abundant way than his less civilized ancestors there is also the enjoyment of more leisure time. In this sense one can answer the question, often raised by philosophers and philanthropists, whether or not economic progress has made men happier. If the productivity of labor were lower than it is in the present capitalist world, man would be forced either to toil more or to forsake many amenities. In establishing this fact the economists do not assert that the only means to attain happiness is to enjoy more material comfort, to live in luxury, or to have more leisure. They simply acknowledge the truth that men are in a position to provide themselves better with what they consider they need.

The fundamental praxeological insight that men prefer what satisfies them more to what satisfies them less and that they value things on the basis of their utility does not need to be corrected or complemented by an additional statement concerning the disutility of labor. These propositions already imply the statement that labor is preferred to leisure only in so far as the yield of labor is more urgently desired than the enjoyment of leisure.

The unique position which the factor labor occupies in our world is due to its nonspecific character. All nature-given primary factors of production — i.e., all those natural things and forces that man can use for improving his state of well-being — have specific powers and virtues. There are ends for whose attainment they are more suitable, ends for which they are less suitable, and ends for which they are altogether unsuitable. But human labor is both suitable and indispensable for the performance of all thinkable processes and modes of production.

It is, of course, impermissible to deal with human labor as such in general. It is a fundamental mistake not to see that men and their abilities to work are different. The work a certain individual can perform is more suitable for some ends, less suitable for other ends, and altogether unsuitable for still other ends. It was one of the deficiencies of classical economics that it did not pay enough attention to this fact and did not take it into account in the construction of its theory of value, prices, and wage rates. Men do not economize labor in general, but the particular kinds of labor available. Wages are not paid for labor expended, but for the achievements of labor, which differ widely in quality and quantity. The production of each particular product requires the employment of workers able to perform the particular kind of labor concerned. It is absurd to justify the failure to consider this point by reference to the alleged fact that the main demand for and supply of labor concerns unskilled common labor which every healthy man is able to perform, and that skilled labor, the labor of people with particular inborn faculties and special training, is by and large an exception. There is no need to investigate whether conditions were such in a remote past or whether even for primitive tribesmen the inequality of inborn and acquired capacities for work was the main factor in economizing labor. In dealing with conditions of civilized peoples it is impermissible to disregard the differences in the quality of labor performed. Work which various people are able to perform is different because men are born unequal and because the skill and experience they acquire in the course of their lives differentiate their capacities still more.

In speaking of the nonspecific character of human labor we certainly do not assert that all human labor is of the same quality. What we want to establish is rather that the differences in the kind of labor required for the production of various commodities are greater than the differences in the inborn capacities of men. (In emphasizing this point we are not dealing with the creative performances of the genius; the work of the genius is outside the orbit of ordinary human action and is like a free gift of destiny which comes to mankind overnight.[6] We furthermore disregard the institutional barriers denying some groups of people access to certain occupations and the training they require.) The innate inequality of various individuals does not break up the zoological uniformity and homogeneity of the species man to such an extent as to divide the supply of labor into disconnected sections. Thus the potential supply of labor available for the per-

6. See below, pp. 139–40.

formance of each particular kind of work exceeds the actual demand for such labor. The supply of every kind of specialized labor could be increased by the withdrawal of workers from other branches and their training. The quantity of need satisfaction is in none of the branches of production permanently limited by a scarcity of people capable of performing special tasks. Only in the short run can there emerge a dearth of specialists. In the long run it can be removed by training people who display the innate abilities required.

Labor is the most scarce of all primary means of production because it is in this restricted sense nonspecific and because every variety of production requires the expenditure of labor. Thus the scarcity of the other primary means of production — i.e., the nonhuman means of production supplied by nature — becomes for acting man a scarcity of those primary material means of production whose utilization requires the smallest expenditure of labor.[7] It is the supply of labor available that determines to what an extent the factor nature in each of its varieties can be exploited for the satisfaction of needs.

If the supply of labor which men are able and ready to perform increases, production increases too. Labor cannot remain unemployed on account of its being useless for the further improvement of need satisfaction. Isolated self-sufficient man always has the opportunity of improving his condition by expending more labor. On the labor market of a market society there are buyers for every supply of labor offered. There can be abundance and superfluity only in segments of the labor market; it results in pushing labor to other segments and in an expansion of production in some other provinces of the economic system. On the other hand, an increase in the quantity of land available — other things being equal — could result in an increase in production only if the additional land is more fertile than the marginal land tilled before.[8] The same is valid with regard to accumulated material equipment for future production. The serviceableness of capital goods also depends on the supply of labor available. It would be wasteful to use the capacity of existing facilities if the labor required could be employed for the satisfaction of more urgent needs.

Complementary factors of production can only be used to the extent allowed by the availability of the most scarce among them. Let us assume that the production of 1 unit of p requires the expenditure

7. Of course, some natural resources are so scarce that they are entirely utilized.
8. Under free mobility of labor it would be wasteful to improve barren soil if the reclaimed area is not so fertile that it compensates for the total cost of the operation.

of 7 units of a and of 3 units of b and that neither a nor b can be used for any production other than that of p. If 49 a and 2,000 b are available, no more than 7 p can be produced. The available supply of a determines the extent of the use of b. Only a is considered an economic good; only for a are people ready to pay prices; the full price of p is allowed for 7 units of a. On the other hand b is not an economic good and no prices are allowed for it. There are quantities of b which remain unused.

We may try to imagine the conditions within a world in which all material factors of production are so fully employed that there is no opportunity to employ all men or to employ all men to the extent that they are ready to work. In such a world labor is abundant; an increase in the supply of labor cannot add any increment whatever to the total amount of production. If we assume that all men have the same capacity and application for work and if we disregard the disutility of labor, labor in such a world would not be an economic good. If this world were a socialist commonwealth, an increase in population figures would be deemed an increase in the number of idle consumers. If it were a market society, wage rates paid would not be enough to prevent starvation. Those seeking employment would be ready to go to work for any wages, however low, even if insufficient for the preservation of their lives. They would be happy to delay for a while death by starvation.

There is no need to dwell upon the paradoxes of this hypothesis and to discuss the problems of such a world. Our world is different. Labor is more scarce than material factors of production. We are not dealing at this point with the problem of optimum population. We are dealing only with the fact that there are material factors of production which remain unused because the labor required is needed for the satisfaction of more urgent needs. In our world there is no abundance, but a shortage of manpower, and there are unused material factors of production, i.e., land, mineral deposits, and even plants and equipment.

This state of affairs could be changed by such an increase in population figures that all material factors required for the production of the foodstuffs indispensable — in the strict meaning of the word — for the preservation of human life are fully exploited. But as long as this is not the case, it cannot be changed by any improvement in technological methods of production. The substitution of more efficient methods of production for less efficient ones does not render labor abundant, provided there are still material factors available whose utilization can increase human well-being. On the contrary, it increases output and thereby the quantity of consumers' goods. "Labor-saving" devices increase supply. They do not bring about "technological unemployment."[9]

Every product is the result of the employment both of labor and of material factors. Man economizes both labor and material factors.

Immediately Gratifying Labor and Mediately Gratifying Labor

As a rule labor gratifies the performer only mediately, namely, through the removal of uneasiness which the attainment of the end brings about. The worker gives up leisure and submits to the disutility of labor in order to enjoy either the product or what other people are ready to give him for it. The expenditure of labor is for him a means for the attainment of certain ends, a price paid and a cost incurred.

But there are instances in which the performance of labor gratifies the worker immediately. He derives immediate satisfaction from the expenditure of labor. The yield is twofold. It consists on the one hand in the attainment of the product and on the other hand in the satisfaction that the performance itself gives to the worker.

People have misinterpreted this fact grotesquely and have based on this misinterpretation fantastic plans for social reforms. One of the main dogmas of socialism is that labor has disutility only within the capitalistic system of production, while under socialism it will be pure delight. We may disregard the effusions of the poor lunatic Charles Fourier. But Marxian "scientific" socialism does not differ in this point from the utopians. Some of its foremost champions, Frederick Engels and Karl Kautsky, expressly declare that a chief effect of a socialist regime will be to transform labor from a pain into a pleasure.[10]

The fact is often ignored that those activities which bring about immediate gratification and are thus direct sources of pleasure and enjoyment, are essentially different from labor and working. Only a very superficial treatment of the facts concerned can fail to recognize these differences. Paddling a canoe as it is practiced on Sundays for amusement on the lakes of public parks can only from the point of view of hydromechanics be likened to the rowing of boatsmen and galley slaves. When judged as a means for the attainment of ends it is as different as is the humming of an aria by a rambler from the recital of the same aria by the singer in the opera. The carefree Sunday paddler and the singing rambler derive immediate gratification from their activities, but not mediate gratification. What they do is therefore not labor, not the employment of their physiological functions for the attainment of ends other than the mere exercise of these functions.

9. See below, pp. 773–74.
10. Karl Kautsky, *Die soziale Revolution* (3d ed. Berlin, 1911), II, 16 ff. About Engels see below, p. 591.

It is merely pleasure. It is an end in itself; it is done for its own sake and does not render any further service. As it is not labor, it is not permissible to call it immediately gratifying labor.[11]

Sometimes a superficial observer may believe that labor performed by other people gives rise to immediate gratification because he himself would like to engage in a kind of play which apparently imitates the kind of labor concerned. As children play school, soldiers, and railroad, so adults too would like to play this and that. They think that the railroad engineer must enjoy operating and steering his engine as much as they would if they were permitted to toy with it. On his hurried way to the office the bookkeeper envies the patrolman who, he thinks, is paid for leisurely strolling around his beat. But the patrolman envies the bookkeeper who, sitting on a comfortable chair in a well-heated room, makes money by some scribbling which cannot seriously be called labor. Yet the opinions of people who misinterpret other people's work and consider it a mere pastime need not be taken seriously.

There are, however, also instances of genuine immediately gratifying labor. There are some kinds of labor of which, under special conditions, small quantities provide immediate gratification. But these quantities are so insignificant that they do not play any role at all in the complex of human action and production for the satisfaction of wants. Our world is characterized by the phenomenon of the disutility of labor. People trade the disutility-bringing labor for the products of labor; labor is for them a source of mediate gratification.

As far as a special kind of labor gives a limited amount of pleasure and not pain, immediate gratification and not disutility of labor, no wages are allowed for its performance. On the contrary, the performer, the "worker," must buy the pleasure and pay for it. Hunting game was and is for many people regular disutility-creating labor. But there are people for whom it is pure pleasure. In Europe amateur hunters buy from the owner of the hunting-ground the right to shoot a definite number of game of a definite type. The purchase of this right is separated from the price to be paid for the bag. If the two purchases are linked together, the price by far exceeds the prices that can be obtained on the market for the bag. A chamois buck still roaming on precipitous rocks has therefore a higher cash value than later when killed, brought down to the valley, and ready for the utilization of the meat, the skin, and the horns, although strenuous climbing and some material must be expended for its killing. One could say that one of the services which a living buck is able to render is to provide the hunter with the pleasure of killing it.

11. Rowing seriously practiced as a sport and singing seriously practiced by an amateur are introversive labor. See below, pp. 587–88.

The Creative Genius

Far above the millions that come and pass away tower the pioneers, the men whose deeds and ideas cut out new paths for mankind. For the pioneering genius [12] to create is the essence of life. To live means for him to create. The activities of these prodigious men cannot be fully subsumed under the praxeological concept of labor. They are not labor because they are for the genius not means, but ends in themselves. He lives in creating and inventing. For him there is not leisure, only intermissions of temporary sterility and frustration. His incentive is not the desire to bring about a result, but the act of producing it. The accomplishment gratifies him neither mediately nor immediately. It does not gratify him mediately because his fellow men at best are unconcerned about it, more often even greet it with taunts, sneers, and persecution. Many a genius could have used his gifts to render his life agreeable and joyful; he did not even consider such a possibility and chose the thorny path without hesitation. The genius wants to accomplish what he considers his mission, even if he knows that he moves toward his own disaster.

Neither does the genius derive immediate gratification from his creative activities. Creating is for him agony and torment, a ceaseless excruciating struggle against internal and external obstacles; it consumes and crushes him. The Austrian poet Grillparzer has depicted this in a touching poem "Farewell to Gastein." [13] We may assume that in writing it he thought not only of his own sorrows and tribulations but also of the greater sufferings of a much greater man, of Beethoven, whose fate resembled his own and whom he understood, through devoted affection and sympathetic appreciation, better than any other of his contemporaries. Nietzsche compared himself to the flame that insatiably consumes and destroys itself.[14] Such agonies are phenomena which have nothing in common with the connotations generally attached to the notions of work and labor, production and success, breadwinning and enjoyment of life.

The achievements of the creative innovator, his thoughts and theories, his poems, paintings, and compositions, cannot be classified praxeologically as products of *labor*. They are not the outcome of

12. Leaders (Führers) are not pioneers. They guide people along the tracks pioneers have laid. The pioneer clears a road through land hitherto inaccessible and may not care whether or not anybody wants to go the new way. The leader directs people toward the goal they want to reach.
13. It seems that there is no English translation of this poem. The book of Douglas Yates (*Franz Grillparzer, a Critical Biography*, Oxford, 1946), I, 57, gives a short English résumé of its content.
14. For a translation of Nietzsche's poem see M. A. Mügge, *Friedrich Nietzsche* (New York, 1911), p. 275.

the employment of labor which could have been devoted to the production of other amenities for the "production" of a masterpiece of philosophy, art, or literature. Thinkers, poets, and artists are sometimes unfit to accomplish any other work. At any rate, the time and toil which they devote to creative activities are not withheld from employment for other purposes. Conditions may sometimes doom to sterility a man who would have had the power to bring forth things unheard of; they may leave him no alternative other than to die from starvation or to use all his forces in the struggle for mere physical survival. But if the genius succeeds in achieving his goals, nobody but himself pays the "costs" incurred. Goethe was perhaps in some respects hampered by his functions at the court of Weimar. But certainly he would not have accomplished more in his official duties as minister of state, theatre manager, and administrator of mines if he had not written his plays, poems, and novels.

It is, furthermore, impossible to substitute other people's work for that of the creators. If Dante and Beethoven had not existed, one would not have been in a position to produce the *Divina Commedia* or the Ninth Symphony by assigning other men to these tasks. Neither society nor single individuals can substantially further the genius and his work. The highest intensity of the "demand" and the most peremptory order of the government are ineffectual. The genius does not deliver to order. Men cannot improve the natural and social conditions which bring about the creator and his creation. It is impossible to rear geniuses by eugenics, to train them by schooling, or to organize their activities. But, of course, one can organize society in such a way that no room is left for pioneers and their path-breaking.

The creative accomplishment of the genius is an ultimate fact for praxeology. It comes to pass in history as a free gift of destiny. It is by no means the result of production in the sense in which economics uses this term.

4   Production

Action, if successful, attains the end sought. It produces the product.

Production is not an act of creation; it does not bring about something that did not exist before. It is a transformation of given elements through arrangement and combination. The producer is not a creator. Man is creative only in thinking and in the realm of imagination. In the world of external phenomena he is only a transformer. All that he can accomplish is to combine the means available in such a way that according to the laws of nature the result aimed at is bound to emerge.

It was once customary to distinguish between the production of tangible goods and the rendering of personal services. The carpenter who made tables and chairs was called productive; but this epithet was denied to the doctor whose advice helped the ailing carpenter to recover his capacity to make tables and chairs. A differentiation was made between the doctor-carpenter nexus and the carpenter-tailor nexus. The doctor, it was asserted, does not himself produce; he makes a living from what other people produce, he is maintained by carpenters and tailors. At a still earlier date the French Physiocrats contended that all labor was sterile unless it extracted something from the soil. Only cultivation, fishing and hunting, and the working of mines and quarries were in their opinion productive. The processing industries did not add to the value of the material employed anything more than the value of the things consumed by the workers.

Present-day economists laugh at their predecessors for having made such untenable distinctions. However, they should rather cast the beam out of their own eyes. The way in which many contemporary writers deal with various problems—for instance, advertising and marketing—is manifestly a relapse into the crude errors which should have disappeared long ago.

Another widely held opinion finds a difference between the employment of labor and that of material factors of production. Nature, it is asserted, dispenses its gifts gratuitously; but labor must be paid for by submitting to its disutility. In toiling and overcoming the disutility of labor man adds something to the universe that did not exist before. In this sense labor was called creative. This too is erroneous. Man's capacity to work is given in the universe as are the original and inherent capacities of the land and the animal substances. Nor does the fact that a part of the potentiality of labor can remain unused differentiate it from the nonhuman factors of production; these too can remain unused. The readiness of individuals to overcome the disutility of labor is the outcome of the fact that they prefer the produce of labor to the satisfaction derived from more leisure.

Only the human mind that directs action and production is creative. The mind too appertains to the universe and to nature; it is a part of the given and existing world. To call the mind creative is not to indulge in any metaphysical speculations. We call it creative because we are at a loss to trace the changes brought about by human action farther back than to the point at which we are faced with the intervention of reason directing human activities. Production is not something physical, material, and external; it is a spiritual and intellectual phenomenon. Its essential requisites are not human labor and external natural forces and things, but the decision of the mind to use these factors as means for the attainment of ends. What produces the product are not toil and trouble in themselves, but the fact that the toiling is guided by reason. The human mind alone has the power to remove uneasiness.

The materialist metaphysics of the Marxians misconstrues these things entirely. The "productive forces" are not material. Production is a spiritual, intellectual, and ideological phenomenon. It is the method that man, directed by reason, employs for the best possible removal of uneasiness. What distinguishes our conditions from those of our ancestors who lived one thousand or twenty thousand years ago is not something material, but something spiritual. The material changes are the outcome of the spiritual changes.

Production is alteration of the given according to the designs of reason. These designs—the recipes, the formulas, the ideologies—are the primary thing; they transform the original factors—both human and nonhuman—into means. Man produces by dint of his reason; he chooses ends and employs means for their attainment. The popular saying according to which economics deals with the material conditions of human life is entirely mistaken. Human action is a manifestation of the mind. In this sense praxeology can be called a moral science (*Geisteswissenschaft*).

Of course, we do not know what mind *is*, just as we do not know what motion, life, electricity *are*. Mind is simply the word to signify the unknown factor that has enabled men to achieve all that they have accomplished: the theories and the poems, the cathedrals and the symphonies, the motorcars and the airplanes.

Action Within the Framework of Society

CHAPTER 8

Human Society

1	Human Cooperation

Society is concerted action, cooperation.

Society is the outcome of conscious and purposeful behavior. This does not mean that individuals have concluded contracts by virtue of which they have founded human society. The actions which have brought about social cooperation and daily bring it about anew do not aim at anything else than cooperation and coadjuvancy with others for the attainment of definite singular ends. The total complex of the mutual relations created by such concerted actions is called society. It substitutes collaboration for the—at least conceivable—isolated life of individuals. Society is division of labor and combination of labor. In his capacity as an acting animal man becomes a social animal.

Individual man is born into a socially organized environment. In this sense alone we may accept the saying that society is—logically or historically—antecedent to the individual. In every other sense this dictum is either empty or nonsensical. The individual lives and acts within society. But society is nothing but the combination of individuals for cooperative effort. It exists nowhere else than in the actions of individual men. It is a delusion to search for it outside the actions of individuals. To speak of a society's autonomous and independent existence, of its life, its soul, and its actions is a metaphor which can easily lead to crass errors.

The questions whether society or the individual is to be considered as the ultimate end, and whether the interests of society should be subordinated to those of the individuals or the interests of the individuals to those of society are fruitless. Action is always action of individual men. The social or societal element is a certain orientation of the actions of individual men. The category *end* makes sense only when applied to action. Theology and the metaphysics of history may discuss the ends of society and the designs which God wants to realize with regard to society in the same way in which they discuss the purpose of all other parts of the created universe. For science,

144 ANDcaCTION WITHIN THE FRAMEWORK OF SOCIETY

which is inseparable from reason, a tool manifestly unfit for the treatment of such problems, it would be hopeless to embark upon speculations concerning these matters.

Within the frame of social cooperation there can emerge between members of society feelings of sympathy and friendship and a sense of belonging together. These feelings are the source of man's most delightful and most sublime experiences. They are the most precious adornment of life; they lift the animal species man to the heights of a really human existence. However, they are not, as some have asserted, the agents that have brought about social relationships. They are fruits of social cooperation, they thrive only within its frame; they did not precede the establishment of social relations and are not the seed from which they spring.

The fundamental facts that brought about cooperation, society, and civilization and transformed the animal man into a human being are the facts that work performed under the division of labor is more productive than isolated work and that man's reason is capable of recognizing this truth. But for these facts men would have forever remained deadly foes of one another, irreconcilable rivals in their endeavors to secure a portion of the scarce supply of means of sustenance provided by nature. Each man would have been forced to view all other men as his enemies; his craving for the satisfaction of his own appetites would have brought him into an implacable conflict with all his neighbors. No sympathy could possibly develop under such a state of affairs.

Some sociologists have asserted that the original and elementary subjective fact in society is a "consciousness of kind."[1] Others maintain that there would be no social systems if there were no "sense of community or of belonging together."[2] One may agree, provided that these somewhat vague and ambiguous terms are correctly interpreted. We may call consciousness of kind, sense of community, or sense of belonging together the acknowledgment of the fact that all other human beings are potential collaborators in the struggle for survival because they are capable of recognizing the mutual benefits of cooperation, while the animals lack this faculty. However, we must not forget that the primary facts that bring about such consciousness or such a sense are the two mentioned above. In a hypothetical world in which the division of labor would not increase productivity, there would not be any society. There would not be any sentiments of benevolence and good will.

---

1. F. H. Giddings, *The Principles of Sociology* (New York, 1926), p. 17.
2. R. M. MacIver, *Society* (New York, 1937), pp. 6–7.

The principle of the division of labor is one of the great basic principles of cosmic becoming and evolutionary change. The biologists were right in borrowing the concept of the division of labor from social philosophy and in adapting it to their field of investigation. There is division of labor between the various parts of any living organism. There are, furthermore, organic entities composed of collaborating animal individuals; it is customary to call metaphorically such aggregations of the ants and bees "animal societies." But one must never forget that the characteristic feature of human society is purposeful cooperation; society is an outcome of human action, i.e., of a conscious aiming at the attainment of ends. No such element is present, as far as we can ascertain, in the processes which have resulted in the emergence of the structure-function systems of plant and animal bodies and in the operation of the societies of ants, bees, and hornets. Human society is an intellectual and spiritual phenomenon. It is the outcome of a purposeful utilization of a universal law determining cosmic becoming, viz., the higher productivity of the division of labor. As with every instance of action, the recognition of the laws of nature is put into the service of man's efforts to improve his conditions.

2 A Critique of the Holistic and Metaphysical View of Society

According to the doctrines of universalism, conceptual realism, holism, collectivism, and some representatives of Gestaltpsychologie, society is an entity living its own life, independent of and separate from the lives of the various individuals, acting on its own behalf and aiming at its own ends which are different from the ends sought by the individuals. Then, of course, an antagonism between the aims of society and those of its members can emerge. In order to safeguard the flowering and further development of society it becomes necessary to master the selfishness of the individuals and to compel them to sacrifice their egoistic designs to the benefit of society. At this point all these holistic doctrines are bound to abandon the secular methods of human science and logical reasoning and to shift to theological or metaphysical professions of faith. They must assume that Providence, through its prophets, apostles, and charismatic leaders, forces men who are constitutionally wicked, i.e., prone to pursue their own ends, to walk in the ways of righteousness which the Lord or *Weltgeist* or history wants them to walk.

This is the philosophy which has characterized from time immemorial the creeds of primitive tribes. It has been an element in all religious teachings. Man is bound to comply with the law issued by a superhuman power and to obey the authorities which this power has entrusted with the enforcement of the law. The order created by this law, human society, is consequently the work of the Deity and not of man. If the Lord had not interfered and had not given enlightenment to erring mankind, society would not have come into existence. It is true that social cooperation is a blessing for man; it is true that man could work his way up from barbarism and the moral and material distress of his primitive state only within the framework of society. However, if left alone he would never have seen the road to his own salvation. For adjustment to the requirements of social cooperation and subordination to the precepts of the moral law put heavy restraints upon him. From the point of view of his wretched intellect he would deem the abandonment of some expected advantage an evil and a privation. He would fail to recognize the incomparably greater, but later, advantages which renunciation of present and visible pleasures will procure. But for supernatural revelation he would never have learned what destiny wants him to do for his own good and that of his offspring.

The scientific theory as developed by the social philosophy of eighteenth-century rationalism and liberalism and by modern economics does not resort to any miraculous interference of superhuman powers. Every step by which an individual substitutes concerted action for isolated action results in an immediate and recognizable improvement in his conditions. The advantages derived from peaceful cooperation and division of labor are universal. They immediately benefit every generation, and not only later descendants. For what the individual must sacrifice for the sake of society he is amply compensated by greater advantages. His sacrifice is only apparent and temporary; he foregoes a smaller gain in order to reap a greater one later. No reasonable being can fail to see this obvious fact. When social cooperation is intensified by enlarging the field in which there is division of labor or when legal protection and the safeguarding of peace are strengthened, the incentive is the desire of all those concerned to improve their own conditions. In striving after his own—rightly understood—interests the individual works toward an intensification of social cooperation and peaceful intercourse. Society is a product of human action, i.e., the human urge to remove uneasiness as far as possible. In order to explain its becoming and its evolution it is not necessary to have recourse to a doctrine, certainly offensive to a truly religious mind, according to which the original creation was so defective that reiterated superhuman intervention is needed to prevent its failure.

The historical role of the theory of the division of labor as elaborated by British political economy from Hume to Ricardo consisted in the complete demolition of all metaphysical doctrines concerning the origin and the operation of social cooperation. It consummated the spiritual, moral and intellectual emancipation of mankind inaugurated by the philosophy of Epicureanism. It substituted an autonomous rational morality for the heteronomous and intuitionist ethics of older days. Law and legality, the moral code and social institutions are no longer revered as unfathomable decrees of Heaven. They are of human origin, and the only yardstick that must be applied to them is that of expediency with regard to human welfare. The utilitarian economist does not say: *Fiat justitia, pereat mundus* [(Latin) Let justice be done, (though) the world be destroyed]. He says: *Fiat justitia, ne pereat mundus* [(Latin) Let justice be done, (so) the world not be destroyed]. He does not ask a man to renounce his well-being for the benefit of society. He advises him to recognize what his rightly understood interests are. In his eyes God's magnificence does not manifest itself in busy interference with sundry affairs of princes and politicians, but in endowing his creatures with reason and the urge toward the pursuit of happiness.[3]

The essential problem of all varieties of universalistic, collectivistic, and holistic social philosophy is: By what mark do I recognize the true law, the authentic apostle of God's word, and the legitimate authority. For many claim that Providence has sent them, and each of these prophets preaches another gospel. For the faithful believer there cannot be any doubt; he is fully confident that he has espoused the only true doctrine. But it is precisely the firmness of such beliefs that renders the antagonisms irreconcilable. Each party is prepared to make its own tenets prevail. But as logical argumentation cannot decide between various dissenting creeds, there is no means left for the settlement of such disputes other than armed conflict. The non-

---

3. Many economists, among them Adam Smith and Bastiat, believed in God. Hence they admired in the facts they had discovered the providential care of "the great Director of Nature." Atheist critics blame them for this attitude. However, these critics fail to realize that to sneer at the references to the "invisible hand" does not invalidate the essential teachings of the rationalist and utilitarian social philosophy. One must comprehend that the alternative is this: Either association is a human process because it best serves the aims of the individuals concerned and the individuals themselves have the ability to realize the advantages they derive from their adjustment to life in social cooperation. Or a superior being enjoins upon reluctant men subordination to the law and to the social authorities. It is of minor importance whether one calls this supreme being God, Weltgeist, Destiny, History, Wotan, or Material Productive Forces and what title one assigns to its apostles, the dictators.

rationalist, nonutilitarian, and nonliberal social doctrines must beget wars and civil wars until one of the adversaries is annihilated or subdued. The history of the world's great religions is a record of battles and wars, as is the history of the present-day counterfeit religions, socialism, statolatry, and nationalism.

Intolerance and propaganda by the executioner's or the soldier's sword are inherent in any system of heteronomous ethics. The laws of God or Destiny claim universal validity, and to the authorities which they declare legitimate all men by rights owe obedience. As long as the prestige of heteronomous codes of morality and of their philosophical corollary, conceptual realism, was intact, there could not be any question of tolerance or of lasting peace. When fighting ceased, it was only to gather new strength for further battling. The idea of tolerance with regard to other people's dissenting views could take root only when the liberal doctrines had broken the spell of universalism. In the light of the utilitarian philosophy, society and state no longer appear as institutions for the maintenance of a world order that for considerations hidden to the human mind pleases the Deity although it manifestly hurts the secular interests of many or even of the immense majority of those living today. Society and state are on the contrary the primary means for all people to attain the ends they aim at of their own accord. They are created by human effort and their maintenance and most suitable organization are tasks not essentially different from all other concerns of human action. The supporters of a heteronomous morality and of the collectivistic doctrine cannot hope to demonstrate by ratiocination the correctness of their specific variety of ethical principles and the superiority and exclusive legitimacy of their particular social ideal. They are forced to ask people to accept credulously their ideological system and to surrender to the authority they consider the right one; they are intent upon silencing dissenters or upon beating them into submission.

Of course, there will always be individuals and groups of individuals whose intellect is so narrow that they cannot grasp the benefits which social cooperation brings them. There are others whose moral strength and will power are so weak that they cannot resist the temptation to strive for an ephemeral advantage by actions detrimental to the smooth functioning of the social system. For the adjustment of the individual to the requirements of social cooperation demands sacrifices. These are, it is true, only temporary and apparent sacrifices as they are more than compensated for by the incomparably greater advantages which living within society provides. However, at the instant, in the very act of renouncing an expected enjoyment, they are painful, and it is not for everybody to realize their later benefits and to behave accordingly. Anarchism believes that education could make all people comprehend what their own interests require them to do; rightly instructed they would of their own accord always comply with the rules of conduct indispensable for the preservation of society. The anarchists contend that a social order in which nobody enjoys privileges at the expense of his fellow-citizens could exist without any compulsion and coercion for the prevention of action detrimental to society. Such an ideal society could do without state and government, i.e., without a police force, the social apparatus of coercion and compulsion.

The anarchists overlook the undeniable fact that some people are either too narrow-minded or too weak to adjust themselves spontaneously to the conditions of social life. Even if we admit that every sane adult is endowed with the faculty of realizing the good of social cooperation and of acting accordingly, there still remains the problem of the infants, the aged, and the insane. We may agree that he who acts antisocially should be considered mentally sick and in need of care. But as long as not all are cured, and as long as there are infants and the senile, some provision must be taken lest they jeopardize society. An anarchistic society would be exposed to the mercy of every individual. Society cannot exist if the majority is not ready to hinder, by the application or threat of violent action, minorities from destroying the social order. This power is vested in the state or government.

State or government is the social apparatus of compulsion and coercion. It has the monopoly of violent action. No individual is free to use violence or the threat of violence if the government has not accorded this right to him. The state is essentially an institution for the preservation of peaceful interhuman relations. However, for the preservation of peace it must be prepared to crush the onslaughts of peace-breakers.

Liberal social doctrine, based on the teachings of utilitarian ethics and economics, sees the problem of the relation between the government and those ruled from a different angle than universalism and collectivism. Liberalism realizes that the rulers, who are always a minority, cannot lastingly remain in office if not supported by the consent of the majority of those ruled. Whatever the system of government may be, the foundation upon which it is built and rests is always the opinion of those ruled that to obey and to be loyal to this government better serves their own interests than insurrection and the establishment of another regime. The majority has the power to do away with an unpopular government and uses this power whenever it becomes convinced that its own welfare requires it. In the long run there is no such thing as an unpopular government. Civil war and revolution are the means by which the discontented majorities overthrow rulers and methods of government which do not suit them. For the sake of domestic peace liberalism aims at democratic government. Democracy is therefore not a revolutionary institution. On the contrary, it is the very means of preventing revolutions and civil wars. It provides a method for the peaceful adjustment of government to the will of the majority. When the men in office and their policies no longer please the majority of the nation, they will—in the next election—be eliminated and replaced by other men espousing different policies.

The principle of majority rule or government by the people as recommended by liberalism does not aim at the supremacy of the mean, of the low-bred, of the domestic barbarians. The liberals too believe that a nation should be ruled by those best fitted for this task. But they believe that a man's ability to rule proves itself better by convincing his fellow-citizens than by using force upon them. There is, of course, no guarantee that the voters will entrust office to the most competent candidate. But no other system could offer such a guarantee. If the majority of the nation is committed to unsound principles and prefers unworthy office-seekers, there is no remedy other than to try to change their mind by expounding more reasonable principles and recommending better men. A minority will never win lasting success by other means.

Universalism and collectivism cannot accept this democratic solution of the problem of government. In their opinion the individual in complying with the ethical code does not directly further his earthly concerns but, on the contrary, foregoes the attainment of his own ends for the benefit of the designs of the Deity or of the collective whole. Moreover reason alone is not capable of conceiving the supremacy of the absolute values and the unconditional validity of the sacred law and of interpreting correctly the canons and commandments. Hence it is in their eyes a hopeless task to try to convince the majority through persuasion and to lead them to righteousness by amicable admonition. Those blessed by heavenly inspiration, to whom their *charisma* has conveyed illumination, have the duty to propagate the gospel to the docile and to resort to violence against the intractable. The charismatic leader is the Deity's vicar, the mandatory of the collective whole, the tool of history. He is infallible and always right. His orders are the supreme norm.

Universalism and collectivism are by necessity systems of theocratic government. The common characteristic of all their varieties is that they postulate the existence of a superhuman entity which the individuals are bound to obey. What differentiates them from one another is only the appellation they give to this entity and the content of the laws they proclaim in its name. The dictatorial rule of a minority cannot find any legitimation other than the appeal to an alleged mandate obtained from a superhuman absolute authority. It does not matter whether the autocrat bases his claims on the divine rights of anointed kings or on the historical mission of the vanguard of the proletariat or whether the supreme being is called *Geist* (Hegel) or *Humanité* (Auguste Comte). The terms society and state as they are used by the contemporary advocates of socialism, planning, and social control of all the activities of individuals signify a deity. The priests of this new creed ascribe to their idol all those attributes which the theologians ascribe to God — omnipotence, omniscience, infinite goodness, and so on.

If one assumes that there exists above and beyond the individual's actions an imperishable entity aiming at its own ends, different from those of mortal men, one has already constructed the concept of a superhuman being. Then one cannot evade the question whose ends take precedence whenever an antagonism arises, those of the state or society or those of the individual. The answer to this question is already implied in the very concept of state or society as conceived by collectivism and universalism. If one postulates the existence of an entity which *ex definitione* is higher, nobler, and better than the individuals, then there cannot be any doubt that the aims of this eminent being must tower above those of the wretched individuals. (It is true that some lovers of paradox — for instance, Max Stirner[4] — took pleasure in turning the matter upside down and for all that asserted the precedence of the individual.) If society or state is an entity endowed with volition and intention and all the other qualities attributed to it by the collectivist doctrine, then it is simply nonsensical to set the shabby individual's trivial aims against its lofty designs.

The quasi-theological character of all collectivist doctrines becomes manifest in their mutual conflicts. A collectivist doctrine does not assert the superiority of a collective whole *in abstracto*; it always proclaims the eminence of a definite collectivist idol, and either flatly denies the existence of other such idols or relegates them to a sub-

4. Cf. Max Stirner (Johann Kaspar Schmidt). *The Ego and His Own*, trans. by S. T. Byington (New York, 1907).

ordinate and ancillary position with regard to its own idol. The worshipers of the state proclaim the excellence of a definite state, i.e., their own; the nationalists, the excellence of their own nation. If dissenters challenge their particular program by heralding the superiority of another collectivist idol, they resort to no objection other than to declare again and again: We are right because an inner voice tells us that we are right and you are wrong. The conflicts of antagonistic collectivist creeds and sects cannot be decided by ratiocination; they must be decided by arms. The alternatives to the liberal and democratic principle of majority rule are the militarist principles of armed conflict and dictatorial oppression.

All varieties of collectivist creeds are united in their implacable hostility to the fundamental political institutions of the liberal system: majority rule, tolerance of dissenting views, freedom of thought, speech, and the press, equality of all men under the law. This collaboration of collectivist creeds in their attempts to destroy freedom has brought about the mistaken belief that the issue in present-day political antagonisms is individualism versus collectivism. In fact it is a struggle between individualism on the one hand and a multitude of collectivist sects on the other hand whose mutual hatred and hostility is no less ferocious than their abomination of the liberal system. It is not a uniform Marxian sect that attacks capitalism, but a host of Marxian groups. These groups—for instance, Stalinists, Trotskyists, Mensheviks, supporters of the Second International, and so on—fight one another with the utmost brutality and inhumanity. And then there are again many other non-Marxian sects which apply the same atrocious methods in their mutual struggles. A substitution of collectivism for liberalism would result in endless bloody fighting.

The customary terminology misrepresents these things entirely. The philosophy commonly called individualism is a philosophy of social cooperation and the progressive intensification of the social nexus. On the other hand the application of the basic ideas of collectivism cannot result in anything but social disintegration and the perpetuation of armed conflict. It is true that every variety of collectivism promises eternal peace starting with the day of its own decisive victory and the final overthrow and extermination of all other ideologies and their supporters. However, the realization of these plans is conditioned upon a radical transformation in mankind. Men must be divided into two classes: the omnipotent godlike dictator on the one hand and the masses which must surrender volition and reasoning in order to become mere chessmen in the plans of the dictator. The masses must be dehumanized in order to make one man their godlike master. Thinking and acting, the foremost characteristics of man as man, would become the privilege of *one* man only. There is no need to point out that such designs are unrealizable. The chiliastic empires of dictators are doomed to failure; they have never lasted longer than a few years. We have just witnessed the breakdown of several of such "millennial" orders. Those remaining will hardly fare better.

The modern revival of the idea of collectivism, the main cause of all the agonies and disasters of our day, has succeeded so thoroughly that it has brought into oblivion the essential ideas of liberal social philosophy. Today even many of those favoring democratic institutions ignore these ideas. The arguments they bring forward for the justification of freedom and democracy are tainted with collectivist errors; their doctrines are rather a distortion than an endorsement of true liberalism. In their eyes majorities are always right simply because they have the power to crush any opposition; majority rule is the dictatorial rule of the most numerous party, and the ruling majority is not bound to restrain itself in the exercise of its power and in the conduct of political affairs. As soon as a faction has succeeded in winning the support of the majority of citizens and thereby attained control of the government machine, it is free to deny to the minority all those democratic rights by means of which it itself has previously carried on its own struggle for supremacy.

This pseudo-liberalism is, of course, the very antithesis of the liberal doctrine. The liberals do not maintain that majorities are godlike and infallible; they do not contend that the mere fact that a policy is advocated by the many is a proof of its merits for the common weal. They do not recommend the dictatorship of the majority and the violent oppression of dissenting minorities. Liberalism aims at a political constitution which safeguards the smooth working of social cooperation and the progressive intensification of mutual social relations. Its main objective is the avoidance of violent conflicts, of wars and revolutions that must disintegrate the social collaboration of men and throw people back into the primitive conditions of barbarism where all tribes and political bodies endlessly fought one another. Because the division of labor requires undisturbed peace, liberalism aims at the establishment of a system of government that is likely to preserve peace, viz., democracy.

Praxeology and Liberalism

Liberalism, in its nineteenth-century sense, is a political doctrine. It is not a theory, but an application of the theories developed by praxeology and especially by economics to definite problems of human action within society.

As a political doctrine liberalism is not neutral with regard to values and the ultimate ends sought by action. It assumes that all men or at least the majority of people are intent upon attaining certain goals. It gives them information about the means suitable to the realization of their plans. The champions of liberal doctrines are fully aware of the fact that their teachings are valid only for people who are committed to these valuational principles.

While praxeology, and therefore economics too, uses the terms happiness and removal of uneasiness in a purely formal sense, liberalism attaches to them a concrete meaning. It presupposes that people prefer life to death, health to sickness, nourishment to starvation, abundance to poverty. It teaches man how to act in accordance with these valuations.

It is customary to call these concerns materialistic and to charge liberalism with an alleged crude materialism and a neglect of the "higher" and "nobler" pursuits of mankind. Man does not live by bread alone, say the critics, and they disparage the meanness and despicable baseness of the utilitarian philosophy. However, these passionate diatribes are wrong because they badly distort the teachings of liberalism.

First: The liberals do not assert that men *ought* to strive after the goals mentioned above. What they maintain is that the immense majority prefer a life of health and abundance to misery, starvation, and death. The correctness of this statement cannot be challenged. It is proved by the fact that all antiliberal doctrines—the theocratic tenets of the various religious, statist, nationalist, and socialist parties—adopt the same attitude with regard to these issues. They all promise their followers a life of plenty. They have never ventured to tell people that the realization of their program will impair their material well-being. They insist—on the contrary—that while the realization of the plans of their rival parties will result in indigence for the majority, they themselves want to provide their supporters with abundance. The Christian parties are no less eager in promising the masses a higher standard of living than the nationalists and the socialists. Present-day churches often speak more about raising wage rates and farm incomes than about the dogmas of the Christian doctrine.

Secondly: The liberals do not disdain the intellectual and spiritual aspirations of man. On the contrary. They are prompted by a passionate ardor for intellectual and moral perfection, for wisdom and for aesthetic excellence. But their view of these high and noble things is far from the crude representations of their adversaries. They do not share the naïve opinion that any system of social organization can directly succeed in encouraging philosophical or scientific thinking, in producing masterpieces of art and literature and in rendering the masses more enlightened. They realize that all that society can achieve in these fields is to provide an environment which does not put insurmountable obstacles in the way of the genius and makes the common man free enough from material concerns to become interested in things other than mere breadwinning. In their opinion the foremost social means of making man more human is to fight poverty. Wisdom and science and the arts thrive better in a world of affluence than among needy peoples.

It is a distortion of facts to blame the age of liberalism for an alleged materialism. The nineteenth century was not only a century of unprecedented improvement in technical methods of production and in the material well-being of the masses. It did much more than extend the average length of human life. Its scientific and artistic accomplishments are imperishable. It was an age of immortal musicians, writers, poets, painters, and sculptors; it revolutionized philosophy, economics, mathematics, physics, chemistry, and biology. And, for the first time in history, it made the great works and the great thoughts accessible to the common man.

Liberalism and Religion

Liberalism is based upon a purely rational and scientific theory of social cooperation. The policies it recommends are the application of a system of knowledge which does not refer in any way to sentiments, intuitive creeds for which no logically sufficient proof can be provided, mystical experiences, and the personal awareness of superhuman phenomena. In this sense the often misunderstood and erroneously interpreted epithets atheistic and agnostic can be attributed to it. It would, however, be a serious mistake to conclude that the sciences of human action and the policy derived from their teachings, liberalism, are antitheistic and hostile to religion. They are radically opposed to all systems of theocracy. But they are entirely neutral with regard to religious beliefs which do not pretend to interfere with the conduct of social, political, and economic affairs.

Theocracy is a social system which lays claim to a superhuman title for its legitimation. The fundamental law of a theocratic regime is an insight not open to examination by reason and to demonstration by logical methods. Its ultimate standard is intuition providing the mind with subjective certainty about things which cannot be conceived by reason and ratiocination. If this intuition refers to one of the traditional systems of teaching concerning the existence of a Divine Creator and Ruler of the universe, we call it a religious belief. If it refers to another system we call it a metaphysical belief. Thus a system of theocratic government need not be founded on one of the great historical religions of the world. It may be the outcome of metaphysical tenets which reject all traditional churches and denominations and take pride in emphasizing their antitheistic and antimetaphysical character. In our time the most powerful theocratic parties are opposed to Christianity and to all other religions which evolved from Jewish monotheism. What characterizes them as theocratic is their craving to organize the earthly affairs of mankind according to the contents of a complex of ideas whose validity cannot be demonstrated by reasoning. They pretend that their leaders are blessed by a knowledge inaccessible to the rest of mankind and contrary to the ideas maintained by those to whom the charisma is denied. The charismatic leaders have been entrusted by a mystical higher power with the office of managing the affairs of erring mankind. They alone are enlightened; all other people are either blind and deaf or malefactors.

It is a fact that many varieties of the great historical religions were affected by theocratic tendencies. Their apostles were inspired by a craving for power and the oppression and annihilation of all dissenting groups. However, we must not confuse the two things, religion and theocracy.

William James calls religious "the feelings, acts and experiences of individual men in their solitude, so far as they apprehend themselves to stand in relation to whatever they may consider the divine."[5] He enumerates the following beliefs as the characteristics of the religious life: That the visible world is part of a more spiritual universe from which it draws its chief significance; that union or harmonious relation with that higher universe is our true end; that prayer or inner communion with the spirit thereof—be that spirit "God" or "law"—is a process wherein work is really done, and spiritual energy flows in and produces effects, psychological or material, within the phenomenal world. Religion, James goes on to say, also includes the following psychological characteristics: A new zest which *adds* itself like a gift to life, and takes the form either of lyrical enchantment or of appeal to earnestness and heroism, and furthermore an assurance of safety and a temper of peace, and, in relation to others, a preponderance of loving affection.[6]

This characterization of mankind's religious experience and feelings does not make any reference to the arrangement of social cooperation. Religion, as James sees it, is a purely personal and individual relation between man and a holy, mysterious, and awe-inspiring divine Reality. It enjoins upon man a certain mode of individual conduct. But it does not assert anything with regard to the problems of social organization.

5. W. James, *The Varieties of Religious Experience* (35th impression, New York, 1925), p. 31.
6. *Ibid.*, pp. 485–86.

St. Francis d'Assisi, the greatest religious genius of the West, did not concern himself with politics and economics. He wanted to teach his disciples how to live piously; he did not draft a plan for the organization of production and did not urge his followers to resort to violence against dissenters. He is not responsible for the interpretation of his teachings by the order he founded.

Liberalism puts no obstacles in the way of a man eager to adjust his personal conduct and his private affairs according to the mode in which he individually or his church or denomination interprets the teachings of the Gospels. But it is radically opposed to all endeavors to silence the rational discussion of problems of social welfare by an appeal to religious intuition and revelation. It does not enjoin divorce or the practice of birth control upon anybody. But it fights those who want to prevent other people from freely discussing the pros and cons of these matters.

In the liberal opinion the aim of the moral law is to impel individuals to adjust their conduct to the requirements of life in society, to abstain from all acts detrimental to the preservation of peaceful social cooperation and to the improvement of interhuman relations. Liberals welcome the support which religious teachings may give to those moral precepts of which they themselves approve, but they are opposed to all those norms which are bound to bring about social disintegration from whatever source they may stem.

It is a distortion of fact to say, as many champions of religious theocracy do, that liberalism fights religion. Where the principle of church interference with secular issues is in force, the various churches, denominations and sects are fighting one another. By separating church and state, liberalism establishes peace among the various religious factions and gives to each of them the opportunity to preach its gospel unmolested.

Liberalism is rationalistic. It maintains that it is possible to convince the immense majority that peaceful cooperation within the framework of society better serves their rightly understood interests than mutual battling and social disintegration. It has full confidence in man's reason. It may be that this optimism is unfounded and that the liberals have erred. But then there is no hope left for mankind's future.

3 The Division of Labor

The fundamental social phenomenon is the division of labor and its counterpart human cooperation.

Experience teaches man that cooperative action is more efficient and productive than isolated action of self-sufficient individuals. The natural conditions determining man's life and effort are such that the division of labor increases output per unit of labor expended. These natural facts are:

First: the innate inequality of men with regard to their ability to perform various kinds of labor. Second: the unequal distribution of the nature-given, nonhuman opportunities of production on the surface of the earth. One may as well consider these two facts as one and the same fact, namely, the manifoldness of nature which makes the universe a complex of infinite varieties. If the earth's surface were such that the physical conditions of production were the same at every point and if one man were as equal to all other men as is a circle to another with the same diameter in Euclidian geometry, men would not have embarked upon the division of labor.

There is still a third fact, viz., that there are undertakings whose accomplishment exceeds the forces of a single man and requires the joint effort of several. Some of them require an expenditure of labor which no single man can perform because his capacity to work is not great enough. Others again could be accomplished by individuals; but the time which they would have to devote to the work would be so long that the result would only be attained late and would not compensate for the labor expended. In both cases only joint effort makes it possible to attain the end sought.

If only this third condition were present, temporary cooperation between men would have certainly emerged. However, such transient alliances to cope with specific tasks which are beyond the strength of an individual would not have brought about lasting social cooperation. Undertakings which could be performed only in this way were not very numerous at the early stages of civilization. Moreover, all those concerned may not often agree that the performance in question is more useful and urgent than the accomplishment of other tasks which they could perform alone. The great human society enclosing all men in all of their activities did not originate from such occasional alliances. Society is much more than a passing alliance concluded for a definite purpose and ceasing as soon as its objective is realized, even if the partners are ready to renew it should an occasion present itself.

The increase in productivity brought about by the division of labor is obvious whenever the inequality of the participants is such that every individual or every piece of land is superior at least in one regard to the other individuals or pieces of land concerned. If A is fit to produce in 1 unit of time 6 p, or 4 q and B only 2 p, but 8 q, they both, when working in isolation, will produce together 4 p + 6 q; when working under the division of labor, each of them producing only that commodity in whose production he is more efficient than his partner, they will produce 6 p + 8 q. But what will happen, if A is more efficient than B not only in the production of p but also in the production of q? This is the problem which Ricardo raised and solved immediately.

4   The Ricardian Law of Association

Ricardo expounded the law of association in order to demonstrate what the consequences of the division of labor are when an individual or a group, more efficient in every regard, cooperates with an individual or a group less efficient in every regard. He investigated the effects of trade between two areas, unequally endowed by nature, under the assumption that the products, but not the workers and the accumulated factors of future production (capital goods), can freely move from each area into the other. The division of labor between two such areas will, as Ricardo's law shows, increase the productivity of labor and is therefore advantageous to all concerned, even if the physical conditions of production for any commodity are more favorable in one of these two areas than in the other. It is advantageous for the better endowed area to concentrate its efforts upon the production of those commodities for which its superiority is greater, and to leave to the less endowed area the production of other goods in which its own superiority is less. The paradox that it is more advantageous to leave more favorable domestic conditions of production unused and to procure the commodities they could produce from areas in which conditions for their production are less favorable, is the outcome of the immobility of labor and capital, to which the more favorable places of production are inaccessible.

Ricardo was fully aware of the fact that his law of comparative cost, which he expounded mainly in order to deal with a special problem of international trade, is a particular instance of the more universal law of association.

If A is in such a way more efficient than B that he needs for the production of 1 unit of the commodity p 3 hours compared with B's 5, and for the production of 1 unit of q 2 hours compared with B's 4, then both will gain if A confines himself to producing q and leaves B to produce p. If each of them gives 60 hours to producing p and 60 hours to producing q, the result of A's labor is 20 p + 30 q; of B's, 12 p + 15 q; and for both together, 32 p + 45 q. If, however, A confines himself to producing q alone, he produces 60 q in 120 hours, while B, if he confines himself to producing p, produces in the same time 24 p. The result of their activities is then 24 p + 60 q, which, as p

has for A a substitution ratio of $\frac{3}{2} q$ and for B one of $\frac{5}{4} q$, signifies a larger output than $32 p + 45 q$. Therefore it is manifest that the division of labor brings advantages to all who take part in it. Collaboration of the more talented, more able, and more industrious with the less talented, less able, and less industrious results in benefit for both. The gains derived from the division of labor are always mutual.

The law of association makes us comprehend the tendencies which resulted in the progressive intensification of human cooperation. We conceive what incentive induced people not to consider themselves simply as rivals in a struggle for the appropriation of the limited supply of means of subsistence made available by nature. We realize what has impelled them and permanently impels them to consort with one another for the sake of cooperation. Every step forward on the way to a more developed mode of the division of labor serves the interests of all participants. In order to comprehend why man did not remain solitary, searching like the animals for food and shelter for himself only and at most also for his consort and his helpless infants, we do not need to have recourse to a miraculous interference of the Deity or to the empty hypostasis of an innate urge toward association. Neither are we forced to assume that the isolated individuals or primitive hordes one day pledged themselves by a contract to establish social bonds. The factor that brought about primitive society and daily works toward its progressive intensification is human action that is animated by the insight into the higher productivity of labor achieved under the division of labor.

Neither history nor ethnology nor any other branch of knowledge can provide a description of the evolution which has led from the packs and flocks of mankind's nonhuman ancestors to the primitive, yet already highly differentiated, societal groups about which information is provided in excavations, in the most ancient documents of history, and in the reports of explorers and travelers who have met savage tribes. The task with which science is faced in respect of the origins of society can only consist in the demonstration of those factors which can and must result in association and its progressive intensification. Praxeology solves the problem. If and as far as labor under the division of labor is more productive than isolated labor, and if and as far as man is able to realize this fact, human action itself tends toward cooperation and association; man becomes a social being not in sacrificing his own concerns for the sake of a mythical Moloch, society, but in aiming at an improvement in his own welfare. Experience teaches that this condition—higher productivity achieved under the division of labor — is present because its cause — the inborn inequality of men and the inequality in the geographical distribution of the natural factors of production — is real. Thus we are in a position to comprehend the course of social evolution.

Current Errors Concerning the Law of Association

People cavil much about Ricardo's law of association, better known under the name *law of comparative cost*. The reason is obvious. This law is an offense to all those eager to justify protection and national economic isolation from any point of view other than the selfish interests of some producers or the issues of war-preparedness.

Ricardo's first aim in expounding this law was to refute an objection raised against freedom of international trade. The protectionist asks: What under free trade will be the fate of a country in which the conditions for any kind of production are less favorable than in all other countries? Now, in a world in which there is free mobility not only for products, but no less for capital goods and for labor, a country so little suited for production would cease to be used as the seat of any human industry. If people fare better without exploiting the — comparatively unsatisfactory — physical conditions of production offered by this country, they will not settle here and will leave it as uninhabited as the polar regions, the tundras and the deserts. But Ricardo deals with a world whose conditions are determined by settlement in earlier days, a world in which capital goods and labor are bound to the soil by definite institutions. In such a milieu free trade, i.e., the free mobility of commodities only, cannot bring about a state of affairs in which capital and labor are distributed on the surface of the earth according to the better or poorer physical opportunities afforded to the productivity of labor. Here the law of comparative cost comes into operation. Each country turns toward those branches of production for which its conditions offer comparatively, although not absolutely, the most favorable opportunities. For the inhabitants of a country it is more advantageous to abstain from the exploitation of some opportunities which — absolutely and technologically — are more propitious and to import commodities produced abroad under conditions which — absolutely and technologically — are less favorable than the unused domestic resources. The case is analogous to that of a surgeon who finds it convenient to employ for the cleaning of the operating room and the instruments a man whom he excels in this performance also and to devote himself exclusively to surgery, in which his superiority is higher.

The theorem of comparative cost is in no way connected with the value theory of classical economics. It does not deal with value or with prices. It is an analytic judgment; the conclusion is implied in the two propositions that the technically movable factors of production differ with regard to their productivity in various places and are institutionally restricted in their mobility. The theorem, without prejudice to the correctness of its conclusions, can disregard problems of valuation because it is free to resort to a set of simple assumptions. These are: that only two products are to be produced; that these products are freely movable; that for the production of each of them two factors are required; that one of these factors (it may be either labor or capital goods) is identical in the production of both, while the other factor (a specific property of the soil) is different for each of the two processes; that the greater scarcity of the factor common to both processes determines the extent of the exploitation of the different factor. In the frame of these assumptions, which make it possible to establish substitution ratios between the expenditure of the common factor and the output, the theorem answers the question raised.

The law of comparative cost is as independent of the classical theory of value as is the law of returns, which its reasoning resembles. In both cases we can content ourselves with comparing only physical input and physical output. With the law of returns we compare the output of the same product. With the law of comparative costs we compare the output of two different products. Such a comparison is feasible because we assume that for the production of each of them, apart from one specific factor, only nonspecific factors of the same kind are required.

Some critics blame the law of comparative cost for this simplification of assumptions. They believe that the modern theory of value would require a reformulation of the law in conformity with the principles of subjective value. Only such a formulation could provide a satisfactory conclusive demonstration. However, they do not want to calculate in terms of money. They prefer to resort to those methods of utility analysis which they consider a means for making value calculations in terms of utility. It will be shown in the further progress of our investigation that these attempts to eliminate monetary terms from economic calculation are delusive. Their fundamental assumptions are untenable and contradictory and all formulas derived from them are vicious. No method of economic calculation is possible other than one based on money prices as determined by the market.[7]

The meaning of the simple assumptions underlying the law of comparative cost is not precisely the same for the modern economists as it was for the classical economists. Some adherents of the classical school considered them as the starting point of a theory of value in international trade. We know now that they were mistaken in this belief. Besides, we realize that with regard to the determination of

7. See below, pp. 201–9.

value and of prices there is no difference between domestic and foreign trade. What makes people distinguish between the home market and markets abroad is only a difference in the data, i.e., varying institutional conditions restricting the mobility of factors of production and of products.

If we do not want to deal with the law of comparative cost under the simplified assumptions applied by Ricardo, we must openly employ money calculation. We must not fall prey to the illusion that a comparison between the expenditure of factors of production of various kinds and of the output of products of various kinds can be achieved without the aid of money calculation. If we consider the case of the surgeon and his handyman we must say: If the surgeon can employ his limited working time for the performance of operations for which he is compensated at $50 per hour, it is to his interest to employ a handyman to keep his instruments in good order and to pay him $2 per hour, although this man needs 3 hours to accomplish what the surgeon could do in 1 hour. In comparing the conditions of two countries we must say: If conditions are such that in England the production of 1 unit of each of the two commodities a and b requires the expenditure of 1 working day of the same kind of labor, while in India with the same investment of capital for a 2 days and for b 3 days are required, and if capital goods and a and b are freely movable from England to India and vice versa, while there is no mobility of labor, wage rates in India in the production of a must tend to be 50 per cent, and in the production of b $33\frac{1}{3}$ per cent, of the English rates. If the English rate is 6 shillings, the rates in India would be the equivalent of 3 shillings in the production of a and the equivalent of 2 shillings in the production of b. Such a discrepancy in the remuneration of labor of the same kind cannot last if there is mobility of labor on the domestic Indian labor market. Workers would shift from the production of b into the production of a; their migration would tend to lower the remuneration in the a industry and to raise it in the b industry. Finally Indian wage rates would be equal in both industries. The production of a would tend to expand and to supplant English competition. On the other hand the production of b would become unprofitable in India and would have to be discontinued, while it would expand in England. The same reasoning is valid if we assume that the difference in the conditions of production consists also or exclusively in the amount of capital investment needed.

It has been asserted that Ricardo's law was valid only for his age and is of no avail for our time which offers other conditions. Ricardo saw the difference between domestic trade and foreign trade in differences in the mobility of capital and labor. If one assumes that capital, labor, and products are movable, then there exists a difference between regional and interregional trade only as far as the cost of transportation comes into play. Then it is superfluous to develop a theory of international trade as distinguished from national trade. Capital and labor are distributed on the earth's surface according to the better or poorer conditions which the various regions offer to production. There are areas more densely populated and better equipped with capital, there are others less densely populated and poorer in capital supply. There prevails on the whole earth a tendency toward an equalization of wage rates for the same kind of labor.

Ricardo, however, starts from the assumption that there is mobility of capital and labor only within each country, and not between the various countries. He raises the question what the consequences of the free mobility of products must be under such conditions. (If there is no mobility of products either, then every country is economically isolated and autarkic, and there is no international trade at all.) The theory of comparative cost answers this question. Now, Ricardo's assumptions by and large held good for his age. Later, in the course of the nineteenth century, conditions changed. The immobility of capital and labor gave way; international transfer of capital and labor became more and more common. Then came a reaction. Today capital and labor are again restricted in their mobility. Reality again corresponds to the Ricardian assumptions.

However, the teachings of the classical theory of interregional trade are above any change in institutional conditions. They enable us to study the problems involved under any imaginable assumptions.

5 The Effects of the Division of Labor

The division of labor is the outcome of man's conscious reaction to the multiplicity of natural conditions. On the other hand it is itself a factor bringing about differentiation. It assigns to the various geographic areas specific functions in the complex of the processes of production. It makes some areas urban, others rural; it locates the various branches of manufacturing, mining, and agriculture in different places. Still more important, however, is the fact that it intensifies the innate inequality of men. Exercise and practice of specific tasks adjust individuals better to the requirements of their performance; men develop some of their inborn faculties and stunt the development of others. Vocational types emerge, people become specialists.

The division of labor splits the various processes of production into minute tasks, many of which can be performed by mechanical devices. It is this fact that made the use of machinery possible and brought about the amazing improvements in technical methods of production. Mechanization is the fruit of the division of labor, its most beneficial achievement, not its motive and fountain spring. Power-driven specialized machinery could be employed only in a social environment under the division of labor. Every step forward on the road toward the use of more specialized, more refined, and more productive machines requires a further specialization of tasks.

6   The Individual Within Society

If praxeology speaks of the solitary individual, acting on his own behalf only and independent of fellow men, it does so for the sake of a better comprehension of the problems of social cooperation. We do not assert that such isolated autarkic human beings have ever lived and that the social stage of man's history was preceded by an age of independent individuals roaming like animals in search of food. The biological humanization of man's nonhuman ancestors and the emergence of the primitive social bonds were effected in the same process. Man appeared on the scene of earthly events as a social being. The isolated asocial man is a fictitious construction.

Seen from the point of view of the individual, society is the great means for the attainment of all his ends. The preservation of society is an essential condition of any plans an individual may want to realize by any action whatever. Even the refractory delinquent who fails to adjust his conduct to the requirements of life within the societal system of cooperation does not want to miss any of the advantages derived from the division of labor. He does not consciously aim at the destruction of society. He wants to lay his hands on a greater portion of the jointly produced wealth than the social order assigns to him. He would feel miserable if antisocial behavior were to become universal and its inevitable outcome, the return to primitive indigence, resulted.

It is illusory to maintain that individuals in renouncing the alleged blessings of a fabulous state of nature and entering into society have foregone some advantages and have a fair claim to be indemnified for what they have lost. The idea that anybody would have fared better under an asocial state of mankind and is wronged by the very existence of society is absurd. Thanks to the higher productivity of social cooperation the human species has multiplied far beyond the margin of subsistence offered by the conditions prevailing in ages with a rudimentary degree of the division of labor. Each man enjoys a standard of living much higher than that of his savage ancestors. The natural condition of man is extreme poverty and insecurity. It is romantic nonsense to lament the passing of the happy days of primitive barbarism. In a state of savagery the complainants would either not have reached the age of manhood, or if they had, they would have lacked the opportunities and amenities provided by civilization. Jean Jacques Rousseau and Frederick Engels, if they had lived in the primitive state which they describe with nostalgic yearning, would not have enjoyed the leisure required for their studies and for the writing of their books.

One of the privileges which society affords to the individual is the privilege of living in spite of sickness or physical disability. Sick animals are doomed. Their weakness handicaps them in their attempts to find food and to repel aggression on the part of other animals. Deaf, nearsighted, or crippled savages must perish. But such defects do not deprive a man of the opportunity to adjust himself to life in society. The majority of our contemporaries are afflicted with some bodily deficiencies which biology considers pathological. Our civilization is to a great extent the achievement of such men. The eliminative forces of natural selection are greatly reduced under social conditions. Hence some people say that civilization tends to deteriorate the hereditary qualities of the members of society.

Such judgments are reasonable if one looks at mankind with the eyes of a breeder intent upon raising a race of men equipped with certain qualities. But society is not a stud-farm operated for the production of a definite type of men. There is no "natural" standard to establish what is desirable and what is undesirable in the biological evolution of man. Any standard chosen is arbitrary, purely subjective, in short a judgment of value. The terms racial improvement and racial degeneration are meaningless when not based on definite plans for the future of mankind.

It is true, civilized man is adjusted to life in society and not to that of a hunter in virgin forests.

The Fable of the Mystic Communion

The praxeological theory of society is assailed by the fable of the mystic communion.

Society, assert the supporters of this doctrine, is not the product of man's purposeful action; it is not cooperation and division of tasks. It stems from unfathomable depths, from an urge ingrained in man's essential nature. It is, says one group, engrossment by the Spirit which is Divine Reality and participation, by virtue of a *unio mystica*, in God's power and love. Another group sees society as a biological phenomenon; it is the work of the voice of the blood, the bond uniting the offspring of common ancestors with these ancestors and with one another, and the mystical harmony between the ploughman and the soil he tills.

That such psychical phenomena are really felt is true. There are people who experience the *unio mystica* and place this experience above everything else, and there are men who are convinced that they hear the voice of the blood and smell with heart and soul the unique scent of the cherished soil of their country. The mystical experience and the ecstatic rapture are facts which psychology must consider real, like any other psychical phenomenon. The error of the communion-doctrines does not consist in their assertion that such phenomena really occur, but in the belief that they are primary facts not dependent on any rational consideration.

The voice of the blood which brings the father close to his child was not heard by those savages who did not know the causal relation between cohabitation and pregnancy. Today, as this relation is known to everybody, a man who has full confidence in his wife's fidelity may perceive it. But if there are doubts concerning the wife's fidelity, the voice of the blood is of no use. Nobody ever ventured to assert that doubts concerning paternity could be resolved by the voice of the blood. A mother who has kept watch over her child since its birth can hear the voice of the blood. If she loses touch with the infant at an early date, she may later identify it by some bodily marks, for instance those moles and scars which once were popular with novel writers. But the blood is mute if such observations and the conclusions derived from them do not make it speak. The voice of the blood, contend the German racists, mysteriously unifies all members of the German people. But anthropology reveals the fact that the German nation is a mixture of the descendants of various races, sub-races, and strains and not a homogeneous stock descended from a common ancestry. The recently germanized Slav who has only a short time since changed his paternal family name for a German-sounding name believes that he is substantially attached to all Germans. But he does not experience any such inner urge impelling him to join the ranks of his brothers or cousins who remained Czechs or Poles.

The voice of the blood is not an original and primordial phenomenon. It is prompted by rational considerations. Because a man believes that he is related to other people by a common ancestry, he develops those feelings and sentiments which are poetically described as the voice of the blood.

The same is true with regard to religious ecstasy and mysticism of the soil. The *unio mystica* of the devout mystic is conditioned by familiarity with the basic teachings of his religion. Only a man who has learned about the greatness and glory of God can experience direct communion with Him. Mysticism of the soil is connected with the development of definite geopolitical ideas. Thus it may happen that inhabitants of the plains or the seashore include in the image of the soil with which they claim to be fervently joined and united also mountain districts which are unfamiliar to them and to whose conditions they could not adapt themselves, only because this territory belongs to the political body of which they are members, or would like to be members. On the other hand they often fail to include in this image of the soil whose voice they claim to hear neighboring areas of a geographic structure very similar to that of their own country if these areas happen to belong to a foreign nation.

The various members of a nation or linguistic group and the clusters they form are not always united in friendship and good will. The history of every nation is a record of mutual dislike and even hatred between its subdivisions. Think of the English and the Scotch, the Yankees and the Southerners, the Prussians and the Bavarians. It was ideologies that overcame such animosities and inspired all members of a nation or linguistic group with those feelings of community and belonging together which present-day nationalists consider a natural and original phenomenon.

The mutual sexual attraction of male and female is inherent in man's animal nature and independent of any thinking and theorizing. It is permissible to call it original, vegetative, instinctive, or mysterious; there is no harm in asserting metaphorically that it makes one being out of two. We may call it a mystic communion of two bodies, a community. However, neither cohabitation, nor what precedes it and follows, generates social cooperation and societal modes of life. The animals too join together in mating, but they have not developed social relations. Family life is not merely a product of sexual intercourse. It is by no means natural and necessary that parents and children live together in the way in which they do in the family. The mating relation need not result in a family organization. The human family is an outcome of thinking, planning, and acting. It is this very fact which distinguishes it radically from those animal groups which we call *per analogiam* animal families.

The mystical experience of communion or community is not the source of societal relations, but their product.

The counterpart of the fable of the mystical communion is the fable of a natural and original repulsion between races or nations. It is asserted that an instinct teaches man to distinguish congeners from strangers and to detest the latter. Scions of noble races abominate any contact with members of lower races. To refute this statement one need only mention the fact of racial mixture. As there are in present-day Europe no pure stocks, we must conclude that between members of the various stocks which once settled in that continent there was sexual attraction and not repulsion. Millions of mulattoes and other half-breeds are living counterevidence to the assertion that there exists a natural repulsion between the various races.

Like the mystical sense of communion, racial hatred is not a natural phenomenon innate in man. It is the product of ideologies. But even if such a thing as a natural and inborn hatred between various races existed, it would not render social cooperation futile and would not invalidate Ricardo's theory of association. Social cooperation has nothing to do with personal love or with a general commandment to love one another. People do not cooperate under the division of labor because they love or should love one another. They cooperate because this best serves their own interests. Neither love nor charity nor any other sympathetic sentiments but rightly understood selfishness is what originally impelled man to adjust himself to the requirements of society, to respect the rights and freedoms of his fellow men and to substitute peaceful collaboration for enmity and conflict.

7   The Great Society

Not every interhuman relation is a social relation. When groups of men rush upon one another in a war of outright extermination, when men fight against men as mercilessly as they crush pernicious animals and plants, there is, between the fighting parties, reciprocal effect and mutual relation, but no society. Society is joint action and cooperation in which each participant sees the other partner's success as a means for the attainment of his own.

The struggles in which primitive hordes and tribes fought one another for watering places, hunting and fishing grounds, pastures and booty were pitiless wars of annihilation. They were total wars. So in the nineteenth century were the first encounters of Europeans with the aborigines of territories newly made accessible. But already in the primeval age, long before the time of which historical records convey information, another mode of procedure began to develop. People preserved even in warfare some rudiments of social relations previously established; in fighting against peoples with whom they never before had had any contact, they began to take into account the idea that between human beings, notwithstanding their immediate enmity, a later arrangement and cooperation is possible. Wars were waged to hurt the foe; but the hostile acts were no longer merciless and pitiless in the full sense of these terms. The belligerents began to respect certain limits which in a struggle against men — as differentiated from that against beasts — should not be transcended. Above the implacable hatred and the frenzy of destruction and annihilation a societal element began to prevail. The idea emerged that every human adversary should be considered as a potential partner in a future cooperation, and that this fact should not be neglected in the conduct of military operations. War was no longer considered the normal state of interhuman relations. People recognized that peaceful cooperation is the best means to carry on the struggle for biological survival. We may even say that as soon as people realized that it is more advantageous to enslave the defeated than to kill them, the warriors, while still fighting, gave thought to the aftermath, the peace. Enslavement was by and large a preliminary step toward cooperation.

The ascendancy of the idea that even in war not every act is to be considered permissible, that there are legitimate and illicit acts of warfare, that there are laws, i.e., societal relationships which are above all nations, even above those momentarily fighting one another, has finally established the Great Society embracing all men and all nations. The various regional societies were merged into one ecumenical society.

Belligerents who do not wage war savagely in the manner of beasts, but according to "human" and social rules of warfare, renounce the use of some methods of destruction in order to attain the same concessions on the part of their foes. As far as such rules are complied with, social relations exist between the fighting parties. The hostile acts themselves are not only asocial, but antisocial. It is inexpedient to define the term *social relationships* in such a way as to include actions which aim at other people's annihilation and at the frustration of their actions.[8] Where the only relations between men are those directed at mutual detriment, there is neither society nor societal relations.

Society is not merely interaction. There is interaction — reciprocal influence — between all parts of the universe: between the wolf and the sheep he devours; between the germ and the man it kills; between the falling stone and the thing upon which it falls. Society, on the other hand, always involves men acting in cooperation with other men in order to let all participants attain their own ends.

8   The Instinct of Aggression and Destruction

It has been asserted that man is a beast of prey whose inborn natural instincts impel him to fight, to kill, and to destroy. Civilization, in creating unnatural humanitarian laxity which alienates man from his animal origin, has tried to quell these impulses and appetites. It has made civilized man a decadent weakling who is ashamed of his animality and proudly calls his depravity true humaneness. In order to prevent further degeneration of the species man, it is imperative to free him from the pernicious effects of civilization. For civilization is merely a cunning invention of inferior men. These underlings are too weak to be a match for the vigorous heroes, they are too cowardly to endure the well-deserved punishment of complete annihilation, and they are too lazy and too insolent to serve the masters as slaves. Thus they have resorted to a tricky makeshift. They have reversed the eternal standards of value, absolutely fixed by the

8. Such is the terminology used by Leopold von Wiese (*Allgemeine Soziologie* [Munich, 1924], I, 10 ff.).

immutable laws of the universe; they have propagated a morality which calls their own inferiority virtue and the eminence of the noble heroes vice. This moral rebellion of the slaves must be undone by a transvaluation of all values. The ethics of the slaves, this shameful product of the resentment of weaklings, must be entirely discarded; the ethics of the strong or, properly speaking, the nullification of any ethical restriction must be substituted for it. Man must become a worthy scion of his ancestors, the noble beasts of days gone by.

It is usual to call such doctrines social or sociological Darwinism. We need not decide here whether this terminology is appropriate or not. At any rate it is a mistake to assign the epithets evolutionary and biological to teachings which blithely disparage the whole of mankind's history from the ages in which man began to lift himself above the purely animal existence of his non-human ancestors as a continuous progression toward degeneration and decay. Biology does not provide any standard for the appraisal of changes occurring within living beings other than whether or not these changes succeeded in adjusting the individuals to the conditions of their environment and thereby in improving their chances in the struggle for survival. It is a fact that civilization, when judged from this point of view, is to be considered a benefit and not an evil. It has enabled man to hold his own in the struggle against all other living beings, both the big beasts of prey and the even more pernicious microbes; it has multiplied man's means of sustenance; it has made the average man taller, more agile, and more versatile and it has stretched his average length of life; it has given man the uncontested mastery of the earth; it has multiplied population figures and raised the standard of living to a level never dreamed of by the crude cave dwellers of prehistoric ages. It is true that this evolution stunted the development of certain knacks and gifts which were once useful in the struggle for survival and have lost their usefulness under changed conditions. On the other hand it developed other talents and skills which are indispensable for life within the frame of society. However, a biological and evolutionary view must not cavil at such changes. For primitive man hard fists and pugnacity were as useful as the ability to be clever at arithmetic and to spell correctly are for modern man. It is quite arbitrary and certainly contrary to any biological standard to call only those characteristics which were useful to primitive man natural and adequate to human nature and to condemn the talents and skills badly needed by civilized man as marks of degeneration and biological deterioration. To advise man to return to the physical and intellectual features of his prehistoric ancestors is no more reasonable than to ask him to renounce his upright gait and to grow a tail again.

It is noteworthy that the men who were foremost in extolling the eminence of the savage impulses of our barbarian forefathers were so frail that their bodies would not have come up to the requirements of "living dangerously." Nietzsche even before his mental breakdown was so sickly that the only climate he could stand was that of the Engadin valley and of some Italian districts. He would not have been in a position to accomplish his work if civilized society had not protected his delicate nerves against the roughness of life. The apostles of violence wrote their books under the sheltering roof of "bourgeois security" which they derided and disparaged. They were free to publish their incendiary sermons because the liberalism which they scorned safeguarded freedom of the press. They would have been desperate if they had had to forego the blessings of the civilization scorned by their philosophy. And what a spectacle was that timid writer Georges Sorel, who went so far in his praise of brutality as to blame the modern system of education for weakening man's inborn tendencies toward violence![9]

One may admit that in primitive man the propensity for killing and destroying and the disposition for cruelty were innate. We may also assume that under the conditions of earlier ages the inclination for aggression and murder was favorable to the preservation of life. Man was once a brutal beast. (There is no need to investigate whether prehistoric man was a carnivore or a herbivore.) But one must not forget that he was physically a weak animal; he would not have been a match for the big beasts of prey if he had not been equipped with a peculiar weapon, reason. The fact that man is a reasonable being, that he therefore does not yield without inhibitions to every impulse, but arranges his conduct according to reasonable deliberation, must not be called unnatural from a zoological point of view. Rational conduct means that man, in face of the fact that he cannot satisfy all his impulses, desires, and appetites, foregoes the satisfaction of those which he considers less urgent. In order not to endanger the working of social cooperation man is forced to abstain from satisfying those desires whose satisfaction would hinder the establishment of societal institutions. There is no doubt that such a renunciation is painful. However, man has made his choice. He has renounced the satisfaction of some desires incompatible with social life and has given priority to the satisfaction of those desires which can be realized only or in a more plentiful way under a system of the division of labor. He has entered upon the way toward civilization, social cooperation, and wealth.

9. Georges Sorel, *Réflexions sur la violence* (3d ed., Paris, 1912), p. 269.

This decision is not irrevocable and final. The choice of the fathers does not impair the sons' freedom to choose. They can reverse the resolution. Every day they can proceed to the transvaluation of values and prefer barbarism to civilization, or, as some authors say, the soul to the intellect, myths to reason, and violence to peace. But they must choose. It is impossible to have things incompatible with one another.

Science, from the point of view of its valuational neutrality, does not blame the apostles of the gospel of violence for praising the frenzy of murder and the mad delights of sadism. Value judgments are subjective, and liberal society grants to everybody the right to express his sentiments freely. Civilization has not extirpated the original tendency toward aggression, bloodthirstiness, and cruelty which characterized primitive man. In many civilized men they are dormant and burst forth as soon as the restraints developed by civilization give way. Remember the unspeakable horrors of the Nazi concentration camps. The newspapers continually report abominable crimes manifesting the latent urges toward bestiality. The most popular novels and moving pictures are those dealing with bloodshed and violent acts. Bull fights and cock fights attract large crowds.

If an author says: the rabble thirst for blood and I with them, he may be no less right than in asserting that primitive man too took delight in killing. But he errs if he passes over the fact that the satisfaction of such sadistic desires impairs the existence of society or if he asserts that "true" civilization and the "good" society are an achievement of people blithely indulging in their passion for violence, murder, and cruelty, that the repression of the impulses toward brutality endangers mankind's evolution and that a substitution of barbarism for humanitarianism would save man from degeneration. The social division of labor and cooperation rests upon conciliatory settlement of disputes. Not war, as Heraclitus said, but peace is the source of all social relations. To man desires other than that for bloodshed are inborn. If he wants to satisfy these other desires, he must forego his urge to kill. He who wants to preserve life and health as well and as long as possible must realize that respect for other people's lives and health better serves his aim than the opposite mode of conduct. One may regret that such is the state of affairs. But no such lamentations can alter the hard facts.

It is useless to censure this statement by referring to irrationality. All instinctive impulses defy examination by reason because reason deals only with the means for attaining ends sought and not with ultimate ends. But what distinguishes man from other animals is precisely that he does not yield without any will of his own to an instinctive urge. Man uses reason in order to choose between the incompatible satisfactions of conflicting desires.

One must not tell the masses: Indulge in your urge for murder; it is genuinely human and best serves your well-being. One must tell them: If you satisfy your thirst for blood, you must forego many other desires. You want to eat, to drink, to live in fine homes, to clothe yourselves, and a thousand other things which only society can provide. You cannot have everything, you must choose. The dangerous life and the frenzy of sadism may please you, but they are incompatible with the security and plenty which you do not want to miss either.

Praxeology as a science cannot encroach upon the individual's right to choose and to act. The final decisions rest with acting men, not with the theorists. Science's contribution to life and action does not consist in establishing value judgments, but in clarification of the conditions under which man must act and in elucidation of the effects of various modes of action. It puts at the disposal of acting man all the information he needs in order to make his choices in full awareness of their consequences. It prepares an estimate of cost and yield, as it were. It would fail in this task if it were to omit from this statement one of the items which could influence people's choices and decisions.

Current Misinterpretations of Modern Natural Science, Especially of Darwinism

Some present-day antiliberals, both of the right-wing and of the left-wing variety, base their teachings on misinterpretations of the achievements of modern biology.

1. *Men are unequal.* Eighteenth-century liberalism and likewise present-day egalitarianism start from the "self-evident truth" that "all men are created equal, and that they are endowed by their Creator with certain unalienable Rights." However, say the advocates of a biological philosophy of society, natural science has demonstrated in an irrefutable way that men are different. There is no room left in the framework of an experimental observation of natural phenomena for such a concept as natural rights. Nature is unfeeling and insensible with regard to any being's life and happiness. Nature is iron necessity and regularity. It is metaphysical nonsense to link together the "slippery" and vague notion of liberty and the unchangeable absolute laws of cosmic order. Thus the fundamental idea of liberalism is unmasked as a fallacy.

Now it is true that the liberal and democratic movement of the eighteenth and nineteenth centuries drew a great part of its strength from the doctrine of natural law and the innate imprescriptible rights of the individual. These ideas, first developed by ancient philosophy and Jewish theology, permeated Christian thinking. Some anti-Catholic sects made them the focal point of their political programs. A long line of eminent philosophers substantiated them. They became popular and were the most powerful moving force in the pro-democratic evolution. They are still supported today. Their advocates do not concern themselves with the incontestable fact that God or nature did not create men equal since many are born hale and hearty while others are crippled and deformed. With them all differences between men are due to education, opportunity, and social institutions.

But the teachings of utilitarian philosophy and classical economics have nothing at all to do with the doctrine of natural right. With them the only point that matters is social utility. They recommend popular government, private property, tolerance, and freedom not because they are natural and just, but because they are beneficial. The core of Ricardo's philosophy is the demonstration that social cooperation and division of labor between men who are in every regard superior and more efficient and men who are in every regard inferior and less efficient is beneficial to both groups. Bentham, the radical, shouted: "*Natural rights* is simple nonsense: natural and imprescriptible rights, rhetorical nonsense." [10] With him "the sole object of government ought to be the greatest happiness of the greatest possible number of the community." [11] Accordingly, in investigating what ought to be right he does not care about preconceived ideas concerning God's or nature's plans and intentions, forever hidden to mortal men; he is intent upon discovering what best serves the promotion of human welfare and happiness. Malthus showed that nature in limiting the means of subsistence does not accord to any living being a right of existence, and that by indulging heedlessly in the natural impulse of proliferation man would never have risen above the verge of starvation. He contended that human civilization and well-being could develop only to the extent that man learned to rein his sexual appetites by moral restraint. The Utilitarians do not combat arbitrary government and privileges because they are against natural law but because they are detrimental to prosperity. They recommend equality under the civil law not because men are equal but because such a policy is beneficial to the commonweal. In rejecting the illusory notions of natural law and human equality modern biology only repeated what the utilitarian champions of liberalism and democracy long before had taught in a much more persuasive way. It is obvious that no biological doctrine can ever invalidate what utilitarian philosophy says about the social utility of democratic government, private property, freedom, and equality under the law.

10. Bentham, *Anarchical Fallacies; being an Examination of the Declaration of Rights issued during the French Revolution,* in *Works* (ed. by Bowring), II, 501.
11. Bentham, *Principles of the Civil Code,* in *Works,* I, 301.

The present-day prevalence of doctrines approving social disintegration and violent conflict is not the result of an alleged adaptation of social philosophy to the findings of biology but of the almost universal rejection of utilitarian philosophy and economic theory. People have substituted an ideology of irreconcilable class conflict and international conflict for the "orthodox" ideology of the harmony of the rightly understood, i.e., long-run, interests of all individuals, social groups, and nations. Men are fighting one another because they are convinced that the extermination and liquidation of adversaries is the only means of promoting their own well-being.

2. *The social implications of Darwinism.* The theory of evolution as expounded by Darwin, says a school of social Darwinism, has clearly demonstrated that in nature there are no such things as peace and respect for the lives and welfare of others. In nature there is always struggle and merciless annihilation of the weak who do not succeed in defending themselves. Liberalism's plans for eternal peace—both in domestic and in foreign relations—are the outcome of an illusory rationalism contrary to the natural order.

However, the notion of the struggle for existence as Darwin borrowed it from Malthus and applied it in his theory, is to be understood in a metaphorical sense. Its meaning is that a living being actively resists the forces detrimental to its own life. This resistance, if it is to succeed, must be appropriate to the environmental conditions in which the being concerned has to hold its own. It need not always be a war of extermination such as in the relations between men and morbific microbes. Reason has demonstrated that, for man, the most adequate means of improving his condition is social cooperation and division of labor. They are man's foremost tool in his struggle for survival. But they can work only where there is peace. Wars, civil wars, and revolutions are detrimental to man's success in the struggle for existence because they disintegrate the apparatus of social cooperation.

3. *Reason and rational behavior called unnatural.* Christian theology deprecated the animal functions of man's body and depicted the "soul" as something outside of all biological phenomena. In an excessive reaction against this philosophy some moderns are prone to disparage everything in which man differs from other animals. In their eyes human reason is inferior to the animal instincts and impulses; it is unnatural and therefore bad. With them the terms rationalism and rational behavior have an opprobrious connotation. The perfect man, the real man, is a being who obeys his primordial instincts more than his reason.

The obvious truth is that reason, man's most characteristic feature, is also a biological phenomenon. It is neither more nor less natural than any other feature of the species *Homo sapiens,* for instance, the upright gait or the hairless skin.

CHAPTER 9

The Role of Ideas

1   Human Reason

Reason is man's particular and characteristic feature. There is no need for praxeology to raise the question whether reason is a suitable tool for the cognition of ultimate and absolute truth. It deals with reason only as far as it enables man to act.

All those objects which are the substratum of human sensation, perception, and observation also pass before the senses of animals. But man alone has the faculty of transforming sensuous stimuli into observation and experience. And man alone can arrange his various observations and experiences into a coherent system.

Action is preceded by thinking. Thinking is to deliberate beforehand over future action and to reflect afterwards upon past action. Thinking and acting are inseparable. Every action is always based on a definite idea about causal relations. He who thinks a causal relation thinks a theorem. Action without thinking, practice without theory are unimaginable. The reasoning may be faulty and the theory incorrect; but thinking and theorizing are not lacking in any action. On the other hand thinking is always thinking of a potential action. Even he who thinks of a pure theory assumes that the theory is correct, i.e., that action complying with its content would result in an effect to be expected from its teachings. It is of no relevance for logic whether such action is feasible or not.

It is always the individual who thinks. Society does not think any more than it eats or drinks. The evolution of human reasoning from the naïve thinking of primitive man to the more subtle thinking of modern science took place within society. However, thinking itself is always an achievement of individuals. There is joint action, but no joint thinking. There is only tradition which preserves thoughts and communicates them to others as a stimulus to their thinking. However, man has no means of appropriating the thoughts of his precursors other than to think them over again. Then, of course, he is in a position to proceed farther on the basis of his forerunners' thoughts. The foremost vehicle of tradition is the word. Thinking is linked up with language and vice versa. Concepts are embodied in terms. Language is a tool of thinking as it is a tool of social action.

The history of thought and ideas is a discourse carried on from generation to generation. The thinking of later ages grows out of the thinking of earlier ages. Without the aid of this stimulation intellectual progress would have been impossible. The continuity of human evolution, sowing for the offspring and harvesting on land cleared and tilled by the ancestors, manifests itself also in the history of science and ideas. We have inherited from our forefathers not only a stock of products of various orders of goods which is the source of our material wealth; we have no less inherited ideas and thoughts, theories and technologies to which our thinking owes its productivity.

But thinking is always a manifestation of individuals.

2   World View and Ideology

The theories directing action are often imperfect and unsatisfactory. They may be contradictory and unfit to be arranged into a comprehensive and coherent system.

If we look at all the theorems and theories guiding the conduct of certain individuals and groups as a coherent complex and try to arrange them as far as is feasible into a system, i.e., a comprehensive body of knowledge, we may speak of it as a world view. A world view is, as a theory, an interpretation of all things, and as a precept for action, an opinion concerning the best means for removing uneasiness as much as possible. A world view is thus, on the one hand, an explanation of all phenomena and, on the other hand, a technology, both these terms being taken in their broadest sense. Religion, metaphysics, and philosophy aim at providing a world view. They interpret the universe and they advise men how to act.

The concept of an ideology is narrower than that of a world view. In speaking of ideology we have in view only human action and social cooperation and disregard the problems of metaphysics, religious dogma, the natural sciences, and the technologies derived from them. Ideology is the totality of our doctrines concerning individual conduct and social relations. Both, world view and ideology, go beyond the limits imposed upon a purely neutral and academic study of things as they are. They are not only scientific theories, but also doctrines about the ought, i.e., about the ultimate ends which man should aim at in his earthly concerns.

Asceticism teaches that the only means open to man for removing pain and for attaining complete quietude, contentment, and happiness is to turn away from earthly concerns and to live without bothering about worldly things. There is no salvation other than to renounce striving after material well-being, to endure submissively the adversities of the earthly pilgrimage and to dedicate oneself exclusively to the preparation for eternal bliss. However, the number of those who consistently and unswervingly comply with the principles of asceticism is so small that it is not easy to instance more than a few names. It seems that the complete passivity advocated by asceticism is contrary to nature. The enticement of life triumphs. The ascetic principles have been adulterated. Even the most saintly hermits made concessions to life and earthly concerns which did not agree with their rigid principles. But as soon as a man takes into account any earthly concerns, and substitutes for purely vegetative ideals an acknowledgment of worldly things, however conditioned and incompatible with the rest of his professed doctrine, he bridges over the gulf which separated him from those who say yes to the striving after earthly ends. Then he has something in common with everyone else.

Human thoughts about things of which neither pure reasoning nor experience provides any knowledge may differ so radically that no agreement can be reached. In this sphere in which the free reverie of the mind is restricted neither by logical thinking nor by sensory experience man can give vent to his individuality and subjectivity. Nothing is more personal than the notions and images about the transcendent. Linguistic terms are unable to communicate what is said about the transcendent; one can never establish whether the hearer conceives them in the same way as the speaker. With regard to things beyond there can be no agreement. Religious wars are the most terrible wars because they are waged without any prospect of conciliation.

But where earthly things are involved, the natural affinity of all men and the identity of the biological conditions for the preservation of their lives come into play. The higher productivity of cooperation under division of labor makes society the foremost means of every individual for the attainment of his own ends whatever they may be. The maintenance and further intensification of social cooperation become a concern of everybody. Every world view and every ideology which is not entirely and unconditionally committed to the practice of asceticism and to a life in anchoritic reclusion must pay heed to the fact that society is the great means for the attainment of earthly ends. But then a common ground is won to clear the way for an agreement concerning minor social problems and the details of society's organization. However various ideologies may conflict with one another, they harmonize in one point, in the acknowledgment of life in society.

People fail sometimes to see this fact because in dealing with philosophies and ideologies they look more at what these doctrines assert with regard to transcendent and unknowable things and less at their statements about action in this world. Between various parts of an ideological system there is often an unbridgeable gulf. For acting man only those teachings are of real importance which result in precepts for action, not those doctrines which are purely academic and do not apply to conduct within the frame of social cooperation. We may disregard the philosophy of adamant and consistent asceticism because such a rigid asceticism must ultimately result in the extinction of its supporters. All other ideologies, in approving of the search for the necessities of life, are forced in some measure to take into account the fact that division of labor is more productive than isolated work. They thus admit the need for social cooperation.

Praxeology and economics are not qualified to deal with the transcendent and metaphysical aspects of any doctrine. But, on the other hand, no appeal to any religious or metaphysical dogmas and creeds can invalidate the theorems and theories concerning social cooperation as developed by logically correct praxeological reasoning. If a philosophy has admitted the necessity of societal links between men, it has placed itself, as far as problems of social action come into play, on ground from which there is no escape into personal convictions and professions of faith not liable to a thorough examination by rational methods.

This fundamental fact is often ignored. People believe that differences in world view create irreconcilable conflicts. The basic antagonisms between parties committed to different world views, it is contended, cannot be settled by compromise. They stem from the deepest recesses of the human soul and are expressive of a man's innate communion with supernatural and eternal forces. There can never be any cooperation between people divided by different world views.

However, if we pass in review the programs of all parties—both the cleverly elaborated and publicized programs and those to which the parties really cling when in power—we can easily discover the fallacy of this interpretation. All present-day political parties strive after the earthly well-being and prosperity of their supporters. They promise that they will render economic conditions more satisfactory to their followers. With regard to this issue there is no difference

THE ROLE OF IDEAS   181

between the Roman Catholic Church and the various Protestant denominations as far as they intervene in political and social questions, between Christianity and the non-Christian religions, between the advocates of economic freedom and the various brands of Marxian materialism, between nationalists and internationalists, between racists and the friends of interracial peace. It is true that many of these parties believe that their own group cannot prosper except at the expense of other groups, and even go so far as to consider the complete annihilation of other groups or their enslavement as the necessary condition of their own group's prosperity. Yet, extermination or enslavement of others is for them not an ultimate end, but a means for the attainment of what they aim at as an ultimate end: their own group's flowering. If they were to learn that their own designs are guided by spurious theories and would not bring about the beneficial results expected, they would change their programs.

The pompous statements which people make about things unknowable and beyond the power of the human mind, their cosmologies, world views, religions, mysticisms, metaphysics, and conceptual phantasies differ widely from one another. But the practical essence of their ideologies, i.e., their teachings dealing with the ends to be aimed at in earthly life and with the means for the attainment of these ends, show much uniformity. There are, to be sure, differences and antagonisms both with regard to ends and means. Yet the differences with regard to ends are not irreconcilable; they do not hinder cooperation and amicable arrangements in the sphere of social action. As far as they concern means and ways only, they are of a purely technical character and as such open to examination by rational methods. When in the heat of party conflicts one of the factions declares: "Here we cannot go on in our negotiations with you because we are faced with a question touching upon our world view; on this point we must be adamant and must cling rigidly to our principles whatever may result," one need only scrutinize matters more carefully to realize that such declarations describe the antagonism as more pointed than it really is. In fact, for all parties committed to pursuit of the people's earthly welfare and thus approving social cooperation, questions of social organization and the conduct of social action are not problems of ultimate principles and of world views, but ideological issues. They are technical problems with regard to which some arrangement is always possible. No party would wittingly prefer social disintegration, anarchy, and a return to primitive barbarism to a solution which must be bought at the price of the sacrifice of some ideological points.

In party programs these technical issues are, of course, of primary importance. A party is committed to certain means, it recommends certain methods of political action and rejects utterly all other methods and policies as inappropriate. A party is a body which combines all those eager to employ the same means for common action. The principle which differentiates men and integrates parties is the choice of means. Thus for the party as such the means chosen are essential. A party is doomed if the futility of the means recommended becomes obvious. Party chiefs whose prestige and political career are bound up with the party's program may have ample reasons for withdrawing its principles from unrestricted discussion; they may attribute to them the character of ultimate ends which must not be questioned because they are based on a world view. But for the people as whose mandataries the party chiefs pretend to act, for the voters whom they want to enlist and for whose votes they canvass, things offer another aspect. They have no objection to scrutinizing every point of a party's program. They look upon such a program only as a recommendation of means for the attainment of their own ends, viz., earthly well-being.

What divides those parties which one calls today world view parties, i.e., parties committed to basic philosophical decisions about ultimate ends, is only seeming disagreement with regard to ultimate ends. Their antagonisms refer either to religious creeds or to problems of international relations or to the problem of ownership of the means of production or to problems of political organization. It can be shown that all these controversies concern means and not ultimate ends.

Let us begin with the problems of a nation's political organization. There are supporters of a democratic system of government, of hereditary monarchy, of the rule of a self-styled elite and of Caesarist dictatorship.[1] It is true that these programs are often recommended by reference to divine institutions, to the eternal laws of the universe, to the natural order, to the inevitable trend of historical evolution, and to other objects of transcendent knowledge. But such statements are merely incidental adornment. In appealing to the electorate, the parties advance other arguments. They are eager to show that the system they support will succeed better than those advocated by other parties in realizing those ends which the citizens aim at. They specify the beneficial results achieved in the past or in other countries; they disparage the other parties' programs by relating their failures.

---

1. Caesarism is today exemplified by the Bolshevik, Fascist, or Nazi type of dictatorship.

They resort both to pure reasoning and to an interpretation of historical experience in order to demonstrate the superiority of their own proposals and the futility of those of their adversaries. Their main argument is always: the political system we support will render you more prosperous and more content.

In the field of society's economic organization there are the liberals advocating private ownership of the means of production, the socialists advocating public ownership of the means of production, and the interventionists advocating a third system which, they contend, is as far from socialism as it is from capitalism. In the clash of these parties there is again much talk about basic philosophical issues. People speak of true liberty, equality, social justice, the rights of the individual, community, solidarity, and humanitarianism. But each party is intent upon proving by ratiocination and by referring to historical experience that only the system it recommends will make the citizens prosperous and satisfied. They tell the people that realization of their program will raise the standard of living to a higher level than realization of any other party's program. They insist upon the expediency of their plans and upon their utility. It is obvious that they do not differ from one another with regard to ends but only as to means. They all pretend to aim at the highest material welfare for the majority of citizens.

The nationalists stress the point that there is an irreconcilable conflict among the interests of various nations, but that, on the other hand, the rightly understood interests of all the citizens within the nation are harmonious. A nation can prosper only at the expense of other nations; the individual citizen can fare well only if his nation flourishes. The liberals have a different opinion. They believe that the interests of various nations harmonize no less than those of the various groups, classes, and strata of individuals within a nation. They believe that peaceful international cooperation is a more appropriate means than conflict for the attainment of the end which they and the nationalists are both aiming at: their own nation's welfare. They do not, as the nationalists charge, advocate peace and free trade in order to betray their own nation's interests to those of foreigners. On the contrary, they consider peace and free trade the best means to make their own nation wealthy. What separates the free traders from the nationalists are not ends, but the means recommended for attainment of the ends common to both.

Dissension with regard to religious creeds cannot be settled by rational methods. Religious conflicts are essentially implacable and irreconcilable. Yet as soon as a religious community enters the field of political action and tries to deal with problems of social organization, it is bound to take into account earthly concerns, however this may conflict with its dogmas and articles of faith. No religion in its exoteric activities ever ventured to tell people frankly: The realization of our plans for social organization will make you poor and impair your earthly well-being. Those consistently committed to a life of poverty withdrew from the political scene and fled into anchoritic seclusion. But churches and religious communities which have aimed at making converts and at influencing political and social activities of their followers have espoused the principles of secular conduct. In dealing with questions of man's earthly pilgrimage they hardly differ from any other political party. In canvassing, they emphasize, more than bliss in the beyond, the material advantages which they have in store for their brothers in faith.

Only a world view whose supporters renounce any earthly activity whatever could neglect to pay heed to the rational considerations which show that social cooperation is the great means for the attainment of all human ends. Because man is a social animal that can thrive only within society, all ideologies are forced to acknowledge the preeminent importance of social cooperation. They must aim at the most satisfactory organization of society and must approve of man's concern for an improvement of his material well-being. Thus they all place themselves upon a common ground. They are separated from one another not by world views and transcendent issues not subject to reasonable discussion, but by problems of means and ways. Such ideological antagonisms are open to a thorough scrutiny by the scientific methods of praxeology and economics.

The Fight Against Error

A critical examination of the philosophical systems constructed by mankind's great thinkers has very often revealed fissures and flaws in the impressive structure of those seemingly consistent and coherent bodies of comprehensive thought. Even the genius in drafting a world view sometimes fails to avoid contradictions and fallacious syllogisms.

The ideologies accepted by public opinion are still more infected by the shortcomings of the human mind. They are mostly an eclectic juxtaposition of ideas utterly incompatible with one another. They cannot stand a logical examination of their content. Their inconsistencies are irreparable and defy any attempt to combine their various parts into a system of ideas compatible with one another.

Some authors try to justify the contradictions of generally accepted ideologies by pointing out the alleged advantages of a compromise, however unsatisfactory from the logical point of view, for the smooth functioning of interhuman relations. They refer to the popular fallacy

THE ROLE OF IDEAS

that life and reality are "not logical"; they contend that a contradictory system may prove its expediency or even its truth by working satisfactorily while a logically consistent system would result in disaster. There is no need to refute anew such popular errors. Logical thinking and real life are not two separate orbits. Logic is for man the only means to master the problems of reality. What is contradictory in theory, is no less contradictory in reality. No ideological inconsistency can provide a satisfactory, i.e., working, solution for the problems offered by the facts of the world. The only effect of contradictory ideologies is to conceal the real problems and thus to prevent people from finding in time an appropriate policy for solving them. Inconsistent ideologies may sometimes postpone the emergence of a manifest conflict. But they certainly aggravate the evils which they mask and render a final solution more difficult. They multiply the agonies, they intensify the hatreds, and make peaceful settlement impossible. It is a serious blunder to consider ideological contradictions harmless or even beneficial.

The main objective of praxeology and economics is to substitute consistent correct ideologies for the contradictory tenets of popular eclecticism. There is no other means of preventing social disintegration and of safeguarding the steady improvement of human conditions than those provided by reason. Men must try to think through all the problems involved up to the point beyond which a human mind cannot proceed farther. They must never acquiesce in any solutions conveyed by older generations, they must always question anew every theory and every theorem, they must never relax in their endeavors to brush away fallacies and to find the best possible cognition. They must fight error by unmasking spurious doctrines and by expounding truth.

The problems involved are purely intellectual and must be dealt with as such. It is disastrous to shift them to the moral sphere and to dispose of supporters of opposite ideologies by calling them villains. It is vain to insist that what we are aiming at is good and what our adversaries want is bad. The question to be solved is precisely what is to be considered as good and what as bad. The rigid dogmatism peculiar to religious groups and to Marxism results only in irreconcilable conflict. It condemns beforehand all dissenters as evildoers, it calls into question their good faith, it asks them to surrender unconditionally. No social cooperation is possible where such an attitude prevails.

No better is the propensity, very popular nowadays, to brand supporters of other ideologies as lunatics. Psychiatrists are vague in drawing a line between sanity and insanity. It would be preposterous for laymen to interfere with this fundamental issue of psychiatry. However, it is clear that if the mere fact that a man shares erroneous views and acts according to his errors qualifies him as mentally disabled, it would be very hard to discover an individual to which the epithet sane or normal could be attributed. Then we are bound to call the past generations lunatic because their ideas about the problems of the natural sciences and concomitantly their techniques differed from ours. Coming generations will call us lunatics for the same reason. Man is liable to error. If to err were the characteristic feature of mental disability, then everybody should be called mentally disabled.

Neither can the fact that a man is at variance with the opinions held by the majority of his contemporaries qualify him as a lunatic. Were Copernicus, Galileo and Lavoisier insane? It is the regular course of history that a man conceives new ideas, contrary to those of other people. Some of these ideas are later embodied in the system of knowledge accepted by public opinion as true. Is it permissible to apply the epithet "sane" only to boors who never had ideas of their own and to deny it to all innovators?

The procedure of some contemporary psychiatrists is really outrageous. They are utterly ignorant of the theories of praxeology and economics. Their familiarity with present-day ideologies is superficial and uncritical. Yet they blithely call the supporters of some ideologies paranoid persons.

There are men who are commonly stigmatized as *monetary cranks*. The monetary crank suggests a method for making everybody prosperous by monetary measures. His plans are illusory. However, they are the consistent application of a monetary ideology entirely approved by contemporary public opinion and espoused by the policies of almost all governments. The objections raised against these ideological errors by the economists are not taken into account by the governments, political parties, and the press.

It is generally believed by those unfamiliar with economic theory that credit expansion and an increase in the quantity of money in circulation are efficacious means for lowering the rate of interest permanently below the height it would attain on a nonmanipulated capital and loan market. This theory is utterly illusory.[2] But it guides the monetary and credit policy of almost every contemporary government. Now, on the basis of this vicious ideology, no valid objection can be raised against the plans advanced by Pierre Joseph Proudhon, Ernest Solvay, Clifford Hugh Douglas and a host of other would-be reformers. They are only more consistent than other people are. They want to reduce the rate of interest to zero and thus to abolish altogether the scarcity of "capital." He who wants to refute them must attack the theories underlying the monetary and credit policies of the great nations.

The psychiatrist may object that what characterizes a man as a lunatic is precisely the fact that he lacks moderation and goes to extremes. While normal man is judicious enough to restrain himself, the paranoid person goes beyond all bounds. This is quite an unsatis-

2. Cf. below, Chapter 20.

factory rejoinder. All the arguments advanced in favor of the thesis that the rate of interest can be reduced by credit expansion from 5 or 4 per cent to 3 or 2 per cent are equally valid for a reduction to zero. The "monetary cranks" are certainly right from the point of view of the monetary fallacies approved by popular opinion.

There are psychiatrists who call the Germans who espoused the principles of Nazism lunatics and want to cure them by therapeutic procedures. Here again we are faced with the same problem. The doctrines of Nazism are vicious, but they do not essentially disagree with the ideologies of socialism and nationalism as approved by other peoples' public opinion. What characterized the Nazis was only the consistent application of these ideologies to the special conditions of Germany. Like all other contemporary nations the Nazis desired government control of business and economic self-sufficiency, i.e., autarky, for their own nation. The distinctive mark of their policy was that they refused to acquiesce in the disadvantages which the acceptance of the same system by other nations would impose upon them. They were not prepared to be forever "imprisoned," as they said, within a comparatively overpopulated area in which physical conditions render the productivity of human effort lower than in other countries. They believed that their nation's great population figures, the strategically propitious geographic situation of their country, and the inborn vigor and gallantry of their armed forces provided them with a good chance to remedy by aggression the evils they deplored.

Now, whoever accepts the ideology of nationalism and socialism as true and as the standard of his own nation's policy, is not in a position to refute the conclusions drawn from them by the Nazis. The only way for a refutation of Nazism left for foreign nations which have espoused these two principles was to defeat the Nazis in war. And as long as the ideology of socialism and nationalism is supreme in the world's public opinion, the Germans or other peoples will try again to succeed by aggression and conquest, should the opportunity ever be offered to them. There is no hope of eradicating the aggression mentality if one does not explode entirely the ideological fallacies from which it stems. This is not a task for psychiatrists, but for economists.[3]

Man has only one tool to fight error: reason.

3   Might

Society is a product of human action. Human action is directed by ideologies. Thus society and any concrete order of social affairs are an outcome of ideologies; ideologies are not, as Marxism asserts, a product of a certain state of social affairs. To be sure, human thoughts and ideas are not the achievement of isolated individuals.

3. Cf. Mises, *Omnipotent Government* (New Haven, 1944), pp. 221–28, 129–31, 135–40.

Thinking too succeeds only through the cooperation of the thinkers. No individual would make headway in his reasoning if he were under the necessity of starting from the beginning. A man can advance in thinking only because his efforts are aided by those of older generations who have formed the tools of thinking, the concepts and terminologies, and have raised the problems.

Any given social order was thought out and designed before it could be realized. This temporal and logical precedence of the ideological factor does not imply the proposition that people draft a complete plan of a social system as the utopians do. What is and must be thought out in advance is not the concerting of individual actions into an integrated system of social organization, but the actions of individuals with regard to their fellow men and of already formed groups of individuals with regard to other groups. Before a man aids his fellow in cutting a tree, such cooperation must be thought out. Before an act of barter takes place, the idea of mutual exchange of goods and services must be conceived. It is not necessary that the individuals concerned become aware of the fact that such mutuality results in the establishment of social bonds and in the emergence of a social system. The individual does not plan and execute actions intended to construct society. His conduct and the corresponding conduct of others generate social bodies.

Any existing state of social affairs is the product of ideologies previously thought out. Within society new ideologies may emerge and may supersede older ideologies and thus transform the social system. However, society is always the creation of ideologies temporally and logically anterior. Action is always directed by ideas; it realizes what previous thinking has designed.

If we hypostatize or anthropomorphize the notion of ideology, we may say that ideologies have might over men. Might is the faculty or power of directing actions. As a rule one says only of a man or of groups of men that they are mighty. Then the definition of might is: might is the power to direct other people's actions. He who is mighty, owes his might to an ideology. Only ideologies can convey to a man the power to influence other people's choices and conduct. One can become a leader only if one is supported by an ideology which makes other people tractable and accommodating. Might is thus not a physical and tangible thing, but a moral and spiritual phenomenon. A king's might rests upon the recognition of the monarchical ideology on the part of his subjects.

He who uses his might to run the state, i.e., the social apparatus of coercion and compulsion, rules. Rule is the exercise of might in the political body. Rule is always based upon might, i.e., the power to direct other people's actions.

Of course, it is possible to establish a government upon the violent oppression of reluctant people. It is the characteristic mark of state and government that they apply violent coercion or the threat of it against those not prepared to yield voluntarily. Yet such violent oppression is no less founded upon ideological might. He who wants to apply violence needs the voluntary cooperation of some people. An individual entirely dependent on himself can never rule by means of physical violence only.[4] He needs the ideological support of a group in order to subdue other groups. The tyrant must have a retinue of partisans who obey his orders of their own accord. Their spontaneous obedience provides him with the apparatus he needs for the conquest of other people. Whether or not he succeeds in making his sway last depends on the numerical relation of the two groups, those who support him voluntarily and those whom he beats into submission. Though a tyrant may temporarily rule through a minority if this minority is armed and the majority is not, in the long run a minority cannot keep the majority in subservience. The oppressed will rise in rebellion and cast off the yoke of tyranny.

A durable system of government must rest upon an ideology acknowledged by the majority. The "real" factor, the "real forces" that are the foundation of government and convey to the rulers the power to use violence against renitent minority groups are essentially ideological, moral, and spiritual. Rulers who failed to recognize this first principle of government and, relying upon the alleged irresistibility of their armed troops, disdained the spirit and ideas have finally been overthrown by the assault of their adversaries. The interpretation of might as a "real" factor not dependent upon ideologies, quite common to many political and historical books, is erroneous. The term *Realpolitik* makes sense only if used to signify a policy taking account of generally accepted ideologies as contrasted with a policy based upon ideologies not sufficiently acknowledged and therefore unfit to support a durable system of government.

He who interprets might as physical or "real" power to carry on and considers violent action as the very foundation of government, sees conditions from the narrow point of view of subordinate officers in charge of sections of an army or police force. To these subordinates a definite task within the framework of the ruling ideology is assigned. Their chiefs commit to their care troops which are not

4. A gangster may overpower a weaker or unarmed fellow. However, this has nothing to do with life in society. It is an isolated antisocial occurrence.

only equipped, armed, and organized for combat, but no less imbued with the spirit which makes them obey the orders issued. The commanders of such subdivisions consider this moral factor a matter of course because they themselves are animated by the same spirit and cannot even imagine a different ideology. The power of an ideology consists precisely in the fact that people submit to it without any wavering and scruples.

However, things are different for the head of the government. He must aim at preservation of the morale of the armed forces and of the loyalty of the rest of the population. For these moral factors are the only "real" elements upon which continuance of his mastery rests. His power dwindles if the ideology that supports it loses force.

Minorities too can sometimes conquer by means of superior military skill and can thus establish minority rule. But such an order of things cannot endure. If the victorious conquerors do not succeed in subsequently converting the system of rule by violence into a system of rule by ideological consent on the part of those ruled, they will succumb in new struggles. All victorious minorities who have established a lasting system of government have made their sway durable by means of a belated ideological ascendancy. They have legitimized their own supremacy either by submitting to the ideologies of the defeated or by transforming them. Where neither of these two things took place, the oppressed many dispossessed the oppressing few either by open rebellion or through the silent but steadfast operation of ideological forces.[5]

Many of the great historical conquests were able to endure because the invaders entered into alliance with those classes of the defeated nation which were supported by the ruling ideology and were thus considered legitimate rulers. This was the system adopted by the Tartars in Russia, by the Turks in the Danube principalities and by and large in Hungary and Transylvania, and by the British and the Dutch in the Indies. A comparatively insignificant number of Britons could rule many hundred millions of Indians because the Indian princes and aristocratic landowners looked upon British rule as a means for the preservation of their privileges and supplied it with the support which the generally acknowledged ideology of India gave to their own supremacy. England's Indian empire was firm as long as public opinion approved of the traditional social order. The Pax Britannica safeguarded the princes' and the landlords' privileges and protected the masses against the agonies of wars between the principalities and of succession wars within them. In our day the

5. Cf. below, pp. 647–51.

infiltration of subversive ideas from abroad has ended British rule and threatens the preservation of the country's age-old social order.

Victorious minorities sometimes owe their success to their technological superiority. This does not alter the case. In the long run it is impossible to withhold the better arms from the members of the majority. Not the equipment of their armed forces, but ideological factors safeguarded the British in India.[6]

A country's public opinion may be ideologically divided in such a way that no group is strong enough to establish a durable government. Then anarchy emerges. Revolutions and civil strife become permanent.

Traditionalism as an Ideology

Traditionalism is an ideology which considers loyalty to valuations, customs, and methods of procedure handed down or allegedly handed down from ancestors both right and expedient. It is not an essential mark of traditionalism that these forefathers were the ancestors in the biological meaning of the term or can be fairly considered such; they were sometimes only the previous inhabitants of the country concerned or supporters of the same religious creed or only precursors in the exercise of some special task. Who is to be considered an ancestor and what is the content of the body of tradition handed down are determined by the concrete teachings of each variety of traditionalism. The ideology brings into prominence some of the ancestors and relegates others to oblivion; it sometimes calls ancestors people who had nothing to do with the alleged posterity. It often constructs a "traditional" doctrine which is of recent origin and is at variance with the ideologies really held by the ancestors.

Traditionalism tries to justify its tenets by citing the success they secured in the past. Whether this assertion conforms with the facts, is another question. Research could sometimes unmask errors in the historical statements of a traditional belief. However, this did not always explode the traditional doctrine. For the core of traditionalism is not real historical facts, but an opinion about them, however mistaken, and a will to believe things to which the authority of ancient origin is attributed.

4 Meliorism and the Idea of Progress

The notions of progress and retrogression make sense only within a teleological system of thought. In such a framework it is sensible to call approach toward the goal aimed at progress and a movement

6. We are dealing here with the preservation of European minority rule in non-European countries. About the prospects of an Asiatic aggression on the West cf. below, pp. 669–70.

in the opposite direction retrogression. Without reference to some agent's action and to a definite goal both these notions are empty and void of any meaning.

It was one of the shortcomings of nineteenth-century philosophies to have misinterpreted the meaning of cosmic change and to have smuggled into the theory of biological transformation the idea of progress. Looking backward from any given state of things to the states of the past one can fairly use the terms development and evolution in a neutral sense. Then evolution signifies the process which led from past conditions to the present. But one must guard against the fatal error of confusing change with improvement and evolution with evolution toward higher forms of life. Neither is it permissible to substitute a pseudoscientific anthropocentrism for the anthropocentrism of religion and the older metaphysical doctrines.

However, there is no need for praxeology to enter into a critique of this philosophy. Its task is to explode the errors implied in current ideologies.

Eighteenth-century social philosophy was convinced that mankind has now finally entered the age of reason. While in the past theological and metaphysical errors were dominant, henceforth reason will be supreme. People will free themselves more and more from the chains of tradition and superstition and will dedicate all their efforts to the continuous improvement of social institutions. Every new generation will contribute its part to this glorious task. With the progress of time society will more and more become the society of free men, aiming at the greatest happiness of the greatest number. Temporary setbacks are, of course, not impossible. But finally the good cause will triumph because it is the cause of reason. People called themselves happy in that they were citizens of an age of enlightenment which through the discovery of the laws of rational conduct paved the way toward a steady amelioration of human affairs. What they lamented was only the fact that they themselves were too old to witness all the beneficial effects of the new philosophy. "I would wish," said Bentham to Philarète Chasles, "to be granted the privilege to live the years which I have still to live, at the end of each of the centuries following my death; thus I could witness the effects of my writing."[7]

All these hopes were founded on the firm conviction, proper to the age, that the masses are both morally good and reasonable. The upper strata, the privileged aristocrats living on the fat of the land, were

7. Philarète Chasles, *Études sur les hommes et les moers du XIXᵉ siècle* (Paris, 1849), p. 89.

thought depraved. The common people, especially the peasants and the workers, were glorified in a romantic mood as noble and unerring in their judgment. Thus the philosophers were confident that democracy, government by the people, would bring about social perfection.

This prejudice was the fateful error of the humanitarians, the philosophers, and the liberals. Men are not infallible; they err very often. It is not true that the masses are always right and know the means for attaining the ends aimed at. "Belief in the common man" is no better founded than was belief in the supernatural gifts of kings, priests, and noblemen. Democracy guarantees a system of government in accordance with the wishes and plans of the majority. But it cannot prevent majorities from falling victim to erroneous ideas and from adopting inappropriate policies which not only fail to realize the ends aimed at but result in disaster. Majorities too may err and destroy our civilization. The good cause will not triumph merely on account of its reasonableness and expediency. Only if men are such that they will finally espouse policies reasonable and likely to attain the ultimate ends aimed at, will civilization improve and society and state render men more satisfied, although not happy in a metaphysical sense. Whether or not this condition is given, only the unknown future can reveal.

There is no room within a system of praxeology for meliorism and optimistic fatalism. Man is free in the sense that he must daily choose anew between policies that lead to success and those that lead to disaster, social disintegration, and barbarism.

The term *progress* is nonsensical when applied to cosmic events or to a comprehensive world view. We have no information about the plans of the prime mover. But it is different with its use in the frame of an ideological doctrine. The immense majority strives after a greater and better supply of food, clothes, homes, and other material amenities. In calling a rise in the masses' standard of living progress and improvement, economists do not espouse a mean materialism. They simply establish the fact that people are motivated by the urge to improve the material conditions of their existence. They judge policies from the point of view of the aims men want to attain. He who disdains the fall in infant mortality and the gradual disappearance of famines and plagues may cast the first stone upon the materialism of the economists.

There is but one yardstick for the appraisal of human action: whether or not it is fit to attain the ends aimed at by acting men.

CHAPTER 10

Exchange Within Society

1   Autistic Exchange and Interpersonal Exchange

Action always is essentially the exchange of one state of affairs for another state of affairs. If the action is performed by an individual without any reference to cooperation with other individuals, we may call it autistic exchange. An instance: the isolated hunter who kills an animal for his own consumption; he exchanges leisure and a cartridge for food.

Within society cooperation substitutes interpersonal or social exchange for autistic exchanges. Man gives to other men in order to receive from them. Mutuality emerges. Man serves in order to be served.

The exchange relation is the fundamental social relation. Interpersonal exchange of goods and services weaves the bond which unites men into society. The societal formula is: *do ut des* [(Latin) I give that you may give]. Where there is no intentional mutuality, where an action is performed without any design of being benefited by a concomitant action of other men, there is no interpersonal exchange, but autistic exchange. It does not matter whether the autistic action is beneficial or detrimental to other people or whether it does not concern them at all. A genius may perform his task for himself, not for the crowd; however, he is an outstanding benefactor of mankind. The robber kills the victim for his own advantage; the murdered man is by no means a partner in this crime, he is merely its object; what is done, is done against him.

Hostile aggression was a practice common to man's nonhuman forebears. Conscious and purposeful cooperation is the outcome of a long evolutionary process. Ethnology and history have provided us with interesting information concerning the beginning and the primitive patterns of interpersonal exchange. Some consider the custom of mutual giving and returning of presents and stipulating a certain return present in advance as a precursory pattern of interpersonal exchange.[1] Others consider dumb barter as the primitive mode of trade. However, to make presents in the expectation of being rewarded

1. Gustav Cassel, *The Theory of Social Economy*, trans. by S. L. Banon (new ed. London, 1932), p. 371.

by the receiver's return present or in order to acquire the favor of a man whose animosity could be disastrous, is already tantamount to interpersonal exchange. The same applies to dumb barter which is distinguished from other modes of bartering and trading only through the absence of oral discussion.

It is the essential characteristic of the categories of human action that they are apodictic and absolute and do not admit of any gradation. There is action or nonaction, there is exchange or nonexchange; everything which applies to action and exchange as such is given or not given in every individual instance according to whether there is or there is not action and exchange. In the same way the boundaries between autistic exchange and interpersonal exchange are sharply distinct. Making one-sided presents without the aim of being rewarded by any conduct on the part of the receiver or of third persons is autistic exchange. The donor acquires the satisfaction which the better condition of the receiver gives to him. The receiver gets the present as a God-sent gift. But if presents are given in order to influence some people's conduct, they are no longer one-sided, but a variety of interpersonal exchange between the donor and the man whose conduct they are designed to influence. Although the emergence of interpersonal exchange was the result of a long evolution, no gradual transition is conceivable between autistic and interpersonal exchange. There were no intermediary modes of exchange between them. The step which leads from autistic to interpersonal exchange was no less a jump into something entirely new and essentially different than was the step from automatic reaction of the cells and nerves to conscious and purposeful behavior, to action.

2 Contractual Bonds and Hegemonic Bonds

There are two different kinds of social cooperation: cooperation by virtue of contract and coordination, and cooperation by virtue of command and subordination or hegemony.

Where and as far as cooperation is based on contract, the logical relation between the cooperating individuals is symmetrical. They are all parties to interpersonal exchange contracts. John has the same relation to Tom as Tom has to John. Where and as far as cooperation is based on command and subordination, there is the man who commands and there are those who obey his orders. The logical relation between these two classes of men is asymmetrical. There is a director and there are people under his care. The director alone chooses and directs; the others—the wards—are mere pawns in his actions.

The power that calls into life and animates any social body is always ideological might, and the fact that makes an individual a member of any social compound is always his own conduct. This is no less valid with regard to a hegemonic societal bond. It is true, people are as a rule born into the most important hegemonic bonds, into the family and into the state, and this was also the case with the hegemonic bonds of older days, slavery and serfdom, which disappeared in the realm of Western civilization. But no physical violence and compulsion can possibly force a man against his will to remain in the status of the ward of a hegemonic order. What violence or the threat of violence brings about is a state of affairs in which subjection as a rule is considered more desirable than rebellion. Faced with the choice between the consequences of obedience and of disobedience, the ward prefers the former and thus integrates himself into the hegemonic bond. Every new command places this choice before him again. In yielding again and again he himself contributes his share to the continuous existence of the hegemonic societal body. Even as a ward in such a system he is an acting human being, i.e., a being not simply yielding to blind impulses, but using his reason in choosing between alternatives.

What differentiates the hegemonic bond from the contractual bond is the scope in which the choices of the individuals determine the course of events. As soon as a man has decided in favor of his subjection to a hegemonic system, he becomes, within the margin of this system's activities and for the time of his subjection, a pawn of the director's actions. Within the hegemonic societal body and as far as it directs its subordinates' conduct, only the director acts. The wards act only in choosing subordination; having once chosen subordination they no longer act for themselves, they are taken care of.

In the frame of a contractual society the individual members exchange definite quantities of goods and services of a definite quality. In choosing subjection in a hegemonic body a man neither gives nor receives anything that is definite. He integrates himself into a system in which he has to render indefinite services and will receive what the director is willing to assign to him. He is at the mercy of the director. The director alone is free to choose. Whether the director is an individual or an organized group of individuals, a directorate, and whether the director is a selfish maniacal tyrant or a benevolent paternal despot is of no relevance for the structure of the whole system.

The distinction between these two kinds of social cooperation is common to all theories of society. Ferguson described it as the contrast between warlike nations and commercial nations;[2] Saint Simon as the contrast between pugnacious nations and peaceful or industrial nations; Herbert Spencer as the contrast between societies of individual freedom and those of a militant structure;[3] Sombart as the contrast between heroes and peddlers.[4] The Marxians distinguish between the "gentile organization" of a fabulous state of primitive society and the eternal bliss of socialism on the one hand and the unspeakable degradation of capitalism on the other hand.[5] The Nazi philosophers distinguish the counterfeit system of bourgeois security from the heroic system of authoritarian *Führertum* [(German) Leadership]. The valuation of both systems is different with the various sociologists. But they fully agree in the establishment of the contrast and no less in recognizing that no third principle is thinkable and feasible.

Western civilization as well as the civilization of the more advanced Eastern peoples are achievements of men who have cooperated according to the pattern of contractual coordination. These civilizations, it is true, have adopted in some respects bonds of hegemonic structure. The state as an apparatus of compulsion and coercion is by necessity a hegemonic organization. So is the family and its household community. However, the characteristic feature of these civilizations is the contractual structure proper to the cooperation of the individual families. There once prevailed almost complete autarky and economic isolation of the individual household units. When interfamilial exchange of goods and services was substituted for each family's economic self-sufficiency, it was, in all nations commonly considered civilized, a cooperation based on contract. Human civilization as it has been hitherto known to historical experience is preponderantly a product of contractual relations.

Any kind of human cooperation and social mutuality is essentially an order of peace and conciliatory settlement of disputes. In the domestic relations of any societal unit, be it a contractual or a hegemonic bond, there must be peace. Where there are violent conflicts and as far as there are such conflicts, there is neither cooperation nor societal bonds. Those political parties which in their eagerness to substitute the hegemonic system for the contractual system point

---

2. Cf. Adam Ferguson, *An Essay on the History of Civil Society* (new ed. Basel, 1789), p. 208.
3. Cf. Herbert Spencer, *The Principles of Sociology* (New York, 1914), III, 575–611.
4. Cf. Werner Sombart, *Haendler und Helden* (Munich, 1915).
5. Cf. Frederick Engels, *The Origin of the Family, Private Property and the State* (New York, 1942), p. 144.

at the rottenness of peace and of bourgeois security, extol the moral nobility of violence and bloodshed and praise war and revolution as the eminently natural methods of interhuman relations, contradict themselves. For their own utopias are designed as realms of peace. The Reich of the Nazis and the commonwealth of the Marxians are planned as societies of undisturbed peace. They are to be created by pacification, i.e., the violent subjection of all those not ready to yield without resistance. In a contractual world various states can quietly coexist. In a hegemonic world there can only be one Reich or commonwealth and only one dictator. Socialism must choose between a renunciation of the advantages of division of labor encompassing the whole earth and all peoples and the establishment of a world-embracing hegemonic order. It is this fact that made Russian Bolshevism, German Nazism, and Italian Fascism "dynamic," i.e., aggressive. Under contractual conditions empires are dissolved into a loose league of autonomous member nations. The hegemonic system is bound to strive after annexation of all independent states.

The contractual order of society is an order of right and law. It is a government under the rule of law (*Rechtsstaat*) as differentiated from the welfare state (*Wohlfahrtsstaat*) or paternal state. Right or law is the complex of rules determining the orbit in which individuals are free to act. No such orbit is left to wards of a hegemonic society. In the hegemonic state there is neither right nor law; there are only directives and regulations which the director may change daily and apply with what discrimination he pleases and which the wards must obey. The wards have one freedom only: to obey without asking questions.

3   Calculative Action

All the praxeological categories are eternal and unchangeable as they are uniquely determined by the logical structure of the human mind and by the natural conditions of man's existence. Both in acting and in theorizing about acting, man can neither free himself from these categories nor go beyond them. A kind of acting categorially different from that determined by these categories is neither possible nor conceivable for man. Man can never comprehend something which would be neither action nor nonaction. There is no history of acting; there is no evolution which would lead from nonaction to action; there are no transitory stages between action and nonaction. There is only acting and nonacting. And for every concrete action all that is rigorously valid which is categorially established with regard to action in general.

Every action can make use of ordinal numbers. For the application of cardinal numbers and for the arithmetical computation based on them special conditions are required. These conditions emerged in the historical evolution of the contractual society. Thus the way was opened for computation and calculation in the planning of future action and in establishing the effects achieved by past action. Cardinal numbers and their use in arithmetical operations are also eternal and immutable categories of the human mind. But their applicability to premeditation and the recording of action depends on certain conditions which were not given in the early state of human affairs, which appeared only later, and which could possibly disappear again.

It was cognition of what is going on within a world in which action is computable and calculable that led men to the elaboration of the sciences of praxeology and economics. Economics is essentially a theory of that scope of action in which calculation is applied or can be applied if certain conditions are realized. No other distinction is of greater significance, both for human life and for the study of human action, than that between calculable action and noncalculable action. Modern civilization is above all characterized by the fact that it has elaborated a method which makes the use of arithmetic possible in a broad field of activities. This is what people have in mind when attributing to it the — not very expedient and often misleading — epithet of rationality.

The mental grasp and analysis of the problems present in a calculating market system were the starting point of economic thinking which finally led to general praxeological cognition. However, it is not the consideration of this historical fact that makes it necessary to start exposition of a comprehensive system of economics by an analysis of the market economy and to place before this analysis an examination of the problem of economic calculation. Neither historical nor heuristic aspects enjoin such a procedure, but the requirements of logical and systematic rigor. The problems concerned are apparent and practical only within the sphere of the calculating market economy. It is only a hypothetical and figurative transfer which makes them utilizable for the scrutiny of other systems of society's economic organization which do not allow of any calculation. Economic calculation is the fundamental issue in the comprehension of all problems commonly called economic.

Economic Calculation

CHAPTER 11

Valuation Without Calculation

1   The Gradation of the Means

Acting man transfers the valuation of ends he aims at to the means. Other things being equal, he assigns to the total amount of the various means the same value he attaches to the end which they are fit to bring about. For the moment we may disregard the time needed for production of the end and its influence upon the relation between the value of the ends and that of the means.

The gradation of the means is, like that of the ends, a process of preferring *a* to *b*. It is preferring and setting aside. It is manifestation of a judgment that *a* is more intensely desired than is *b*. It opens a field for application of ordinal numbers, but it is not open to application of cardinal numbers and arithmetical operations based on them. If somebody gives me the choice among three tickets entitling one to attend the operas *Aïda*, *Falstaff*, and *Traviata* and I take, if I can only take one of them, *Aïda*, and if I can take one more, *Falstaff* also, I have made a choice. That means: under given conditions I prefer *Aïda* and *Falstaff* to *Traviata*; if I could only choose one of them, I would prefer *Aïda* and renounce *Falstaff*. If I call the admission to *Aïda* *a*, that to *Falstaff* *b* and that to *Traviata* *c*, I can say: I prefer *a* to *b* and *b* to *c*.

The immediate goal of acting is frequently the acquisition of countable and measurable supplies of tangible things. Then acting man has to choose between countable quantities; he prefers, for example, 15 *r* to 7 *p*; but if he had to choose between 15 *r* and 8 *p*, he might prefer 8 *p*. We can express this state of affairs by declaring that he values 15 *r* less than 8 *p*, but higher than 7 *p*. This is tantamount to the statement that he prefers *a* to *b* and *b* to *c*. The substitution of 8 *p* for *a*, of 15 *r* for *b* and of 7 *p* for *c* changes neither the meaning of the statement nor the fact that it describes. It certainly does not render reckoning with cardinal numbers possible. It does not open a field for economic calculation and the mental operations based upon such calculation.

2   The Barter-Fiction of the Elementary Theory of Value and Prices

The elaboration of economic theory is heuristically dependent on the logical processes of reckoning to such an extent that the economists failed to realize the fundamental problem involved in the methods of economic calculation. They were prone to take economic calculation as a matter of course; they did not see that it is not an ultimate given, but a derivative requiring reduction to more elementary phenomena. They misconstrued economic calculation. They took it for a category of all human action and ignored the fact that it is only a category inherent in acting under special conditions. They were fully aware of the fact that interpersonal exchange, and consequently market exchange effected by the intermediary of a common medium of exchange—money, and therefore prices, are special features of a certain state of society's economic organization which did not exist in primitive civilizations and could possibly disappear in the further course of historical change.[1] But they did not comprehend that money prices are the only vehicle of economic calculation. Thus most of their studies are of little use. Even the writings of the most eminent economists are vitiated to some extent by the fallacies implied in their ideas about economic calculation.

The modern theory of value and prices shows how the choices of individuals, their preferring of some things and setting aside of other things, result, in the sphere of interpersonal exchange, in the emergence of market prices.[2] These masterful expositions are unsatisfactory in some minor points and disfigured by unsuitable expressions. But they are essentially irrefutable. As far as they need to be amended, it must be done by a consistent elaboration of the fundamental thoughts of their authors rather than by a refutation of their reasoning.

In order to trace back the phenomena of the market to the universal category of preferring *a* to *b*, the elementary theory of value and prices is bound to use some imaginary constructions. The use of imaginary constructions to which nothing corresponds in reality is an indispensable tool of thinking. No other method would have contributed anything to the interpretation of reality. But one of the most

1. The German Historical School expressed this by asserting that private ownership of the means of production, market exchange, and money are "historical categories."

2. Cf. especially Eugen von Böhm-Bawerk, *Kapital und Kapitalzins*, Pt. II, Bk. III. [It should be noted that Böhm-Bawerk's *Kapital und Kapitalzins* was translated into English by Hans F. Sennholz and published as *Capital and Interest* (South Holland, Ill.: Libertarian Press, 1959). See p. 133n. above. This note refers specifically to Volume II, Book II, Parts A & B, *Value and Price*, pp. 121–256; published separately as *Value and Price* (1962).]

important problems of science is to avoid the fallacies which ill-considered employment of such constructions can entail.

The elementary theory of value and prices employs, apart from other imaginary constructions to be dealt with later,[3] the construction of a market in which all transactions are performed in direct exchange. There is no money; goods and services are directly bartered against other goods and services. This imaginary construction is necessary. One must disregard the intermediary role played by money in order to realize that what is ultimately exchanged is always economic goods of the first order against other such goods. Money is nothing but a medium of interpersonal exchange. But one must carefully guard oneself against the delusions which this construction of a market with direct exchange can easily engender.

A serious blunder that owes its origin and its tenacity to a misinterpretation of this imaginary construction was the assumption that the medium of exchange is a neutral factor only. According to this opinion the only difference between direct and indirect exchange was that only in the latter was a medium of exchange used. The interpolation of money into the transaction, it was asserted, did not affect the main features of the business. One did not ignore the fact that in the course of history tremendous alterations in the purchasing power of money have occurred and that these fluctuations often convulsed the whole system of exchange. But it was believed that such events were exceptional facts caused by inappropriate policies. Only "bad" money, it was said, can bring about such disarrangements. In addition people misunderstood the causes and effects of these disturbances. They tacitly assumed that changes in purchasing power occur with regard to all goods and services at the same time and to the same extent. This is, of course, what the fable of money's neutrality implies. The whole theory of catallactics, it was held, can be elaborated under the assumption that there is direct exchange only. If this is once achieved, the only thing to be added is the "simple" insertion of money terms into the complex of theorems concerning direct exchange. However, this final completion of the catallactic system was considered of minor importance only. It was not believed that it could alter anything essential in the structure of economic teachings. The main task of economics was conceived as the study of direct exchange. What remained to be done besides this was at best only a scrutiny of the problems of "bad" money.

Complying with this opinion, economists neglected to lay due stress upon the problems of indirect exchange. Their treatment of

3. See below, pp. 236–56.

monetary problems was superficial; it was only loosely connected with the main body of their scrutiny of the market process. About the beginning of the twentieth century the problems of indirect exchange were by and large relegated to a subordinate place. There were treatises on catallactics which dealt only incidentally and cursorily with monetary matters, and there were books on currency and banking which did not even attempt to integrate their subject into the structure of a catallactic system. At the universities of the Anglo-Saxon countries there were separate chairs for economics and for currency and banking, and at most of the German universities monetary problems were almost entirely disregarded.[4] Only later economists realized that some of the most important and most intricate problems of catallactics are to be found in the field of indirect exchange and that an economic theory which does not pay full regard to them is lamentably defective. The coming into vogue of investigations concerning the relation between the "natural rate of interest" and the "money rate of interest," the ascendancy of the monetary theory of the trade cycle, and the entire demolition of the doctrine of the simultaneousness and evenness of the changes in the purchasing power of money were marks of the new tenor of economic thought. Of course, these new ideas were essentially a continuation of the work gloriously begun by David Hume, the British Currency School, John Stuart Mill and Cairnes.

Still more detrimental was a second error which emerged from the careless use of the imaginary construction of a market with direct exchange.

An inveterate fallacy asserted that things and services exchanged are of equal value. Value was considered as objective, as an intrinsic quality inherent in things and not merely as the expression of various people's eagerness to acquire them. People, it was assumed, first established the magnitude of value proper to goods and services by an act of measurement and then proceeded to barter them against quantities of goods and services of the same amount of value. This fallacy frustrated Aristotle's approach to economic problems and, for almost

---

4. Neglect of the problems of indirect exchange was certainly influenced by political preposessions. People did not want to give up the thesis according to which economic depressions are an evil inherent in the capitalist mode of production and are in no way caused by attempts to lower the rate of interest by credit expansion. Fashionable teachers of economics deemed it "unscientific" to explain depressions as a phenomenon originating "only" out of events in the sphere of money and credit. There were even surveys of the history of business cycle theory which omitted any discussion of the monetary thesis. Cf., e.g., Eugen von Bergmann, *Geschichte der nationalökonomischen Krisentheorien* (Stuttgart, 1895).

two thousand years, the reasoning of all those for whom Aristotle's opinions were authoritative. It seriously vitiated the marvelous achievements of the classical economists and rendered the writings of their epigones, especially those of Marx and the Marxian school, entirely futile. The basis of modern economics is the cognition that it is precisely the disparity in the value attached to the objects exchanged that results in their being exchanged. People buy and sell only because they appraise the things given up less than those received. Thus the notion of a measurement of value is vain. An act of exchange is neither preceded nor accompanied by any process which could be called a measuring of value. An individual may attach the same value to two things; but then no exchange can result. But if there is a diversity in valuation, all that can be asserted with regard to it is that one a is valued higher, that it is preferred to one b. Values and valuations are intensive quantities and not extensive quantities. They are not susceptible to mental grasp by the application of cardinal numbers.

However, the spurious idea that values are measurable and are really measured in the conduct of economic transactions was so deeply rooted that even eminent economists fell victim to the fallacy implied. Even Friedrich von Wieser and Irving Fisher took it for granted that there must be something like measurement of value and that economics must be able to indicate and to explain the method by which such measurement is effected.[5] Most of the lesser economists simply maintained that money serves "as a measure of values."

Now, we must realize that valuing means to prefer a to b. There is—logically, epistemologically, psychologically, and praxeologically—only one pattern of preferring. It does not matter whether a lover prefers one girl to other girls, a man one friend to other people, an amateur one painting to other paintings, or a consumer a loaf of bread to a piece of candy. Preferring always means to love or to desire a more than b. Just as there is no standard and no measurement of sexual love, of friendship and sympathy, and of aesthetic enjoyment, so there is no measurement of the value of commodities. If a man exchanges two pounds of butter for a shirt, all that we can assert with regard to this transaction is that he—at the instant of the transaction and under the conditions which this instant offers to him—prefers one shirt to two pounds of butter. It is certain that every act

5. For a critical analysis and refutation of Fisher's argument, cf. Mises, *The Theory of Money and Credit*, [pp. 55–58 in the Liberty Fund reprint (1980)]; for the same with regard to Wieser's argument, Mises, *Nationalökonomie* (Geneva, 1940), pp. 192–94.

of preferring is characterized by a definite psychic intensity of the feelings it implies. There are grades in the intensity of the desire to attain a definite goal and this intensity determines the psychic profit which the successful action brings to the acting individual. But psychic quantities can only be felt. They are entirely personal, and there is no semantic means to express their intensity and to convey information about them to other people.

There is no method available to construct a unit of value. Let us remember that two units of a homogeneous supply are necessarily valued differently. The value attached to the nth unit is lower than that attached to the $(n - 1)$th unit.

In the market society there are money prices. Economic calculation is calculation in terms of money prices. The various quantities of goods and services enter into this calculation with the amount of money for which they are bought and sold on the market or for which they could prospectively be bought and sold. It is a fictitious assumption that an isolated self-sufficient individual or the general manager of a socialist system, i.e., a system in which there is no market for means of production, could calculate. There is no way which could lead one from the money computation of a market economy to any kind of computation in a non-market system.

The Theory of Value and Socialism

Socialists, Institutionalists and the Historical School have blamed economists for having employed the imaginary construction of an isolated individual's thinking and acting. This Robinson Crusoe pattern, it is asserted, is of no use for the study of the conditions of a market economy. The rebuke is somewhat justified. Imaginary constructions of an isolated individual and of a planned economy without market exchange become utilizable only through the implication of the fictitious assumption, self-contradictory in thought and contrary to reality, that economic calculation is possible also within a system without a market for the means of production.

It was certainly a serious blunder that economists did not become aware of this difference between the conditions of a market economy and a non-market economy. Yet the socialists had little reason for criticizing this fault. For it consisted precisely in the fact that the economists tacitly implied the assumption that a socialist order of society could also resort to economic calculation and that they thus asserted the possibility of the realization of the socialist plans.

The classical economists and their epigones could not, of course, recognize the problems involved. If it were true that the value of things is determined by the quantity of labor required for their production or reproduction, then there is no further problem of economic calculation. The supporters of the labor theory of value cannot be blamed for having misconstrued the problems of a socialist system. Their fateful failure was their untenable doctrine of value. That some of them were ready to consider the imaginary construction of a socialist economy as a useful and realizable pattern for a thorough reform of social organization did not contradict the essential content of their theoretical analysis. But it was different with subjective catallactics. It was unpardonable for the modern economists to have failed to recognize the problems involved.

Wieser was right when he once declared that many economists have unwittingly dealt with the value theory of communism and have on that account neglected to elaborate that of the present state of society.[6] It is tragic that he himself did not avoid this failure.

The illusion that a rational order of economic management is possible in a society based on public ownership of the means of production owed its origin to the value theory of the classical economists and its tenacity to the failure of many modern economists to think through consistently to its ultimate conclusions the fundamental theorem of the subjectivist theory. Thus the socialist utopias were generated and preserved by the shortcomings of those schools of thought which the Marxians reject as "an ideological disguise of the selfish class interest of the exploiting bourgeoisie." In truth it was the errors of these schools that made the socialist ideas thrive. This fact clearly demonstrates the emptiness of the Marxian teachings concerning "ideologies" and its modern offshoot, the sociology of knowledge.

3   The Problem of Economic Calculation

Acting man uses knowledge provided by the natural sciences for the elaboration of technology, the applied science of action possible in the field of external events. Technology shows what could be achieved if one wanted to achieve it, and how it could be achieved provided people were prepared to employ the means indicated. With the progress of the natural sciences technology progressed too; many would prefer to say that the desire to improve technological methods prompted the progress of the natural sciences. The quantification of the natural sciences made technology quantitative. Modern technology is essentially the applied art of quantitative prediction of the outcome of possible action. One calculates with a reasonable degree of precision the outcome of planned actions, and one calculates in order to arrange an action in such a way that a definite result emerges.

6. Cf. Friedrich von Wieser, *Der natürliche Wert* (Vienna, 1889), p. 60, n. 3. [English translation: *Natural Value*. Translation by Christian A. Malloch. Edited with a Preface (1893) and Analysis by William Smart. New York: Kellely & Millman, 1956.]

However, the mere information conveyed by technology would suffice for the performance of calculation only if all means of production—both material and human—could be perfectly substituted for one another according to definite ratios, or if they all were absolutely specific. In the former case all means of production would be fit, although according to different ratios, for the attainment of all ends whatever; things would be as if only one kind of means—one kind of economic goods of a higher order existed. In the latter case each means could be employed for the attainment of one end only; one would attach to each group of complementary factors of production the value attached to the respective good of the first order. (Here again we disregard provisionally the modifications brought about by the time factor.) Neither of these two conditions is present in the universe in which man acts. The means can only be substituted for one another within narrow limits; they are more or less specific means for the attainment of various ends. But, on the other hand, most means are not absolutely specific; most of them are fit for various purposes. The facts that there are different classes of means, that most of the means are better suited for the realization of some ends, less suited for the attainment of some other ends and absolutely useless for the production of a third group of ends, and that therefore the various means allow for various uses, set man the task of allocating them to those employments in which they can render the best service. Here computation in kind as applied by technology is of no avail. Technology operates with countable and measurable quantities of external things and effects; it knows causal relations between them, but it is foreign to their relevance to human wants and desires. Its field is that of objective use-value only. It judges all problems from the disinterested point of view of a neutral observer of physical, chemical, and biological events. For the notion of subjective use-value, for the specifically human angle, and for the dilemmas of acting man there is no room in the teachings of technology. It ignores the economic problem: to employ the available means in such a way that no want more urgently felt should remain unsatisfied because the means suitable for its attainment were employed—wasted—for the attainment of a want less urgently felt. For the solution of such problems technology and its methods of counting and measuring are unfit. Technology tells how a given end could be attained by the employment of various means which can be used together in various combinations, or how various available means could be employed for certain purposes. But it is at a loss to tell man which procedures he should choose out of the infinite variety of imaginable and possible modes of production. What acting man wants to know is how he must employ the available means for the best possible—the most economic — removal of felt uneasiness. But technology provides him with nothing more than statements about causal relations between external things. It tells, for example, $7\,a + 3\,b + 5\,c + \ldots x\,n$ are liable to bring about $8\,P$. But although it knows the value attached by acting man to the various goods of the first order, it cannot decide whether this formula or any other out of the infinite multitude of similarly constructed formulas best serves the attainment of the ends sought by acting man. The art of engineering can establish how a bridge must be built in order to span a river at a given point and to carry definite loads. But it cannot answer the question whether or not the construction of such a bridge would withdraw material factors of production and labor from an employment in which they could satisfy needs more urgently felt. It cannot tell whether or not the bridge should be built at all, where it should be built, what capacity for bearing burdens it should have, and which of the many possibilities for its construction should be chosen. Technological computation can establish relations between various classes of means only to the extent that they can be substituted for one another in the attempts to attain a definite goal. But action is bound to discover relations among all means, however dissimilar they may be, without any regard to the question whether or not they can replace one another in performing the same services.

Technology and the considerations derived from it would be of little use for acting man if it were impossible to introduce into their schemes the money prices of goods and services. The projects and designs of engineers would be purely academic if they could not compare input and output on a common basis. The lofty theorist in the seclusion of his laboratory does not bother about such trifling things; what he is searching for is causal relations between various elements of the universe. But the practical man, eager to improve human conditions by removing uneasiness as far as possible, must know whether, under given conditions, what he is planning is the best method, or even a method, to make people less uneasy. He must know whether what he wants to achieve will be an improvement when compared with the present state of affairs and with the advantages to be expected from the execution of other technically realizable projects which cannot be put into execution if the project he has in mind absorbs the available means. Such comparisons can only be made by the use of money prices.

Thus money becomes the vehicle of economic calculation. This is not a separate function of money. Money is the universally used medium of exchange, nothing else. Only because money is the common medium of exchange, because most goods and services can be sold and bought on the market against money, and only as far as this is the case, can men use money prices in reckoning. The exchange ratios between money and the various goods and services as established on the market of the past and as expected to be established on the market of the future are the mental tools of economic planning. Where there are no money prices, there are no such things as economic quantities. There are only various quantitative relations between various causes and effects in the external world. There is no means for man to find out what kind of action would best serve his endeavors to remove uneasiness as far as possible.

There is no need to dwell upon the primitive conditions of the household economy of self-sufficient farmers. These people performed only very simple processes of production. For them no calculation was needed, as they could directly compare input and output. If they wanted shirts, they grew hemp, they spun, wove, and sewed. They could, without any calculation, easily make up their minds whether or not the toil and trouble expended were compensated by the product. But for civilized mankind a return to such a life is out of the question.

4   Economic Calculation and the Market

The quantitative treatment of economic problems must not be confused with the quantitative methods applied in dealing with the problems of the external universe of physical and chemical events. The distinctive mark of economic calculation is that it is neither based upon nor related to anything which could be characterized as measurement.

A process of measurement consists in the establishment of the numerical relation of an object with regard to another object, viz., the unit of the measurement. The ultimate source of measurement is that of spatial dimensions. With the aid of the unit defined in reference to extension one measures energy and potentiality, the power of a thing to bring about changes in other things and relations, and the passing of time. A pointer-reading is directly indicative of a spatial relation and only indirectly of other quantities. The assumption underlying measurement is the immutability of the unit. The unit of length is the rock upon which all measurement is based. It is assumed that man cannot help considering it immutable.

The last decades have witnessed a revolution in the traditional epistemological setting of physics, chemistry, and mathematics. We are on the eve of innovations whose scope cannot be foreseen. It may be that the coming generations of physicists will have to face problems in some way similar to those with which praxeology must deal. Perhaps they will be forced to drop the idea that there is something unaffected by cosmic changes which the observer can use as a standard of measurement. But however that may come, the logical structure of the measurement of earthly entities in the macroscopic or molar field of physics will not alter. Measurement in the orbit of microscopic physics too is made with meter scales, micrometers, spectrographs—ultimately with the gross sense organs of man, the observer and experimenter, who himself is molar.[7] It cannot free itself from Euclidian geometry and from the notion of an unchangeable standard.

There are monetary units and there are measurable physical units of various economic goods and of many—but not of all—services bought and sold. But the exchange ratios which we have to deal with are permanently fluctuating. There is nothing constant and invariable in them. They defy any attempt to measure them. They are not facts in the sense in which a physicist calls the establishment of the weight of a quantity of copper a fact. They are historical events, expressive of what happened once at a definite instant and under definite circumstances. The same numerical exchange ratio may appear again, but it is by no means certain whether this will really happen and, if it happens, the question is open whether this identical result was the outcome of preservation of the same circumstances or of a return to them rather than the outcome of the interplay of a very different constellation of price-determining factors. Numbers applied by acting man in economic calculation do not refer to quantities measured but to exchange ratios as they are expected—on the basis of understanding—to be realized on the markets of the future to which alone all acting is directed and which alone counts for acting man.

We are not dealing at this point of our investigation with the problem of a "quantitative science of economics," but with the analysis of the mental processes performed by acting man in applying quantitative distinctions when planning conduct. As action is always directed toward influencing a future state of affairs, economic calculation always deals with the future. As far as it takes past events and exchange ratios of the past into consideration, it does so only for the sake of an arrangement of future action.

The task which acting man wants to achieve by economic calculation is to establish the outcome of acting by contrasting input and output. Economic calculation is either an estimate of the expected

7. Cf. A. Eddington, *The Philosophy of Physical Science*, pp. 70–79, 168–69.

outcome of future action or the establishment of the outcome of past action. But the latter does not serve merely historical and didactic aims. Its practical meaning is to show how much one is free to consume without impairing the future capacity to produce. It is with regard to this problem that the fundamental notions of economic calculation — capital and income, profit and loss, spending and saving, cost and yield — are developed. The practical employment of these notions and of all notions derived from them is inseparably linked with the operation of a market in which goods and services of all orders are exchanged against a universally used medium of exchange, viz., money. They would be merely academic, without any relevance for acting within a world with a different structure of action.

CHAPTER 12

The Sphere of Economic Calculation

1   The Character of Monetary Entries

Economic calculation can comprehend everything that is exchanged against money.

The prices of goods and services are either historical data describing past events or anticipations of probable future events. Information about a past price conveys the knowledge that one or several acts of interpersonal exchange were effected according to this ratio. It does not convey directly any knowledge about future prices. We may often assume that the market conditions which determined the formation of prices in the recent past will not change at all or at least not change considerably in the immediate future so that prices too will remain unchanged or change only slightly. Such expectations are reasonable if the prices concerned were the result of the interaction of many people ready to buy or to sell provided the exchange ratios seemed propitious to them and if the market situation was not influenced by conditions which are considered as accidental, extraordinary, and not likely to return. However, the main task of economic calculation is not to deal with the problems of unchanging or only slightly changing market situations and prices, but to deal with change. The acting individual either anticipates changes which will occur without his own interference and wants to adjust his actions to this anticipated state of affairs; or he wants to embark upon a project which will change conditions even if no other factors produce a change. The prices of the past are for him merely starting points in his endeavors to anticipate future prices.

Historians and statisticians content themselves with prices of the past. Practical man looks at the prices of the future, be it only the immediate future of the next hour, day, or month. For him the prices of the past are merely a help in anticipating future prices. Not only in his preliminary calculation of the expected outcome of planned action, but no less in his attempts to establish the result of his past transactions, he is primarily concerned with future prices.

In balance sheets and in profit-and-loss statements the result of past action becomes visible as the difference between the money equiv-

alent of funds owned (total assets minus total liabilities) at the beginning
and at the end of the period reported, and as the difference between the
money equivalent of costs incurred and gross proceeds earned. In such
statements it is necessary to enter the estimated money equivalent of all
assets and liabilities other than cash. These items should be appraised according to the prices at which they could probably be sold in the future
or, as is especially the case with equipment for production processes, in
reference to the prices to be expected in the sale of merchandise manu-
factured with their aid. However, old business customs and the provisions
of commercial law and of the tax laws have brought about a deviation
from sound principles of accounting which aim merely at the best attain-
able degree of correctness. These customs and laws are not so much concerned with correctness in balance sheets and profit-and-loss statements as
with the pursuit of other aims. Commercial legislation aims at a method
of accounting which could indirectly protect creditors against loss. It tends
more or less to an appraisal of assets below their estimated market value
in order to make the net profit and the total funds owned appear smaller
than they really are. Thus a safety margin is created which reduces the
danger that, to the prejudice of creditors, too much might be withdrawn
from the firm as alleged profit and that an already insolvent firm might go
on until it had exhausted the means available for the satisfaction of its
creditors. Contrariwise tax laws often tend toward a method of computation which makes earnings appear higher than an unbiased method
would. The idea is to raise effective tax rates without making this raise visible in the nominal tax rate schedules. We must therefore distinguish between economic calculation as it is practiced by businessmen planning future transactions and those computations of business facts which serve
other purposes. The determination of taxes due and economic calculation
are two different things. If a law imposing a tax upon the keeping of domestic servants prescribes that one male servant should be counted as two
female servants, nobody would interpret such a provision as anything other
than a method for determining the amount of tax due. Likewise if an inheritance tax law prescribes that securities should be appraised at the stock
market quotation on the day of the decedent's death, we are merely provided with a way of determining the amount of the tax.

The duly kept accounts in a system of correct bookkeeping are ac-
curate as to dollars and cents. They display an impressive precision,
and the numerical exactitude of their items seems to remove all doubts.
In fact, the most important figures they contain are speculative antic-

ipations of future market constellations. It is a mistake to compare the items of any commercial account to the items used in purely technological reckoning, e.g., in the design for the construction of a machine. The engineer — as far as he attends to the technological side of his job — applies only numerical relations established by the methods of the experimental natural sciences; the businessman cannot avoid numerical terms which are the outcome of his understanding of future human conduct. The main thing in balance sheets and in profit-and-loss statements is the evaluation of assets and liabilities not embodied in cash. All such balances and statements are virtually interim balances and interim statements. They describe as well as possible the state of affairs at an arbitrarily chosen instant while life and action go on and do not stop. It is possible to wind up individual business units, but the whole system of social production never ceases. Nor are the assets and liabilities consisting in cash exempt from the indeterminacy inherent in all business accounting items. They depend on the future constellation of the market no less than any item of inventory or equipment. The numerical exactitude of business accounts and calculations must not prevent us from realizing the uncertainty and speculative character of their items and of all computations based on them.

Yet, these facts do not detract from the efficiency of economic calculation. Economic calculation is as efficient as it can be. No reform could add to its efficiency. It renders to acting man all the services which he can obtain from numerical computation. It is, of course, not a means of knowing future conditions with certainty, and it does not deprive action of its speculative character. But this can be considered a deficiency only by those who do not come to recognize the facts that life is not rigid, that all things are perpetually fluctuating, and that men have no certain knowledge about the future.

It is not the task of economic calculation to expand man's information about future conditions. Its task is to adjust his actions as well as possible to his present opinion concerning want-satisfaction in the future. For this purpose acting man needs a method of computation, and computation requires a common denominator to which all items entered are to be referable. The common denominator of economic calculation is money.

2   The Limits of Economic Calculation

Economic calculation cannot comprehend things which are not sold and bought against money.

There are things which are not for sale and for whose acquisition sacrifices other than money and money's worth must be expended. He who wants to train himself for great achievements must employ many means, some of which may require expenditure of money. But the essential things to be devoted to such an endeavor are not purchasable. Honor, virtue, glory, and likewise vigor, health, and life itself play a role in action both as means and as ends, but they do not enter into economic calculation.

There are things which cannot at all be evaluated in money, and there are other things which can be appraised in money only with regard to a fraction of the value assigned to them. The appraisal of an old building must disregard its artistic and historical eminence as far as these qualities are not a source of proceeds in money or goods vendible. What touches a man's heart only and does not induce other people to make sacrifices for its attainment remains outside the pale of economic calculation.

However, all this does not in the least impair the usefulness of economic calculation. Those things which do not enter into the items of accountancy and calculation are either ends or goods of the first order. No calculation is required to acknowledge them fully and to make due allowance for them. All that acting man needs in order to make his choice is to contrast them with the total amount of costs their acquisition or preservation requires. Let us assume that a town council has to decide between two water supply projects. One of them implies the demolition of a historical landmark, while the other at the cost of an increase in money expenditure spares this landmark. The fact that the feelings which recommend the conservation of the monument cannot be estimated in a sum of money does not in any way impede the councilmen's decision. The values that are not reflected in any monetary exchange ratio are, on the contrary, by this very fact lifted into a particular position which makes the decision rather easier. No complaint is less justified than the lamentation that the computation methods of the market do not comprehend things not vendible. Moral and aesthetic values do not suffer any damage on account of this fact.

Money, money prices, market transactions, and economic calculation based upon them are the main targets of criticism. Loquacious sermonizers disparage Western civilization as a mean system of mongering and peddling. Complacency, self-righteousness, and hypocrisy exult in scorning the "dollar-philosophy" of our age. Neurotic reformers, mentally unbalanced literati, and ambitious demagogues take pleasure in indicting "rationality" and in preaching the gospel of the "irrational." In the eyes of these babblers money and calculation are the source of the most serious evils. However, the fact that men have developed a method of ascertaining as far as possible the expediency of their actions and of removing uneasiness in the most practical and economic way does not prevent anybody from arranging his conduct according to the principle he considers to be right. The "materialism" of the stock exchange and of business accountancy does not hinder anybody from living up to the standards of Thomas à Kempis or from dying for a noble cause. The fact that the masses prefer detective stories to poetry and that it therefore pays better to write the former than the latter, is not caused by the use of money and monetary accounting. It is not the fault of money that there are gangsters, thieves, murderers, prostitutes, corruptible officials and judges. It is not true that honesty does not "pay." It pays for those who prefer fidelity to what they consider to be right to the advantages which they could derive from a different attitude.

Other critics of economic calculation fail to realize that it is a method available only to people acting in the economic system of the division of labor in a social order based upon private ownership of the means of production. It can only serve the considerations of individuals or groups of individuals operating in the institutional setting of this social order. It is consequently a calculation of private profits and not of "social welfare." This means that the prices of the market are the ultimate fact for economic calculation. It cannot be applied for considerations whose standard is not the demand of the consumers as manifested on the market but the hypothetical valuations of a dictatorial body managing all national or earthly affairs. He who seeks to judge actions from the point of view of a pretended "social value," i.e., from the point of view of the "whole society," and to criticize them by comparison with the events in an imaginary socialist system in which his own will is supreme, has no use for economic calculation. Economic calculation in terms of money prices is the calculation of entrepreneurs producing for the consumers of a market society. It is of no avail for other tasks.

He who wants to employ economic calculation must not look at affairs in the manner of a despotic mind. Prices can be used for calculation by the entrepreneurs, capitalists, landowners, and wage earners of a capitalist society. For matters beyond the pursuits of these categories it is inadequate. It is nonsensical to evaluate in money objects which are not negotiated on the market and to employ in calculations arbitrary items which do not refer to reality. The law determines the amount which ought to be paid as indemnification for having caused a man's death. But the statute enacted for the determination of the amends due does not mean that there is a price for human life. Where there is slavery, there are market prices of slaves. Where there is no slavery man, human life, and health are *res extra commercium* [(Latin) thing or things outside of business or commercial transactions]. In a society of free men the preservation of life and health are ends, not means. They do not enter into any process of accounting means.

It is possible to determine in terms of money prices the sum of the income or the wealth of a number of people. But it is nonsensical to reckon national income or national wealth. As soon as we embark upon considerations foreign to the reasoning of a man operating within the pale of a market society, we are no longer helped by monetary calculation methods. The attempts to determine in money the wealth of a nation or of the whole of mankind are as childish as the mystic efforts to solve the riddles of the universe by worrying about the dimensions of the pyramid of Cheops. If a business calculation values a supply of potatoes at $100, the idea is that it will be possible to sell it or to replace it against this sum. If a whole entrepreneurial unit is estimated at $1,000,000, it means that one expects to sell it for this amount. But what is the meaning of the items in a statement of a nation's total wealth? What is the meaning of the computation's final result? What must be entered into it and what is to be left outside? Is it correct or not to enclose the "value" of the country's climate and the people's innate abilities and acquired skills? The businessman can convert his property into money, but a nation cannot.

The money equivalents as used in acting and in economic calculation are money prices, i.e., exchange ratios between money and other goods and services. The prices are not measured in money; they consist in money. Prices are either prices of the past or expected prices of the future. A price is necessarily a historical fact either of the past or of the future. There is nothing in prices which permits one to liken them to the measurement of physical and chemical phenomena.

3   The Changeability of Prices

Exchange ratios are subject to perpetual change because the conditions which produce them are perpetually changing. The value that an individual attaches both to money and to various goods and services is the outcome of a moment's choice. Every later instant may generate something new and bring about other considerations and valuations. Not that prices are fluctuating, but that they do not alter more quickly could fairly be deemed a problem requiring explanation.

Daily experience teaches people that the exchange ratios of the market are mutable. One would assume that their ideas about prices would take full account of this fact. Nevertheless all popular notions of production and consumption, marketing and prices are more or less contaminated by a vague and contradictory notion of price rigidity. The layman is prone to consider the preservation of yesterday's price structure both as normal and as fair, and to condemn changes in the exchange ratios as a violation of the rules of nature and of justice.

It would be a mistake to explain these popular beliefs as a precipitate of old opinions conceived in earlier ages of more stable conditions of production and marketing. It is questionable whether or not prices were less changeable in those older days. On the contrary, it could rather be asserted that the merger of local markets into larger national markets, the final emergence of a world embracing world market, and the evolution of commerce aiming at continuously supplying the consumers have made price changes less frequent and less sharp. In precapitalistic times there was more stability in technological methods of production, but there was much more irregularity in supplying the various local markets and in adjusting supply to their changing demands. But even if it were true that prices were somewhat more stable in a remote past, it would be of little avail for our age. The popular notions about money and money prices are not derived from ideas formed in the past. It would be wrong to interpret them as atavistic remnants. Under modern conditions every individual is daily faced with so many problems of buying and selling that we are right in assuming that his thinking about these matters is not simply a thoughtless reception of traditional ideas.

It is easy to understand why those whose short-run interests are hurt by a change in prices resent such changes, emphasize that the previous prices were not only fairer but also more normal, and maintain that price stability is in conformity with the laws of nature and of morality. But every change in prices furthers the short-run interests of other people. Those favored will certainly not be prompted by the urge to stress the fairness and normalcy of price rigidity.

Neither atavistic reminiscences nor the state of selfish group interests can explain the popularity of the idea of price stability. Its roots are to be seen in the fact that notions concerning social relations have been constructed according to the pattern of the natural sciences. The economists and sociologists who aimed at shaping the social sciences according to the pattern of physics or physiology only indulged in a way of thinking which popular fallacies had adopted long before.

Even the classical economists were slow to free themselves from this error. With them value was something objective, i.e., a phenomenon of the external world and a quality inherent in things and therefore measurable. They utterly failed to comprehend the purely human and voluntaristic character of value judgments. As far as we can see today, it was Samuel Bailey who first disclosed what is going on in preferring one thing to another.[1] But his book was overlooked as were the writings of other precursors of the subjective theory of value.

It is not only a task of economic science to discard the errors concerning measurability in the field of action. It is no less a task of economic policy. For the failures of present-day economic policies are to some extent due to the lamentable confusion brought about by the idea that there is something fixed and therefore measurable in interhuman relations.

4   Stabilization

An outgrowth of all these errors is the idea of stabilization.

Shortcomings in the governments' handling of monetary matters and the disastrous consequences of policies aimed at lowering the rate of interest and at encouraging business activities through credit expansion gave birth to the ideas which finally generated the slogan "stabilization." One can explain its emergence and its popular appeal, one can understand it as the fruit of the last hundred and fifty years' history of currency and banking, one can, as it were, plead extenuating circumstances for the error involved. But no such sympathetic appreciation can render its fallacies any more tenable.

Stability, the establishment of which the program of stabilization aims at, is an empty and contradictory notion. The urge toward action, i.e., improvement of the conditions of life, is inborn in man. Man himself changes from moment to moment and his valuations, volitions, and acts change with him. In the realm of action there is nothing perpetual but change. There is no fixed point in this ceaseless fluctuation other than the eternal aprioristic categories of action. It is vain to sever valuation and action from man's unsteadiness and the changeability of his conduct and to argue as if there were in the universe eternal values independent of human value judgments and suitable to serve as a yardstick for the appraisal of real action.[2]

All methods suggested for a measurement of the changes in the

---

1. Cf. Samuel Bailey, A *Critical Dissertation on the Nature, Measures and Causes of Values.* London, 1825. No. 7 in Series of Reprints of Scarce Tracts in Economics and Political Science, London School of Economics (London, 1931).
2. For the propensity of the mind to view rigidity and unchangeability as the essential thing and change and motion as the accidental, cf. Bergson, *La Pensée et le mouvant,* pp. 85 ff.

monetary unit's purchasing power are more or less unwittingly founded on the illusory image of an eternal and immutable being who determines by the application of an immutable standard the quantity of satisfaction which a unit of money conveys to him. It is a poor justification of this ill-thought idea that what is wanted is merely to measure changes in the purchasing power of money. The crux of the stability notion lies precisely in this concept of purchasing power. The layman, laboring under the ideas of physics, once considered money as a yardstick of prices. He believed that fluctuations of exchange ratios occur only in the relations between the various commodities and services and not also in the relation between money and the "totality" of goods and services. Later, people reversed the argument. It was no longer money to which constancy of value was attributed, but the "totality" of things vendible and purchasable. People began to devise methods for working up complexes of commodity units to be contrasted to the monetary unit. Eagerness to find indexes for the measurement of purchasing power silenced all scruples. Both the doubtfulness and the incomparability of the price records employed and the arbitrary character of the procedures used for the computation of averages were disregarded.

Irving Fisher, the eminent economist, who was the champion of the American stabilization movement, contrasts with the dollar a basket containing all the goods the housewife buys on the market for the current provision of her household. In the proportion in which the amount of money required for the purchase of the content of this basket changes, the purchasing power of the dollar has changed. The goal assigned to the policy of stabilization is the preservation of the immutability of this money expenditure.[3] This would be all right if the housewife and her imaginary basket were constant elements, if the basket were always to contain the same goods and the same quantity of each and if the role which this assortment of goods plays in the family's life were not to change. But we are living in a world in which none of these conditions is realized.

First of all there is the fact that the quality of the commodities produced and consumed changes continuously. It is a mistake to identify wheat with wheat, not to speak of shoes, hats, and other manufactures. The great price differences in the synchronous sales of commodities which mundane speech and statistics arrange in the same class clearly evidence this truism. An idiomatic expression asserts that two peas are alike; but buyers and sellers distinguish

3. Cf. Irving Fisher, *The Money Illusion* (New York, 1928), pp. 19–20.

various qualities and grades of peas. A comparison of prices paid at different places or at different dates for commodities which technology or statistics calls by the same name, is useless if it is not certain that their qualities—but for the place difference—are perfectly the same. Quality means in this connection: all those properties to which the buyers and would-be-buyers pay heed. The mere fact that the quality of all goods and services of the first order is subject to change explodes one of the fundamental assumptions of all index number methods. It is irrelevant that a limited amount of goods of the higher orders—especially metals and chemicals which can be uniquely determined by a formula—are liable to a precise description of their characteristic features. A measurement of purchasing power would have to rely upon the prices of the goods and services of the first order and, what is more, of *all* of them. To employ the prices of the producers' goods is not helpful because it could not avoid counting the various stages of the production of one and the same consumers' good several times and thus falsifying the result. A restriction to a group of selected goods would be quite arbitrary and therefore vicious.

But even apart from all these insurmountable obstacles the task would remain insoluble. For not only do the technological features of commodities change but new kinds of goods appear while many old ones disappear. Valuations change too, and they cause changes in demand and production. The assumptions of the measurement doctrine would require men whose wants and valuations are rigid. Only if people were to value the same things always in the same way, could we consider price changes as expressive of changes in the power of money to buy things.

As it is impossible to establish the total amount of money spent at a given fraction of time for consumers' goods, statisticians must rely upon the prices paid for individual commodities. This raises two further problems for which there is no apodictic solution. It becomes necessary to attach to the various commodities coefficients of importance. It would be manifestly wrong to let the prices of various commodities enter into the computation without taking into account the different roles they play in the total system of the individuals' households. But the establishment of such proper weighting is again arbitrary. Secondly, it becomes necessary to compute averages out of the data collected and adjusted. But there exist different methods for the computation of averages. There are the arithmetic, the geometric, the harmonic averages, there is the quasi-average known as the median. Each of them leads to different results. None of them can be recognized as the unique way to attain a logically unassailable answer. The decision in favor of one of these methods of computation is arbitrary.

If all human conditions were unchangeable, if all people were always to repeat the same actions because their uneasiness and their ideas about its removal were constant, or if we were in a position to assume that changes in these factors occurring with some individuals or groups are always outweighed by opposite changes with other individuals or groups and therefore do not affect total demand and total supply, we would live in a world of stability. But the idea that in such a world money's purchasing power could change is contradictory. As will be shown later, changes in the purchasing power of money must necessarily affect the prices of different commodities and services at different times and to different extents; they must consequently bring about changes in demand and supply, in production and consumption.[4] The idea implied in the inappropriate term *level of prices*, as if—other things being equal—all prices could rise or drop evenly, is untenable. Other things cannot remain equal if the purchasing power of money changes.

In the field of praxeology and economics no sense can be given to the notion of measurement. In the hypothetical state of rigid conditions there are no changes to be measured. In the actual world of change there are no fixed points, dimensions, or relations which could serve as a standard. The monetary unit's purchasing power never changes evenly with regard to all things vendible and purchasable. The notions of stability and stabilization are empty if they do not refer to a state of rigidity and its preservation. However, this state of rigidity cannot even be thought out consistently to its ultimate logical consequences; still less can it be realized.[5] Where there is action, there is change. Action is a lever of change.

The pretentious solemnity which statisticians and statistical bureaus display in computing indexes of purchasing power and cost of living is out of place. These index numbers are at best rather crude and inaccurate illustrations of changes which have occurred. In periods of slow alterations in the relation between the supply of and the demand for money they do not convey any information at all. In periods of inflation and consequently of sharp price changes they provide a rough image of events which every individual experiences in his daily life. A judicious housewife knows much more about price changes as far as they affect her own household than the statistical

4. See below, pp. 411–13.
5. See below, pp. 247–50.

averages can tell. She has little use for computations disregarding changes both in quality and in the amount of goods which she is able or permitted to buy at the prices entering into the computation. If she "measures" the changes for her personal appreciation by taking the prices of only two or three commodities as a yardstick, she is no less "scientific" and no more arbitrary than the sophisticated mathematicians in choosing their methods for the manipulation of the data of the market.

In practical life nobody lets himself be fooled by index numbers. Nobody agrees with the fiction that they are to be considered as measurements. Where quantities are measured, all further doubts and disagreements concerning their dimensions cease. These questions are settled. Nobody ventures to argue with the meteorologists about their measurements of temperature, humidity, atmospheric pressure, and other meteorological data. But on the other hand nobody acquiesces in an index number if he does not expect a personal advantage from its acknowledgment by public opinion. The establishment of index numbers does not settle disputes; it merely shifts them into a field in which the clash of antagonistic opinions and interests is irreconcilable.

Human action originates change. As far as there is human action there is no stability, but ceaseless alteration. The historical process is a sequence of changes. It is beyond the power of man to stop it and to bring about an age of stability in which all history comes to a standstill. It is man's nature to strive after improvement, to beget new ideas, and to rearrange the conditions of his life according to these ideas.

The prices of the market are historical facts expressive of a state of affairs that prevailed at a definite instant of the irreversible historical process. In the praxeological orbit the concept of measurement does not make any sense. In the imaginary—and, of course, unrealizable—state of rigidity and stability there are no changes to be measured. In the actual world of permanent change there are no fixed points, objects, qualities or relations with regard to which changes could be measured.

5 The Root of the Stabilization Idea

Economic calculation does not require monetary stability in the sense in which this term is used by the champions of the stabilization movement. The fact that rigidity in the monetary unit's purchasing power is unthinkable and unrealizable does not impair the methods of economic calculation. What economic calculation requires is a monetary system whose functioning is not sabotaged by government interference. The endeavors to expand the quantity of money in circulation either in order to increase the government's capacity to spend or in order to bring about a temporary lowering of the rate of interest disintegrate all currency matters and derange economic calculation. The first aim of monetary policy must be to prevent governments from embarking upon inflation and from creating conditions which encourage credit expansion on the part of banks. But this program is very different from the confused and self-contradictory program of stabilizing purchasing power.

For the sake of economic calculation all that is needed is to avoid great and abrupt fluctuations in the supply of money. Gold and, up to the middle of the nineteenth century, silver served very well all the purposes of economic calculation. Changes in the relation between the supply of and the demand for the precious metals and the resulting alterations in purchasing power went on so slowly that the entrepreneur's economic calculation could disregard them without going too far afield. Precision is unattainable in economic calculation quite apart from the shortcomings emanating from not paying due consideration to monetary changes.[6] The planning businessman cannot help employing data concerning the unknown future; he deals with future prices and future costs of production. Accounting and bookkeeping in their endeavors to establish the result of past action are in the same position as far as they rely upon the estimation of fixed equipment, inventories, and receivables. In spite of all these uncertainties economic calculation can achieve its tasks. For these uncertainties do not stem from deficiencies of the system of calculation. They are inherent in the essence of acting that always deals with the uncertain future.

The idea of rendering purchasing power stable did not originate from endeavors to make economic calculation more correct. Its source is the wish to create a sphere withdrawn from the ceaseless flux of human affairs, a realm which the historical process does not affect. Endowments which were designed to provide in perpetuity for an ecclesiastic body, for a charitable institution, or for a family were long established in land or in disbursement of agricultural prod-

---

6. No practical calculation can ever be precise. The formula underlying the process of calculation may be exact; the calculation itself depends on the approximate establishment of quantities and is therefore necessarily inaccurate. Economics is, as has been shown above (p. 39), an exact science of real things. But as soon as price data are introduced into the chain of thought, exactitude is abandoned and economic history is substituted for economic theory.

ucts in kind. Later annuities to be settled in money were added. Endowers and beneficiaries expected that an annuity determined in terms of a definite amount of precious metals would not be affected by changes in economic conditions. But these hopes were illusory. Later generations learned that the plans of their ancestors were not realized. Stimulated by this experience they began to investigate how the aims sought could be attained. Thus they embarked upon attempts to measure changes in purchasing power and to eliminate such changes.

The problem assumed much greater importance when governments initiated their policies of long-term irredeemable and perpetual loans. The state, this new deity of the dawning age of statolatry, this eternal and superhuman institution beyond the reach of earthly frailties, offered to the citizen an opportunity to put his wealth in safety and to enjoy a stable income secure against all vicissitudes. It opened a way to free the individual from the necessity of risking and acquiring his wealth and his income anew each day in the capitalist market. He who invested his funds in bonds issued by the government and its subdivisions was no longer subject to the inescapable laws of the market and to the sovereignty of the consumers. He was no longer under the necessity of investing his funds in such a way that they would best serve the wants and needs of the consumers. He was secure, he was safeguarded against the dangers of the competitive market in which losses are the penalty of inefficiency; the eternal state had taken him under its wing and guaranteed him the undisturbed enjoyment of his funds. Henceforth his income no longer stemmed from the process of supplying the wants of the consumers in the best possible way, but from the taxes levied by the state's apparatus of compulsion and coercion. He was no longer a servant of his fellow citizens, subject to their sovereignty; he was a partner of the government which ruled the people and exacted tribute from them. What the government paid as interest was less than the market offered. But this difference was far outweighed by the unquestionable solvency of the debtor, the state whose revenue did not depend on satisfying the public, but on insisting on the payment of taxes.

In spite of the unpleasant experiences with public debts in earlier days, people were ready to trust freely the modernized state of the nineteenth century. It was generally assumed that this new state would scrupulously meet its voluntarily contracted obligations. Capitalists and entrepreneurs were fully aware of the fact that in the market society there is no means of preserving acquired wealth other than by acquiring it anew each day in tough competition with everybody, with the already existing firms as well as with newcomers "operating on a shoe string." The entrepreneur, grown old and weary and no longer prepared to risk his hard-earned wealth by new attempts to meet the wants of consumers, and the heir of other people's profits, lazy and fully conscious of his own inefficiency, preferred investment in bonds of the public debt because they wanted to be free from the law of the market.

Now, the irredeemable perpetual public debt presupposes the stability of purchasing power. Although the state and its compulsion may be eternal, the interest paid on the public debt could be eternal only if based on a standard of unchanging value. In this form the investor who for security's sake shuns the market, entrepreneurship, and investment in free enterprise and prefers government bonds is faced again with the problem of the changeability of all human affairs. He discovers that in the frame of a market society there is no room left for wealth not dependent upon the market. His endeavors to find an inexhaustible source of income fail.

There are in this world no such things as stability and security and no human endeavors are powerful enough to bring them about. There is in the social system of the market society no other means of acquiring wealth and of preserving it than successful service to the consumers. The state is, of course, in a position to exact payments from its subjects and to borrow funds. However, even the most ruthless government in the long run is not able to defy the laws determining human life and action. If the government uses the sums borrowed for investment in those lines in which they best serve the wants of the consumers, and if it succeeds in these entrepreneurial activities in free and equal competition with all private entrepreneurs, it is in the same position as any other businessman; it can pay interest because it has made surpluses. But if the government invests funds unsuccessfully and no surplus results, or if it spends the money for current expenditure, the capital borrowed shrinks or disappears entirely, and no source is opened from which interest and principal could be paid. Then taxing the people is the only method available for complying with the articles of the credit contract. In asking taxes for such payments the government makes the citizens answerable for money squandered in the past. The taxes paid are not compensated by any present service rendered by the government's apparatus.

The government pays interest on capital which has been consumed and no longer exists. The treasury is burdened with the unfortunate results of past policies.

A good case can be made out for short-term government debts under special conditions. Of course, the popular justification of war loans is nonsensical. All the materials needed for the conduct of a war must be provided by restriction of civilian consumption, by using up a part of the capital available and by working harder. The whole burden of warring falls upon the living generation. The coming generations are only affected to the extent to which, on account of the war expenditure, they will inherit less from those now living than they would have if no war had been fought. Financing a war through loans does not shift the burden to the sons and grandsons.[7] It is merely a method of distributing the burden among the citizens. If the whole expenditure had to be provided by taxes, only those who have liquid funds could be approached. The rest of the people would not contribute adequately. Short-term loans can be instrumental in removing such inequalities, as they allow for a fair assessment on the owners of fixed capital.

The long-term public and semipublic credit is a foreign and disturbing element in the structure of a market society. Its establishment was a futile attempt to go beyond the limits of human action and to create an orbit of security and eternity removed from the transitoriness and instability of earthly affairs. What an arrogant presumption to borrow and to lend money for ever and ever, to make contracts for eternity, to stipulate for all times to come! In this respect it mattered little whether the loans were in a formal manner made irredeemable or not; intentionally and practically they were as a rule considered and dealt with as such. In the heyday of liberalism some Western nations really retired parts of their long-term debt by honest reimbursement. But for the most part new debts were only heaped upon old ones. The financial history of the last century shows a steady increase in the amount of public indebtedness. Nobody believes that the states will eternally drag the burden of these interest payments. It is obvious that sooner or later all these debts will be liquidated in some way or other, but certainly not by payment of interest and principal according to the terms of the contract. A host

7. Loans, in this context, mean funds borrowed from those who have money available for lending. We do not refer here to credit expansion of which the main vehicle in present-day America is borrowing from the commercial banks.

of sophisticated writers are already busy elaborating the moral palliation for the day of final settlement.[8]

The fact that economic calculation in terms of money is unequal to the tasks which are assigned to it in these illusory schemes for establishment of an unrealizable realm of calm removed from the inescapable limitations of human action and providing eternal security cannot be called a deficiency. There are no such things as eternal, absolute, and unchanging values. The search for a standard of such values is vain. Economic calculation is not imperfect because it does not correspond to the confused ideas of people yearning for a stable income not dependent on the productive processes of men.

8. The most popular of these doctrines is crystallized in the phrase: A public debt is no burden because we owe it to ourselves. If this were true, then the wholesale obliteration of the public debt would be an innocuous operation, a mere act of bookkeeping and accountancy. The fact is that the public debt embodies claims of people who have in the past entrusted funds to the government against all those who are daily producing new wealth. It burdens the producing strata for the benefit of another part of the people. It is possible to free the producers of new wealth from this burden by collecting the taxes required for the payments exclusively from the bondholders. But this means undisguised repudiation.

CHAPTER 13

Monetary Calculation as a Tool of Action

1 Monetary Calculation as a Method of Thinking

Monetary calculation is the guiding star of action under the social system of division of labor. It is the compass of the man embarking upon production. He calculates in order to distinguish the remunerative lines of production from the unprofitable ones, those of which the sovereign consumers are likely to approve from those of which they are likely to disapprove. Every single step of entrepreneurial activities is subject to scrutiny by monetary calculation. The premeditation of planned action becomes commercial precalculation of expected costs and expected proceeds. The retrospective establishment of the outcome of past action becomes accounting of profit and loss.

The system of economic calculation in monetary terms is conditioned by certain social institutions. It can operate only in an institutional setting of the division of labor and private ownership of the means of production in which goods and services of all orders are bought and sold against a generally used medium of exchange, i.e., money.

Monetary calculation is the method of calculating employed by people acting within the frame of society based on private control of the means of production. It is a device of acting individuals; it is a mode of computation designed for ascertaining private wealth and income and private profits and losses of individuals acting on their own behalf within a free enterprise society.[1] All its results refer to the actions of individuals only. When statisticians summarize these results, the outcome shows the sum of the autonomous actions of a plurality of self-directing individuals, but not the effect of the action of a collective body, of a whole, or of a totality. Monetary calculation is entirely inapplicable and useless for any consideration which does not look at things from the point of view of individuals. It involves calculating the individuals' profits, not imaginary "social" values and "social" welfare.

1. In partnerships and corporations it is always individuals who act, although not only one individual.

Monetary calculation is the main vehicle of planning and acting in the social setting of a society of free enterprise directed and controlled by the market and its prices. It developed in this frame and was gradually perfected with the improvement of the market mechanism and with the expansion of the scope of things which are negotiated on markets against money. It was economic calculation that assigned to measurement, number, and reckoning the role they play in our quantitative and computing civilization. The measurements of physics and chemistry make sense for practical action only because there is economic calculation. It is monetary calculation that made arithmetic a tool in the struggle for a better life. It provides a mode of using the achievements of laboratory experiments for the most efficacious removal of uneasiness.

Monetary calculation reaches its full perfection in capital accounting. It establishes the money prices of the available means and confronts this total with the changes brought about by action and by the operation of other factors. This confrontation shows what changes occurred in the state of the acting men's affairs and the magnitude of those changes; it makes success and failure, profit and loss ascertainable. The system of free enterprise has been dubbed capitalism in order to deprecate and to smear it. However, this term can be considered very pertinent. It refers to the most characteristic feature of the system, its main eminence, viz., the role the notion of capital plays in its conduct.

There are people to whom monetary calculation is repulsive. They do not want to be roused from their daydreams by the voice of critical reason. Reality sickens them; they long for a realm of unlimited opportunity. They are disgusted by the meanness of a social order in which everything is nicely reckoned in dollars and pennies. They call their grumbling the noble deportment worthy of the friends of the spirit, of beauty, and virtue as opposed to the ignoble baseness and villainy of Babbittry. However, the cult of beauty and virtue, wisdom and the search for truth are not hindered by the rationality of the calculating and computing mind. It is only romantic reverie that cannot thrive in a milieu of sober criticism. The cool-headed reckoner is the stern chastiser of the ecstatic visionary.

Our civilization is inseparably linked with our methods of economic calculation. It would perish if we were to abandon this most precious intellectual tool of acting. Goethe was right in calling bookkeeping by double entry "one of the finest inventions of the human mind." [2]

2. Cf. Goethe, *Wilhelm Meister's Apprenticeship*, Bk. I, chap. x.

2   Economic Calculation and the
     Science of Human Action

The evolution of capitalist economic calculation was the necessary condition
for the establishment of a systematic and logically coherent science of human
action. Praxeology and economics have a definite place in the evolution of human history and in the process of scientific research. They could only emerge
when acting man had succeeded in creating methods of thinking that made it
possible to calculate his actions. The science of human action was at the beginning merely a discipline dealing with those actions which can be tested by
monetary calculation. It dealt exclusively with what we may call the orbit of
economics in the narrower sense, that is, with those actions which within a
market society are transacted by the intermediary of money. The first steps on
the way to its elaboration were odd investigations concerning currency,
moneylending, and the prices of various goods. The knowledge conveyed by
Gresham's Law, the first crude formulations of the quantity theory of money —
such as those of Bodin and Davanzati — and the Law of Gregory King mark
the first dawn of the cognition that regularity of phenomena and inevitable
necessity prevail in the field of action. The first comprehensive system of economic theory, that brilliant achievement of the classical economists, was
essentially a theory of calculated action. It drew implicitly the borderline between what is to be considered economic and what extra-economic along the
line which separates action calculated in monetary terms from other action.
Starting from this basis, the economists were bound to widen step by step the
field of their studies until they finally developed a system dealing with all
human choices, a general theory of action.